A PEOPLE'S GUIDE TO THE
SAN FRANCISCO
BAY AREA

THE PUBLISHER AND THE UNIVERSITY OF CALIFORNIA PRESS FOUNDATION
GRATEFULLY ACKNOWLEDGE THE GENEROUS SUPPORT OF THE
PETER BOOTH WILEY ENDOWMENT FUND IN HISTORY.

UNIVERSITY OF CALIFORNIA PRESS
PEOPLE'S GUIDES

Los Angeles
Greater Boston
San Francisco Bay Area

Forthcoming

New York City
Orange County, California
Richmond and Central Virginia
New Orleans

About the Series

Tourism is one of the largest and most profitable industries in the world today, especially for cities. Yet the vast majority of tourist guidebooks focus on the histories and sites associated with a small, elite segment of the population and encourage consumption and spectacle as the primary way to experience a place. These representations do not reflect the reality of life for most urban residents— including people of color, the working class and poor, immigrants, indigenous people, and LGBTQ communities—nor are they embedded within a systematic analysis of power, privilege, and exploitation. The *People's Guide* series was born from the conviction that we need a different kind of guidebook: one that explains power relations in a way everyone can understand, and that shares stories of struggle and resistance to inspire and educate activists, students, and critical thinkers.

Guidebooks in the series uncover the rich and vibrant stories of political struggle, oppression, and resistance in the everyday landscapes of metropolitan regions. They reveal an alternative view of urban life and history by flipping the script of the conventional tourist guidebook. These books not only tell histories from the bottom up, but also show how *all* landscapes and places are the product of struggle. Each book features a range of sites where the powerful have dominated and exploited other people and resources, as well as places where ordinary people have fought back in order to create a more just world. Each book also includes carefully curated thematic tours through which readers can explore specific urban processes and their relation to metropolitan geographies in greater detail. The photographs model how to read space, place, and landscape critically, while the maps, nearby sites of interest, and additional learning resources create a resource that is highly usable. By mobilizing the conventional format of the tourist guidebook in these strategic ways, books in the series aim to cultivate stronger public understandings of how power operates spatially.

A PEOPLE'S GUIDE TO THE
SAN FRANCISCO BAY AREA

Rachel Brahinsky and Alexander Tarr

Photography by Bruce Rinehart

University of California Press

University of California Press
Oakland, California

Library of Congress Cataloging-in-Publication Data

Names: Brahinsky, Rachel, 1974– author. | Tarr, Alexander, 1981– author. |
    Rinehart, Bruce, 1961– photographer.
Title: A people's guide to the San Francisco Bay Area / Rachel Brahinsky
    and Alexander Tarr ; photography by Bruce Rinehart.
Description: Oakland, California : University of California Press, [2020] |
    Includes bibliographical references and index.
Identifiers: LCCN 2019042832 (print) | LCCN 2019042833 (ebook) |
    ISBN 9780520288379 (paperback) | ISBN 9780520963320 (ebook)
Subjects: LCSH: San Francisco Bay Area (Calif.)—Description and travel.
Classification: LCC F868.S156 B69 2020 (print) | LCC F868.S156 (ebook) |
    DDC 917.94/604--dc23
LC record available at https://lccn.loc.gov/2019042832
LC ebook record available at https://lccn.loc.gov/2019042833

Designer and compositor: Nicole Hayward
Text: 10/14.5 Dante
Display: Museo Sans and Museo Slab
Prepress: Embassy Graphics
Indexer: Susan Storch
Cartographer: Alexander Tarr
Printer and binder: Sheridan Books, Inc.

Printed in the United States of America

29   28   27   26   25   24   23   22   21   20
10   9   8   7   6   5   4   3   2   1

For our families, given and chosen

Contents

Maps

924 GILMAN STREE
VOLUNTEER IRON
ALL AGES

NO ALCOHOL
NO DRUGS
NO VIOLENCE
NO STAGEDIVING
NO DOGS
NO FUCKED-UP
BEHAVIOR:
NO RACISM
NO MISOGYNY/SEXISM
NO HOMOPHOBIA
NO TRANSPHOBIA

$2 MEMBERSHIP

VOLUNTEER

NO Outside
Beverages
minus BLOOD
(you dirty vampire's)

HEY PUNK!
YES you with the forty
in your backpac/jacket/orfice
Take your drinks 2 blocks away
and make sure to get rid of
your empties properly.
Thanx! - Gilman Trash Ki...

EGGPLANT EATS RAMAN NODLES

Introduction

You might begin in West Oakland, a place that reflects a remarkable spectrum of the Bay Area's culture and politics, its historical contradictions and challenges, and perhaps its hope for the future. Traverse these streets and you'll see Victorian cottages hand-built by workers in the late nineteenth century. You'll pass by community gardens where locals are claiming their right to urban spaces while remaking the meaning of urbanism. You'll maneuver streets where midcentury urban redevelopment tore through, devastating the neighborhood, and where people responded by building movements calling for self-determination and community control that echoed around the world.

In wandering here, you will inevitably intersect with the BART train tracks, as they swoop from under the San Francisco Bay, shuttling thousands daily into San Francisco and out to the "east county" suburbs. In the distance, you can probably see some of the cranes at the Port of Oak-land, the Bay Area's stalwart economic gateway to the world. You may notice tent camps under the freeway overpasses or in the in-between places where uneven development has produced gaps in the urban fabric. Not far from where houseless folks find shelter, you'll also see slickly painted homes with high-end cars and new fences. These are the now-ubiquitous poles of the Bay Area's economic extremes, visible block to block.

You can't see it today, but if you'd looked down 7th Street toward the San Francisco Bay a century ago, you would have been facing the last stop on the first transcontinental railroad. That train looms large in narratives of the conquest of the West and the fortunes that it brought to the rapacious capitalists known as the Big Four (Stanford, Huntington, Hopkins, and Crocker, the core investors and figureheads of the Central Pacific Railroad). Ultimately, however, the majority of the people that these trains

SANTA ROSA

Napa Co.
Solano Co.

Sonoma Co.
Marin Co.

PETALUMA

4 | NORTH BAY & ISLANDS

VALLEJO

Sacramento Co.

*San Pablo
Bay*

SAN RAFAEL   RICHMOND

1 | EAST BAY

SAUSALITO   BERKELEY

3 | SAN FRANCISCO   OAKLAND

SAN FRANCISCO

Contra Costa Co.
Alameda Co.

DALY CITY   SOUTH S.F.

*San
Francisco
Bay*   HAYWARD

SAN MATEO   FREMONT

Pacific Ocean   Santa Clara Co.

PALO ALTO

2 | SOUTH BAY   SAN JOSE
& PENINSULA

San Mateo Co.
Santa Cruz Co.

<u>10 Miles</u> N̂

carried to the Bay Area—Chinese, Black, and working-class whites—represent a very different narrative about this place.

Here in West Oakland, for example, you'll be treading the same ground walked by the African American employees of the Pullman Company, who in the 1920s organized the Brotherhood of Sleeping Car Porters. It was the first Black-run union chartered by the AFL-CIO and a bedrock in the development of neighborhoods like this one. Its presence on these streets helped create the historical possibility for social justice movements years later, like the Black Panther Party for Self Defense, and the contemporary Movement for Black Lives. This historical legacy still lives in these streets; it is part of why these blocks hold places where antiforeclosure activism has had some success, with residents banding together to save each other's homes from predatory bank actions, building community organizations for broader resilience along the way.

There are older histories here that can be even harder to see, but they too shape the everyday life of this neighborhood and the broader city. Before the Age of Conquest carved its urban patterns into the land, Native American tribes that thrived here for thousands of years knew it as Huichin, among other names. At least one of the dozens of sacred shellmounds that circled the bay was here, near the water's edge. Though most visual evidence of this and other shellmounds has been buried by settler-colonial urbanization, Native activists and allies continue to fight for recognition and respect for these sites.

As we write this book, Oakland has been getting a lot of attention as the new "it" place to visit or move to, especially for people priced out of the San Francisco housing market. For many communities that had already made Oakland their home, from the working-class families of color who stuck with the city across multiple generations to the radicals and outsiders who found a base at the fringe of mainstream society here, this newfound attention is a blessing and a curse. Economically, Oakland—particularly the flatlands and downtown—has been under-invested for a long time, and a boost of some kind is certainly needed. But in many neighborhoods, things have shifted from boost to booting-out terrifyingly fast. Longtime residents and businesses are displaced seemingly overnight, and traces of their impact quickly hidden under the patina of recently flipped houses, a coat of new battleship-gray paint that signals "welcome, open for consumption" to a different class of people.

We start the book in West Oakland, not because it is hip or transit accessible to SF, as the boosters will tell you. Instead, we begin here because in many ways this is one of the historic centers for so much of what we think of as "San Francisco." From the activism mentioned already, to the "urban renewal" that crisscrossed this neighborhood with freeways; from the Victorian visuals, to the colorful muralized storytelling that seems to grow each year, West Oakland reflects diverse narratives of connection across the region. It's a good place from which to ask one of the questions at the heart of this book: How and why did the Bay Area come to be what it is now?

A Path Around the San Francisco Bay

Oakland sits at the geographic center of this book, but the life of this city is only one piece of the larger story that *A People's Guide to the San Francisco Bay Area* tells about people and place. From our starting point, the Bay Region spirals in all directions: You can travel via train and bus to the South Bay, passing south through the working-class flatland neighborhoods, with larger houses and redwood parks perched above in the hills. In the South Bay, you'll traverse dense residential suburbs arranged in a maze of cul-de-sacs and manicured tech "campuses." A different train will take you north from San Jose's perpetually aspirational downtown, out through the industrial end of the once-fertile Santa Clara (now Silicon) Valley, and along the sparkling estuaries of the South Bay. When you reach the city of San Francisco, you step into a thickly settled urbanism, the densest in the region. If you catch a ferry to the north, past the island-prison of Alcatraz, the rolling open spaces of Marin, Sonoma, and Napa will rise up out of the fog, fiercely guarded by the communities tucked into its valleys. If you ride BART in any direction, you can watch the landscape change in fascinating ways.

These places are rich with struggle and beauty, sometimes on full display and other times carefully hidden. This region is home to social movements that have sparked local and international change, and to people whose ideas and values are embedded in the urban landscape. This book is a guide to finding those ideas, to reading the landscape for clues as to where and why it came to be. It is an invitation to recognize and preserve the histories of how people produced the geography of the Bay Area.

In this spirit, this book has four main aims: First, we investigate the ways the Bay Area has been made through the efforts of people who lived, struggled, and thrived here. This is a special place where communities have challenged the abuse of power and built their own kinds of strength, generating wide webs of activism and humane creativity that continues to produce life-giving ideas. Second, we argue for the Bay Area to be understood not as San Francisco and its surroundings, but as an integrated region where, over time, communities intersect and shape each other, challenge each other, and forge the networks of power and identity that give shape to this place.

More broadly, the book is a guide to using a geographic lens on a place to understand its history and social movements. That is, through seeing and learning about spatial patterns and the situated histories of people, you can better understand how the Bay Area (or any place) came to be, and how social struggles produced and continue to produce places like this. Finally, this book asks you to put the book down and wander on your own. We want to show you some of the things that we see and how we understand them. We hope you'll also find your own path through these places.

There is continual debate about how to define the Bay Area. One way to draw a circle around the region is to include the nine counties that touch the San Francisco Bay. These counties all share a watershed and have interlinking political histories and overlapping experiences of urbanization, development, and demographic change. This is a regional vision long used by urban planners, and it encompasses over seven million residents and 101 cities. Within that framework, we offer a curated tour of the nine-county region that draws out largely undertold sociopolitical histories. These are places and stories tucked into a zone that extends no more than a two-hour car drive from the center of Oakland, and much of the book encourages and includes walkable, rollable, bikeable, and transit-friendly wandering.

Throughout the text, we view the region's interdependence as an elemental part of its character. Depictions of historical periods like the rush for gold and the rise of banking or tourism often cast San Francisco as the dominant cultural and economic force in the region, which it certainly has been at times. But the mythology of "San Francisco" can overshadow both the unique histories of each urban node and, more important to this volume, how the people and places of the region are connected through economic, political, cultural, and ecological configurations. Each of the four main chapters opens with a brief introduction that lays out more detailed contours of these histories and relationships.

The first four chapters each address a geographic region, first the East Bay, then the South Bay plus the Peninsula, followed by San Francisco, then the North Bay along with several key islands. These chapters are organized geographically and alphabetically; most essays are titled by the place in which events occurred, rather than with descriptive titles that suggest what took place there. Also, watch for the "nearby" and "related" sites after many entries. Chapter 5 offers suggestions for creating thematic tours out of the material in the first four chapters. Finally, two appendixes offer further resources for wandering and thinking critically about geography, history, politics, and culture in the Bay Area, as well as a timeline of key historical moments that frame the text.

Everyday Places, and Power

This book seeks to simultaneously document and engage. We aim to make disappearing and long-gone landscapes more visible in social memory, and to combat the erasure of visual clues to the past. The guidebook format offers a practical approach through which to connect to readers as more than consumers of words on a page. We hope you will travel these streets, seeking clues to the past that help explain the present; these are real places where people have sought to make the world as they would want it.

The "people's guide" approach to geography is not ours alone. This work is part of a series initiated by 2013's *A People's Guide to Los Angeles,* by Laura Pulido, Laura Barraclough, and Wendy Cheng, who now serve as the editors for the series. Along with them, we are interested in how people have created longstanding institutions and the spaces in which ephemeral acts of politics, revolt, care, and hope take place. We are concerned with histories of oppression and with struggle, as well as moments of power-building and success of movements in transforming political-economic conditions toward a more human scale. We wrote this guide with an eye to understanding the past in support of developing a broader social memory that, in turn, can lend itself to the creation of a more just world in the present and over the long haul. We write from a tradition within cultural geography that emphasizes political economy, and are indebted to scholars who look to the landscape for narratives of power with central attention to the connections between race and place, and with an interest in finding new ways to understand communities on their own terms.[1]

One of the amazing things about the Bay Area is the continued commitment by everyday people to forging new ways of life and politics. Given that, a tremendous array of organizations, from grassroots to formal nonprofit to corporate and beyond—have emerged over the years. Since we're looking at the whole region in the span of one relatively short book, however, we can't begin to claim to cover it all. This is not a comprehensive history; it is a curated tour of places and people, and often we've chosen sites or stories that get less attention in other texts, which means that we pass over many important (and sometimes better-known) people and moments. This is a guide to using observations of the landscape as a way to understand larger structures and social problems, so we offer the book as a set of examples from which to build.

In studying these landscapes, we emphasize power, both top-down and bottom-up. The sites we select do not overlook the extraordinarily powerful men—and it was usually men—who ruled the region over the past two and a half centuries. Indeed, they are embedded into the very place names of the region: Vallejo, Fremont, Geary, and the name San Francisco itself memorialize the Spanish, Mexican, and Anglo conquerors, generals, and others who violently carved the region from a network of indigenous communities into bounded ranches, missions, and pueblos. Unlike some guides to Bay Area cities, however, this book is not primarily about the names that have been prominent for a century or more. Instead, we often focus on the workers, the marginalized, and the everyday people who fought, struggled, made art, survived, and even triumphed to make home out of the Bay Area, in the face of many forms of violence, dispossession, and both literal and figurative erasures.

In unraveling stories of the Bay Region, we share interconnected social-movement histories, to think about how people have worked collectively, locally and globally, to challenge the status quo. Sometimes these are long-fought battles like labor strikes and civil rights campaigns; other times they are small acts of resistance or compassion that keep a person or community alive and whole. These histories reveal multiple expressions of power and its challengers, specifically the ways that the relationships between political leaders, capitalists, and countermovements interact and respond to each other.

To that end, this book draws on and engages the robust existing literature on Bay Area social movements and activism. Although Big Tech is rapidly becoming the global image of the region, the Bay Area may still be best known as a place of cultural openness and social liberalism. Branded as the iconic hearth of the 1960s cultural revolutions and thought of as the seat of LGBTQ+ acceptance, the Bay Area has also been one of the early homes for environmentalism, a center for both union labor and anticorporate organizing, and a catalyst for a variety of other people-driven movements for social change. Pop culture, however, often treats this social history as a quirky backdrop for consumption following an expected path toward inclusion, acceptance, and inevitable comfort for all. This idea produces a paradoxical misperception—that the Bay Area simply is and has always been progressive, even though it springs from the capitalist histories of the gold rush to the largest global corporations in Big Tech.

In contrast to a monolithic progressive march across time and space, however, we see a complicated mosaic of struggles, wins, and losses, a patchwork of places in which social movements have been both crushed and nurtured. Rather than only the power of a few capitalists in local history, we also want to understand power building from below. The region has undeniably attracted and fostered new waves of justice movements, but each wave has come from the work of people who were committed to a cause, in spite of—or because of—major challenges.

At the same time, viewing the region through a push-and-pull framework may help explain why racial and economic inequalities remain entrenched here, in spite of progressivism on issues like the environment and sexuality, and even on race and class. In fact, we argue in this book that big moments that shape the public sensibility about the Bay Area as politically radical also had roots in authoritarian state control or corporate power. The immigrants' rights movement, for example, has had a strong base in the Bay Area—both because of anti-immigrant crackdowns, and strong traditions of fighting back. Similarly, Berkeley's Free Speech Movement was not simply a product of UC Berkeley's progressiveness, but a direct outgrowth of the university's attempt to limit free speech on campus, by force if necessary. These relationships of oppression and resistance continue into the present, each producing new cultural dynamics embedded in place.

We have chosen the stories in this book to tease out the complexities and intersec-

PERSONAL REFLECTION FROM NTANYA LEE, LONGTIME ORGANIZER IN BLACK AND LATINX WORKING-CLASS COMMUNITIES, AND NATIONAL ORGANIZER FOR LEFTROOTS[2]

Reflecting on twenty years of organizing in the Bay Area, I was drawn here because of the history of progressive struggle and movement building. As a queer person of color and a leftist, I was drawn to the density of organizing here. Looking back, I now better understand the ways in which this environment was historically produced. If you learn the history of Left, working-class, people of color in particular, over many decades and generations throughout the twentieth century to the present, it becomes clear how this unique situation was actually produced—through struggle. This changes how you see the Bay Area. When people think about the "Bay Area bubble," they're often thinking more of the hippies of Berkeley than the communists in Chinatown, the Marxists in Oakland who started the Black Panther Party, or the feminists of color that created all kinds of local institutions in the 1980s. Understanding these stories gives us a window into what kinds of leadership and struggle are required for the transformation of the whole country. It shows us what makes the Bay Area both special and not so different from elsewhere.

tions between social movement and their geographies—people and their places—while also highlighting the reasons for the persistence of social movements. Thus, many of the landscapes we find significant are what you might think of as counter-spaces, those off-the-beaten-path or inconspicuous places where political and social movements took shape, created a home for people and communities, or openly rebelled against oppressions and the status quo. Counter-spaces tend to have less longevity than more "official" parts of the landscape, and some of these places are much changed or no longer visible. But we still find that visiting those spaces, and perhaps contemplating their partial or complete erasure in the context of the landscape that surrounds them, provides an important opportunity to consider how political, cultural, and economic legacies linger.

A Guide Book in the Age of Google

As you well know, you can google "San Francisco Bay Area" and in milliseconds receive images, maps, Wikipedia pages, tour guides, travel blogs, and restaurant recommendations—a near-infinite algorithmically generated and profit-motivated smorgasbord of information about this place. You may find something to eat or get the ferry schedule to Richmond, for example, but ultimately you won't know much about Richmond itself. There was a time not so long ago, though, before the Bay Area turned *google* into a verb, when accessing even a fraction of that kind of information required being in a place. This book contends that there is still today a much deeper knowledge of a place—not simply information—to be gained from traveling its streets and paths, and talking with the people who have made it.

The information found on the Internet can feel precise, but it's incomplete. For example, you can easily find the address for the Facebook campus (that's One Hacker Way). But a search algorithm won't likely tell you about how Facebook and other companies built their campuses without much regard to where employees would live or how they would get to work. Nor will it direct you to the corner of 24th and Mission Streets in San Francisco where in the 2010s, housing and transit organizers physically blocked private buses— bureaucratically known as tech shuttles but colloquially called "Google buses"—in acts of political street theater that drew international attention. These activists showed how high-tech-worker salaries were funneled into the hands of developers and landlords, who were in turn gutting rent-controlled housing, businesses, and community spaces to make way for affluent tenants, many of whom work down near Hacker Way.

The algorithm can offer you facts and reviews covering the neighborhoods that people are willing to risk jail to protect. But it can't show you what it feels like to hear infectious K-pop beats coming from a second-floor dance studio that was saved from eviction by community protests, while you eat lunch in a local taqueria where conversations still take place in Spanish. Perhaps the table to one side of you hosts what sounds like a venture-capital start-up meeting laced with plans of civic disruption, and the other side is brimming with conversations about a labor-rights action where community members stepped up to support their neighbors. These are the contradictions and polarities of today's

Bay Area toward which this book directs your attention.

A Book for Tourists and for Locals

The Bay Area is a major destination for domestic and international tourists, with some 16.5 million visitors annually (for an average of 45,200 each day) in San Francisco alone, according to the San Francisco Travel Association. People are drawn here for all kinds of reasons, from stories of Northern California's magical qualities—like giant trees and beautiful sunsets—to its famed epicurean offerings, from the promise of experiencing any number of social-cultural liberations, to striking it rich in a boom industry. In turn, the dozens of guidebooks to San Francisco and the Bay Area—documenting the mythos and spectacle of well-worn spots like Union Square, Fisherman's Wharf, and the wealth of restaurants that flourish in enclaves from Berkeley's gourmet corridors to wine country and beyond—are hardly homogenous. Because of the draw that the Bay Area has for alternative lifestyles, some guides emphasize the city's reputation as a home to "edgy" people or institutions. Other guides focus on specific communities, like LGBTQ San Francisco. Niche groups—like geologists, bird-watchers, or streetcar enthusiasts—are also well served. Few texts in the guidebook genre, however, tread deep into broad intersecting political-economic contexts. Rebecca Solnit's *Infinite City* atlas does this; it is not a guidebook, but is a dear cousin to our work.

The *People's Guide* series is interested in an ethically oriented public-geography approach to urbanism. Our curiosity about the connection between how people shape the landscape and are shaped by it themselves has taken the form of a guidebook because, in our experience, walking and moving through a place is critical to one's ability to understand it. This is a long tradition within our academic discipline of geography and is shared with community historians and those interested in participatory forms of urban design and planning. Many of the contributors to this book teach urban-field courses at universities in the region and elsewhere, implementing this philosophy as a core way to teach and learn. In fact, we are inspired by a variety of politically oriented walking tours of Bay Area cities that have been bringing a similar kind of bottom-up education to the broader public for some time, like Shaping San Francisco and others (see appendix B for more).

Finally, this is an academic effort, exhaustively researched and reviewed, but it is also a work that seeks to connect across communities. If you are visiting the region, we want to help you both enjoy *and* see beyond the beauty of the hills, the boats, the bay, and yes, the food. But this book is not for tourists only; we hope it may be a useful tool for students, researchers, activists, and organizers in the Bay Area. Whether you are one of the many new migrants or a longtime resident, we hope to help you better understand and engage with the geography and stories that surround you.

On Restaurants

The Bay Area birthed what is known as California cuisine, and the diversity of the region feeds a rich restaurant culture with foods from all around the world. We believe that an important entry into understanding a place comes through sampling its culinary offerings—subtleties of menus, unexpected combinations of flavors, and well-worn tables all reveal a great deal. So we encourage you to eat your way around the Bay Area, but we aren't recommending specific eateries for a couple of reasons. A longtime favorite may have been pushed out by rent increases, or some new amazing pop-up run by second-generation migrants may be the best thing in a neighborhood—you can only really know by being there.

Wandering and perusing menus (whether they're taped to a window or painted on the side of a truck) is almost always a good method, but asking around is the most surefire way to get the most interesting local recommendations (not always the best food, but usually the most educational about a place). Online recommendation sites certainly offer guidance, but their algorithms tend to highlight paying clients and middle-of-the-road tastes. We suggest finding the community newspapers and blogs to see what local reviewers are excited about. For a meal that explicitly supports the rights of food workers, check the Restaurant Opportunity Center United's diners guide at chapters.rocunited.org/diners-guide/.

On the "Sharing Economy" and Getting Around

In the 2000s, the rise of the so-called "sharing economy" has had a huge impact on mobility and everyday life in the Bay Area; we'd like to encourage travelers and locals to be mindful of their socioeconomic impact. Drivers use Uber, Lyft, and other ride-hailing companies for essential income, and some riders use these services for safe mobility, but it's also important to be aware of the impact they have on the city. For example, these companies have explicitly sought to replace public transportation and the more regulated taxi industry, while increasing traffic in cities and undercutting wages for drivers. Meanwhile, among the many Internet start-ups fostered in the Bay Area, Airbnb is high on any list of impact and global recognition. Unfortunately, the effect in its hometown—as well as in many other cities around the world—has contributed to an accelerated pace of neighborhood change, exacerbating the instability of urban life. With the option to use homes as hotels, for example, landlords initiated a wave of evictions across the region as they sought to clear the way for lucrative short-term rentals.

If you want to avoid the above modes of travel and shelter, you have some options. Public train and bus service are relatively accessible across the region and offer unique opportunities to meet other people or see the landscape from a different angle and pace than a private car. Admittedly, transit can get crowded at times, certain systems get delayed so you need extra time, and not every chance meeting is a good one. If you like to ride bicycles, rentals are easy to find, and a regional bike-share system (that is, bike rental by the hour) is now widely available and can be good for short jaunts around or between neighborhoods. There are also niche programs for certain communities, like the Homobiles ride-hailing car service for LGBTQ people and their allies.

Housing can be a trickier issue to handle ethically. If you have the funds for a hotel, we recommend searching through the Fair Hotel site fairhotel.com for a unionized hotel. If you choose Airbnb, it may be possible to sort out which rentals are rooms in an active household; this could suggest that it is a genuine short-term rental that isn't displacing tenants, rather than a whole apartment that has been removed from the rental market for the higher profits of hoteling. The latter is the larger political and social problem with the use of that and related services.

On Authorship

The majority of this book is written by Rachel Brahinsky, Alexander Tarr, or the two of us together. Our individual and collective work has no additional byline. We are honored to also include the contributions of a wonderful group of Bay Area geographers, researchers, and public historians. Their names are noted at the end of any site entry that they authored or contributed to, with the caveat that we have edited the whole book for consistency. They are also listed in the acknowledgments.

Reflections on Finishing *A People's Guide to the San Francisco Bay Area*

One of our aims as we worked on this book was to embrace what scholar Katherine McKittrick describes as "the geographical imperatives in the struggle for social justice."[3] That is, we wanted to look at the role of place and geography in understanding the bounds of justice and we wanted to better understand how communities have reshaped those boundaries over time. Literary legend Toni Morrison writes about this sort of work, through the metaphor of mapping. As she put it, "I want to draw a map, so to speak, of a critical geography and use that map to open as much space for discovery, intellectual adventure, and close exploration as did the original charting of the New World—without the mandate for conquest."[4] This approach has driven our research and work on the Bay Area *People's Guide*.

We wrote this book over the course of many years, and in that time so much of the world seemed to change. We began writing in the ambivalent afterglow of the Occupy movement, and we completed most of it during—and were influenced by—the dual arrival of the Black Lives Matter movement and the now-widespread antigentrification political work that has centered around evictions and housing. We completed the text amid the global rise of authoritarianism and the radical, white-supremacist Right. We saw the most dramatic impacts of climate change to date, such that the term *climate change* began to morph into *climate emergency* just as we set out to edit our final text. The movement of that crisis was so rapid that we expect there to be new words and new terrible milestones (deadliest fires, biggest floods, hottest summers, hottest winters) before this book makes it to your hands.

In that same period in California, we saw the birth and expansion of the app-fueled gig economy, which was just a small techno-dream when we began to write. By this book's end, Airbnb, Uber, Lyft, and the like had transformed communities around the globe, accelerating the visibility of the economic instability that was already on the rise. More generally, economic inequality fueled huge changes in the landscape, and many places and people that have formed our idea of the Bay Area have disappeared, pushed out by rising rents, demolitions, and a fraying social-safety net. As we finished writing, the horrors of US detention camps for migrant children grew in scale. Sometimes these events made it hard to focus on writing. We wondered: Does this book matter in the midst of so much inhumanity and crisis?

But as we worked on these essays, we continually rediscovered connections between the stories about the difficult past with our knowledge of the difficult present. And we were reminded that the relationships between oppression and activism are not chance meetings. As geographer and prison-abolitionist Ruth Wilson Gilmore writes, "We simultaneously make places, things, and selves, although not under conditions of our own choosing. . . . If agency is the human ability to craft opportunity from the wherewithal of everyday life, then agency and structure are products of each other. Without their mutual interaction, there would be no drama, no dynamic, no story to tell."[5]

Indeed, as we argue throughout this book, the Bay Area is a place with entrenched injustices—racism, economic violence, homophobia. This means that the work of understanding what has come before and how people have survived, fought back, reimagined, and dreamed is essential here, and beyond here. What this book shows is that, from San Jose to Oakland to Petaluma, people continue to seek and strategize for a better world. These people persist, they are creative, sometimes they are victorious. When they get tired, there must be others to step in and take the baton. We hope that this book can contribute a small part to sustaining communities engaged in these struggles, offering lessons about the enduring realities of oppression alongside true stories of the geographies of hope and activism that offer necessary inspiration.

As we closed out our work on *A People's Guide to the Bay Area* in the summer of 2019, we came back to the idea that investigations into the two-way relationship between people and place matter deeply for dreaming a new future. In his novel on Native American Oakland, Tommy Orange writes that this may be the very thing that saves communities in enduringly challenging times. He writes, for example, that the mid-twentieth-century government relocation of young Native Americans to cities was an attempt to eliminate Native culture. Instead, in the hands of his community, he observes that a forced migration was ultimately transformed as people forged new possibilities out of the ashes of the past. Even through dark times, as he puts it, "The city made us new, and we made it ours."[6]

Endnotes

1. We have learned so much from Richard Walker and Paul Groth, key analysts of Bay Area cultural and economic landscapes. We also follow in the footsteps of scholars of race, place, and power, particularly Katherine McKittrick, Laura Pulido, Ruth Wilson Gilmore, and Clyde Woods.

2. We often use the ending x for ethnic terms like *Latino/a* or *Filipino /a*, following new conventions by writers and activists seeking to develop nonbinary language around gender. The x suggests that the term is not solely male or female and that other gender expressions are included.

3. Katherine McKittrick, *Demonic Grounds: Black Women and the Cartographies of Struggle.* Minneapolis: University of Minnesota Press, 2006, p. xix.

4. Toni Morrison, *Playing in the Dark: Whiteness and the Literary Imagination.* Cambridge, MA: Harvard University Press, 1992, p. 3.

5. Ruth Wilson Gilmore, *Golden Gulag: Prisons, Surplus, Crisis, and Opposition in Globalizing California.* Berkeley: University of California Press, 2007, p. 27.

6. Tommy Orange, *There There.* New York: Alfred A. Knopf, 2018, p. 8.

The East Bay

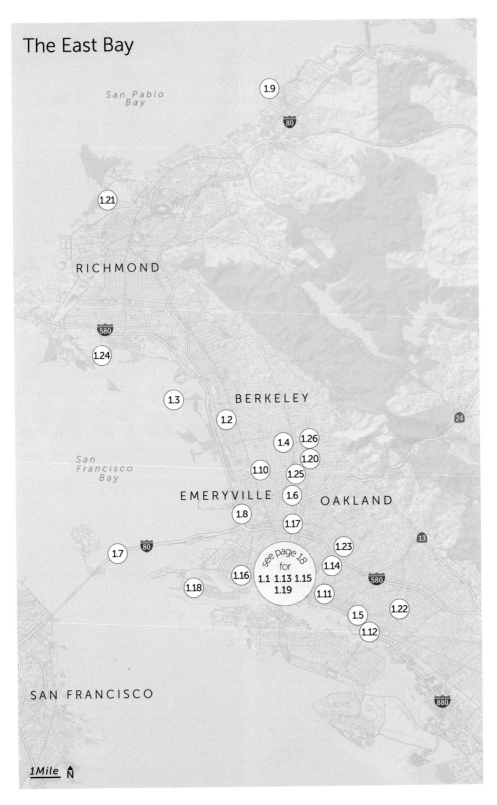

The East Bay

San Pablo
Bay

1.9

80

1.21

RICHMOND

580

1.24

1.3

BERKELEY

1.2

1.4   1.26

San
Francisco
Bay

1.10   1.25

1.20

EMERYVILLE

1.6

OAKLAND

1.8

1.17

24

1.7   80

1.23

1.14

580

13

1.16

see page 18
for
1.1 1.13 1.15
1.19

1.11

1.18

1.5

1.22

1.12

SAN FRANCISCO

880

1Mile N

Introduction

On a recent holiday weekend, Lake Merritt—the tidal-lagoon-turned-lake that serves as a central community park for the city of Oakland—sparkled in the East Bay light. On this sunny day with clear, blue skies, Oakland's social diversity was fully on display. There were picnics dotting the grassy lakeshore in all directions; people of varied ethnic and class backgrounds, gender expressions, and cultural affiliations filled the 3.4-mile circumference of the park. Languages from around the world dotted the soundscape. In the near distance the skyscrapers of downtown Oakland and the residential hills revealed a variety of architectural styles signaling multiple cycles of capital investment over the last century or so. This diversity represents the East Bay: The lived experience of interculturalism makes Oakland, and the East Bay more broadly, come to life.

Of course, this isn't the only experience of the East Bay. There are important differences evident in struggles over power and rights, often along race-class lines drawn from the legacies of segregation and inequality that pervade US cities. The geography of these divisions, in fact, is textbook: The flatlands have historically been the location of industrial development, alongside the houses of the working class and poor, and have been home to communities of color (the demographics differ across the city). Meanwhile, the hills have long been developed as wealthier residential-only spaces, and with a higher concentration of white people. This split was essentially established by the end of the nineteenth century, reinforced by restrictive housing covenants and redlining, and then later expanded by continued race-class segregation.

Across the region there are other divisions. The East Bay includes the college-town

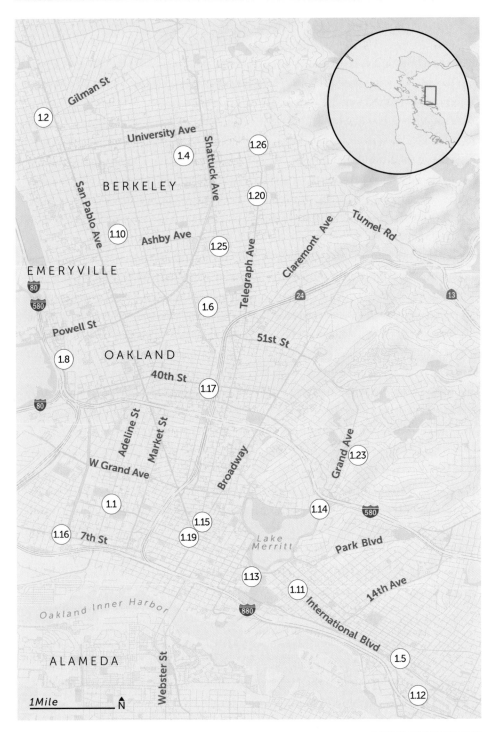

DETAIL FROM PAGE 16

urbanism of Berkeley, the historically industrial cities of Emeryville and Richmond, residential hills that cross several urban boundaries, as well as the suburban sprawl and crawl to the east of the hills, which reaches out through Walnut Creek and Livermore. In this chapter, we walk you through the places where these divisions have been cemented, and where they have been fought, with an eye to the ways that interconnected social and political movements shape people and place.

In the long saga of the Bay Area, the East Bay is often cast in a secondary role to the more famous San Francisco. Perhaps best known as the place where UC Berkeley thrives, the East Bay is home to decades of urban and industrial growth that brought the whole region to global prominence under the moniker "San Francisco." Though much writing on the region follows this line—that San Francisco is the central city of the larger region—we are interested in the ways that the East Bay is also, and has always been, central. At this book's writing the entire East Bay was experiencing intense and rapid change as Silicon Valley tech firms moved in, and as Oakland sought to fast-track housing development to serve the broader regional economic boom. Meanwhile, the East Bay is home to a broad spectrum of communities, who collectively speak some 125 languages and who have forged social movements that shape national and even international politics, from the Left to the Right.

A Shifting Center

We center many of the stories of this chapter in The Town, which is the affectionate local name for the city of Oakland, but we'll also take you out to Emeryville, for a quick stroll through Berkeley, and north to the cities of Albany and Richmond. In choosing sites for this chapter, we were interested in broad representation, but we also looked for places that are suggestive of some of the larger struggles of the area, from policing to racial justice, economic development and cycles of displacement. We're interested in the ways that today's built environment reveals layers of the past—including important traces of the long history of human habitation prior to the Spanish and Anglo conquests.

As the original terminus of the transcontinental railroad in the nineteenth century, Oakland could have emerged as the socioeconomic powerhouse of the region. Instead, urban developers logged Oakland's forests and capitalists built wealth around San Francisco's deep-water port first, leaving Oakland to persist as a "second city" culturally, politically, and economically—even as the two cities shared workers, families, and ecosystems. The 1906 San Francisco quake and fire, which destroyed San Francisco's downtown and nearby neighborhoods, could have shifted the regional urban core east to Oakland. But even though a large share of San Francisco's industry and residents left at that time to populate the East Bay—Oakland's Chinatown expanded, for example—and even though the educational powerhouse of UC Berkeley fostered generations of public intellectuals and planted the seeds of activist movements with global influence, San Francisco remained the capital city of the region.

Two of the key drivers of this ongoing dynamic are the wicked problems of race and class. Race-class exclusions drove post–World War II disinvestment, which meant that capitalist and middle-class wealth withdrew from Oakland. This flight-by-capital left the once-vibrant downtown relatively vacant for decades and weakened the urban tax base, even as urban-fringe neighborhoods boomed. By the 1960s, African Americans had made Oakland a central home, having been both displaced by San Francisco's redevelopment of the Fillmore District and excluded from East Bay suburbs. At the same time, Oakland leaders also pursued urban redevelopment, uprooting those same communities to make way for freeways and mega-developments. These projects improved regional mobility, but they left gaping wounds in the cityscape across Oakland's multiracial working-class communities, disproportionately hitting Black, and later Latinx, homes and businesses.

These urban rearrangements intersected with the social configurations of the time. Before WWII, white violence was, at its most extreme, embodied by the Ku Klux Klan's growth in Oakland and the island city of Alameda. After WWII it continued in the practices of the police and sheriff departments. The counterforce of groups like the Black Panther Party and the Brown Berets emerged in part as a response to those conditions—and more. Though pop culture narratives tend to remember them for posing with guns in front of Oakland City Hall, for example, the Panthers' "Ten Point Platform" included an emphasis on universal literacy and feeding people. It was a stance that emerged out of members' everyday experiences of poverty and over-policing in The Town. These politics also grew from members' intellectual investigations that crossed urban borders throughout the East Bay, with the public university and college systems playing a fundamental role in offering young people the chance to develop their ideas, and with intersecting social movements—including South Asian, Chicano, and labor movements—all learning from each other and in some cases joining together to demand better education at UC Berkeley and beyond. These earlier struggles set the stage for today's Oakland and greater East Bay, in which the collective lived experience of people, across ethnic and racial lines, includes the apparent paradox of deep poverty alongside the riches of successive booms. With each force comes a counterforce.

Community struggles over access to affordable and safe housing offer a lesson in the complexity of the East Bay and its place in the region. In the 2010s, for example, the cost of housing rose sharply, housing development didn't match job creation, and new proposals lacked sufficient affordable housing or enough protection for vulnerable residents in redeveloped neighborhoods. Oakland moved from the police blotter to the travel section of big city papers in the 2000s, and its reputation was reshaped by commercial boosters who encouraged a renaissance of new, young transplants to the area. But the housing crisis of the gentrification era was a problem with deeper historical roots. Outside of the urban cores, much (though not all) of the East Bay was first developed as a series of low-density urban-fringe neighborhoods, initiating a pattern of housing inequity that remains. Meanwhile, the capital that fled the Oakland core fifty years ago has returned quite unevenly.

Wealth's renewed interest in Oakland has meant that some areas are receiving much-needed upgrades to dilapidated housing and commercial building stock, as well as city services, but often in forms that push out longtime Oaklanders, sparking revivals of housing-centered social movements. In fact, community members' efforts to remain in their homes and neighborhoods are central to their role in making the East Bay. Indeed, the East Bay's legacy of political organizing and creativity is quite alive, and community organizations have pushed for a vision of "development without displacement," motivating a regional coalition to push for expansions of state and local rent protections, widening the geography of protest and struggle. These efforts intersect with energized local campaigns in many Bay Area cities, including the relatively small city of Richmond to the north. There, a long-growing progressive coalition turned ideals into pragmatic policy. Aiming to curb the toxic impact of local refineries, Richmond residents organized to raise the local minimum wage, bought back guns to remove them from the streets, and threatened the use of eminent domain (which is the city's power to retake private property) as a way to help stop foreclosure-related displacement.

The stories of housing struggles thus link to the larger challenges of urban life and the balancing act between encouraging needed investment and supporting existing communities. With that in mind, this chapter raises issues and tells stories that are rooted in place, but tries to do so in a way that treads lightly on the very same landscapes that we find so interesting; we are aware of the mixed blessings of tourist attentions.

There are many other stories and paths that we trace in this chapter, stories of culture and art, innovations in everyday life, and long-buried histories that come to light. For us it adds up to this: it's time to see and listen to the East Bay. Listen to the stories of the people who have built and fostered its many cultures and communities, giving these cities their character and sense of place. Dig deeper to understand the geographies that make and continue to remake these places from the ground up.

■ ■ ■

1.1 1500 Block of Adeline Street

Adeline Street Between 14th and 15th Streets, Oakland 94607

The fallout from the foreclosure crisis of the 2000s is written in the streets of Oakland.

Residents of the 1500 block of Adeline Street successfully fought to save their homes from bank foreclosure.

Much of that story is a painful one of displacement, but there are some important legacies of community organizing and resistance, and this block of West Oakland represents one epicenter for organizing where some residents used mass community pressure to save their homes. On December 6, 2011, for example, Adeline Street resident Gayla Newsome decided to put the rallying cry of a nationwide "Occupy Our Homes Day" into action. Together with a group of about a hundred activists from Occupy Oakland and ACCE (Alliance of Californians for Community Empowerment), Newsome and her three daughters successfully reclaimed their home of fifteen years, which was under active foreclosure. The family lived on this block, at the heart of one of the long-

Black Panther Party members renamed DeFremery Park "Li'l Bobby Hutton Park," after BPP treasurer Robert James Hutton, who was killed by police in this neighborhood at the age of seventeen.

contested residential spaces of West Oakland, where waves of eviction and foreclosure compounded upon decades of disinvestment. We're not including her exact address here to maintain residential privacy.

Between 2005 and 2015, banks foreclosed on well over twenty thousand homes across Oakland, according to research by the Anti-Eviction Mapping Project (AEMP). The mass evictions of small property owners and renters that ensued were largely the result of predatory lending practices actively targeting low-income communities of color, as was later widely uncovered by researchers across the country. A report conducted by the nonprofit Urban Strategies Council in 2011 found that 42 percent of homes foreclosed in Oakland between 2007 and 2011 were acquired by large institutional investors, many of whom are based outside of Oakland. Some of them had previously been mortgage brokers, meaning they not only had access to valuable insider knowledge, but might have also played a part in creating the crisis in the first place. Others would later be prosecuted by the FBI for conspiring to rig foreclosure auctions in their own favor.

West Oakland saw a thick concentration of foreclosures and large-investor accumulation. Neill Sullivan's REO Homes LLC, for example, snapped up over one hundred foreclosed homes in West Oakland alone. Sullivan focused on single-family homes, which are exempt from rent control by California state law; he followed those acquisitions with a round of evictions, serving 357 eviction notices between 2010 and 2016, according to public Rent Board data collected by AEMP researchers. The evictions helped clear the way for a neighborhood rebranding as West Oakland was sold as the "eclectic West Side" and the "new edge of Silicon Valley."

Even as investors like Sullivan were taking control of the neighborhood, activists turned their energy toward the foreclosures and joined in to support Newsome and other neighborhood leaders. They formed the Foreclosure Defense Group, which sought to disrupt foreclosure auctions at the Alameda County Courthouse. The group worked to reclaim the homes of community members through direct action by reoccupying emptied homes; they would initiate a campaign of community pressure, garnering media attention and rallying a mass phone campaign to pressure the banks. Newsome's home on Adeline Street was one of the success stories of this tactic. Organizers also used the foreclosure activism as a base-building effort, which meant that each home they reoccupied was an opportunity to knock on doors and talk to neighbors. Through this process they sought to develop stronger networks for community solidarity and support. (Katja Schwaller)

NEARBY SITES OF INTEREST

DeFremery Park
1651 Adeline Street, 94607
The Black Panther Party gathered here for rallies, training, and celebrations over several decades. The park today hosts important annual festivals, like "Life is Living," which links politics and culture.

Murals throughout the neighborhood
Murals like the one at Martin Luther King Jr. Elementary School (960 10th Street) testify to the long tradition of community resistance and the continuing struggle for development without displacement.

TO LEARN MORE

Anti-Eviction Mapping Project. *Counterpoints: Stories and Data for Resisting Displacement*, 2016. http://www.antievictionmappingproject.net/ALAMEDA-Report.pdf

Arnold, Eric K. "Foreclosure Crisis Meets Occupy Effect," *Race, Poverty and the Environment* 19, no. 1 (2012): 67–70.

Causa Justa, Just Cause. "Development without Displacement: Resisting Gentrification in the Bay Area," 2014.

King, Steve. *Who Owns Your Neighborhood? The Roles of Investors in Post-Foreclosure Oakland*. Oakland, CA: Urban Strategies Council, 2012.

Strike Debt. *The Debt Resisters' Operations Manual*. Oakland, CA: PM Press, 2014.

Posted: No alcohol . . . No racism. The 924 Gilman rules announce a radically inclusive safe space for overlapping subcultures.

1.2 924 Gilman

924 Gilman Street, Berkeley 94710

Having survived two decades of wealth flooding the Bay Area, 924 Gilman is a unique, radical subcultural space. It would be easy to miss the place during the day, tucked under the sign of the long-standing Caning Shop that owns the building. There is no marquee, only the occasional graffiti-covered recycling bin out front, to hint at the presence here of a multidecade center of music, culture, and politics organized around the anti-establishment culture of punk music. Known both as the heart of a fiercely independent local music scene and a global source of major trends in popular music, 924 Gilman communicates its central philosophy on a sign just inside the door (see photo, this page).

These rules, slightly expanded since Gilman first opened in 1986, keep the venue safe for people of any age and persuasion—a rarity among music venues normally run on alcohol-driven profits and, frequently, unsafe sexual politics. For several generations, Gilman has acted as much as a community center and gathering place for young people who do not fit into mainstream social norms—as well as for older folks and seemingly straitlaced people—as it has as a hearth for punk music.

Not listed in the rules, but equally enforced, is a long-standing policy that prohibits bands on major record labels from playing in the venue. As corporate media companies monetized most subgenres of popular music in the 1990s and 2000s, Gilman continued to provide a space for radical, loud, and often political music, for people making zines and art in the face of mass-media-dominated culture, and for an active do-it-yourself culture that permeated the region. Many of the bands playing Gilman put together their own labels or connected to independent labels through the scene there. The Gilman membership committee famously banned mega-successful group Green Day, which had emerged from the 1980s Gilman milieu, after Green Day signed with a major label in 1993. One brief exception was made in 2015, when the band returned to perform in a fundraiser for local anarchist publisher AK Press and printer 1984 Printing after their shared warehouse burned.

Part of what makes Gilman unique, in contrast to both large formal rock venues and informal, temporary "punk houses," is its permanent structure as a not-for-profit and volunteer-run space. Under the auspices of the Alternative Music Foundation, Gilman members run all dimensions of the venue via open, biweekly membership meetings. Organizers chose the location on Gilman Street as an accessible but out-of-the-way and affordable spot in what used to be a semi-abandoned part of industrial west Berkeley—a great place for young punks to hang out without being hassled. In the intervening decades, the

PERSONAL REFLECTION FROM IVY JEANNE, BAY AREA ARTIST AND PUNK SINGER (INTERVIEWED BY JOHN STEHLIN)

As a teenager, I was a Gilman rat. I was at Gilman almost every weekend for a couple years. There were so many amazing and unforgettable shows and gatherings to make new friends and find community. Seeing Blatz, Tribe 8, and Bikini Kill on the same bill singing about radical feminism and queerness when I was fifteen changed my life. I saw that it was possible for me to make music about my life as a teenage runaway trying to create new worlds. In the summer of '93, I squatted across the street from Gilman with my old punk band Los Canadians in a massive abandoned warehouse that was formerly a lift-and-pulley machining shop. We just walked around back and the door was open. It really speaks to the area, which was a desolate and forgotten industrial zone. I think that's why Gilman was able to really plant roots and stay open. Gilman booked shows Thursday through Sunday, and I would find the runaways, the weirdos, the travelers, and invite them to stay across the street, saying, "Hey, you've got a place."

venue has been surrounded by high-rent development. Members of the Gilman collective have organized to keep their rent affordable and have drawn on extended networks to raise funds to keep the doors open, all while maintaining the nonprofit, volunteer-run organization dedicated to affordable shows (tickets are usually less than $8) and youth space.

The impact of the place over many years goes beyond youth culture; generations have now come up through Gilman: Some are now progressive elected officials, others are professors, many are still musicians and DJs, others bring their own teenage children to events, and some who have moved far away still donate to keep the space open. Shows continue every Friday, Saturday, and Sunday; the $2 membership is required for attendance.

TO LEARN MORE

Edge, Brian. *924 Gilman: The Story So Far.* Berkeley, CA: Maximum Rocknroll, 2004.

Gonzales, Michelle Cruz, Martín Sorrondeguy, and Mimi Thi Nguyen. *The Spitboy Rule: Tales of a Xicana in a Female Punk Band.* Oakland, CA: PM Press, 2016.

Turn It Around: The Story of East Bay Punk. Directed by Corbett Redford. New York: Abramorama, 2017.

RELATED SITE OF INTEREST

KPFA Radio Station
1929 MLK Jr. Way, Berkeley 94704
Alternative music, and nearly every other subculture that has come through the East Bay, have at one point or another been featured on this homegrown radio station—the very first noncommercial, listener-supported station in the country. The hosts and guests are often at the leading edge of Left political and cultural movements, and the station has helped nurture careers of hundreds of beloved cultural forces, including (among so many) the comic Richard Pryor and science-fiction writer Philip K. Dick, both onetime Berkeley residents.

1.3 Albany Bulb

1 Buchanan Street, Albany, CA 94706

The Albany Bulb is a place literally made from the ruins of Bay Area urbanization. This former landfill turned quasi-public park represents the alternative lives that capitalist cities inevitably produce through redevelopment and continual creation of consumer detritus. At the same time, the Albany Bulb is a phenomenally beautiful place to visit and offers a fascinating story about a Bay Area place that remains a bit less regulated and controlled than just about everywhere else.

Views from every corner of this park provide a panorama of the region. San Francisco looms misty and dreamlike across the bay. The trails teem with a wild mix of grasses, flowers, overgrown fennel—and art. Freestanding murals once dotted the edge of the marshy shoreline, and a mix of large sculpture and other installations, all of which can change year to year, is typically scattered throughout the park. The space has also often been home to people—disaffected, houseless, seeking connection that they couldn't find in the urbanized parts of the region—those who, long before the Occupy movement, found ways to reclaim and reuse public spaces.

For many years the city of Albany used this site to dump construction debris and municipal waste. The result was a thirty-one-acre lollipop-shaped peninsula colloquially known as the Bulb, with a landscape of twisted metal, slag left over from nearby mining, rusty pipes, and chunks of redeveloped streets, sometimes retaining their yel-

This is one of many works of art made from found and scrap materials at the Albany Bulb. Berkeley attorney Osha Neumann, who is known for representing houseless people, created this one, called *The Beseeching Woman* (foreground, photographed 2019).

low lane-stripes. The landfill that produced the Bulb was one of several major sites along the East Bay waterfront that inspired the creation of the environmental nonprofit Save the Bay, which targeted the Bulb's landfill for closure in the early 1980s. The closing of the landfill in 1983 both created an opportunity for artists and coincided with the modern period of rising homelessness, so it is no surprise that people without homes adopted its knolls and tucks as their own. In between the chaotic beauty of wildflowers and trash-turned-art, people built outdoor kitchens, small homes from driftwood, and other shelter.

A move to incorporate the Bulb into the larger McLaughlin Eastshore State Park—named for Save the Bay cofounder Sylvia McLaughlin—has been underway since the early 2000s. This shift toward park formalization has raised the challenging question of which public has the right to use the space as they want. Those who found shelter here note that they improved the land, having built many of the long-used trails and gardens. City and state officials argue they must enforce regulations against overnight camping and off-leash dogs. Artists and hikers often enjoy the place for its unregulated surprises. The struggle has inspired feisty artistic responses to the exercise of state power. In 1999, for example, the landfill's residents faced a highly publicized eviction. After the eviction, artists erected a monument to the homeless: a massive pile of shopping carts that was later mined for

PERSONAL REFLECTION BY SUSAN MOFFAT, PROJECT DIRECTOR, UC BERKELEY GLOBAL URBAN HUMANITIES INITIATIVE, AND FOUNDER OF LOVE THE BULB

The Bulb kind of holds up a mirror to the urbanization that has happened around the bay. Everything that got torn up in order to make room for change in the urban fabric got dumped out here. It's where the waste created in the process of development is made visible. When we build something new, we forget about the old stuff that has to go away. But the chunks of highway and bathroom tile and pieces of rebar sticking out here remind us that there is no "away." So it's kind of urbanization in your face. It's naked in a way that capped landfill can't ever be. But it's embroidered with all of these flowers and trees and art and layers of human habitation and memories.

sculptural work across the park. However, in 2014 the most definitive of the many rounds of eviction took place, with the city paying people to leave with the signed promise of never returning.

Creative resistance to formalize the landscape into a planned conservation district has been taken up by the nonprofit Love the Bulb, which organizes art and cultural programming and walking tours that emphasize the unregulated nature of the place. Free-range artists continue to make and remake the place. Enter from the parking lot at the end of Buchanan, near the Golden Gate Fields racetrack; bring extra layers, as it's typically colder out on the Bulb than in the parking lot.

NEARBY SITE OF INTEREST

San Francisco Bay Trail

The trail spanned more than 350 miles in 2019 and was planned to expand to 500, making a pedestrian- and bike-friendly ring around the entire bay that will touch nine counties. Already, the trail passes through many formerly and still-industrial landscapes at the water's edge. See www.baytrail.org.

TO LEARN MORE

Moffat, Susan. "The Battle of the Bulb: Nature, Culture and Art at a San Francisco Bay Landfill," *Boom: A Journal of California* 6, 3 (2016): 68–79.

1.4 Berkeley High School

1980 Allston Way, Berkeley 94704

Infuriatingly, many US schools are more segregated now than any time since the end of the Jim Crow era, a fact that undermines the narrative of civil rights progress that many hold dear. That's part of what makes the Berkeley High School story unique. Back in 1994, the *New York Times* labeled Berkeley High the "most integrated school in America." The school reflected the city's diverse population, making the institution fertile ground for political and cultural debate and home to the country's first and longest-running high school African American studies department. But all of this did not come easily—even in Berkeley. It was hard fought, and keeping programs like this alive continues to be a conscious struggle in a rapidly changing Bay Area.

In the heat of the civil rights struggle, Berkeley Unified School District launched a 1968 desegregation campaign titled Integration '68 and became one of the first districts

Joshua Redman is one of several alumni featured on the art boxes that surround Berkeley High, which has a history of student and teacher activism.

in the country to voluntarily integrate its elementary and middle schools by busing children of color from neighborhoods in the south and west areas of the city to schools in the overwhelmingly white north and east. The impact of the busing tactic here, as across the country, was mixed, and it was hard for parents to remain involved or feel that their kids were learning in culturally appropriate ways. Although the busing program was not aimed directly at Berkeley High, the new racial landscape profoundly impacted education there. That same year, educators inspired both by the national call for Afrocentric education (see Nairobi School System, p. 104), and by the intersecting struggles of the Free Speech and Ethnic Studies movements underway at the college level, founded African American studies at Berkeley High. The school was already racially integrated, but it lacked an inclusive curriculum, and educators sought to give Berkeley's students a sense of racial equity that busing could not address. This was part of a wave

of new Black studies and African American economics curricula at Bay Area institutions, from grade schools to universities.

At its height, Berkeley High's program offered courses in African American literature and history, the Black Social Experience (later to be called Black Male-Female Relations), Black Psychology, African American Economics, and African-Haitian Dance. Students took Kiswahili language courses, and enrolled in a youth empowerment class called Black Soul, Black Gold, Black Dynamite. The program produced its own newspaper, *Ujama*. Inspired by this legacy, in the early 1990s students successfully pushed to expand this programming to include Chicano and Asian American studies courses. Implementation of this programming, however, has always been contested by more conservative residents and administrators, in what the Reverend Robert McKnight, former teacher and chair of African American studies, has described as a "perpetual struggle" to maintain the programming.

The social and racial justice activism of the student body has remained a cornerstone of the school's identity. In 2000, a group of immigrant students—primarily South Asian girls—formed a group called Cultural Unity to reflect the diversity of the English Language Learner student body and to highlight their relative isolation within it. In the months after 9/11, harassment of Muslim and Sikh students increased, with two documented on-campus assaults on Cultural Unity members. In response, South Asian students wrote and published a short book of stories and poetry for use in the school's curriculum. They also organized free legal clinics for the local Muslim community and organized "Unity Assemblies" that emphasized cultural performance and cross-cultural political dialogue. The legacy of diversity and struggle at Berkeley High is commemorated in visible ways. One can begin by visiting the utility boxes along the perimeter of the high school, illustrated by the Arts and Humanities Academy Class of 2012, which depict some of the school's famed activist alumni, including Black Panther Bobby Seale, writers Ursula K. Le Guin and Chinaka Hodge, as well as musicians Phil Lesh and Joshua Redman. (Diana Negrín da Silva)

NEARBY SITES OF INTEREST

Martin Luther King Jr. Civic Center Park
Allston Way at Martin Luther King Jr. Way, Berkeley 94704
Also called Provo Park in honor of the Dutch counterculture movement and Ho Chi Minh Park during the Vietnam War era, this park has been at the center of many of Berkeley's historic protests.

Ohlone Murals and Park
Milvia Street and Hearst Avenue, Berkeley 94704
Murals painted by Indigenous artist and activist Jean LaMarr in 1995 adorn a BART vent building at the east end of the park. This is the beginning of the four-and-a-half-mile Ohlone Greenway, which traces old railroad rights-of-way to Richmond.

Berkeley Post Office
2000 Allston Way, Berkeley 94704
A threat to New Deal–era murals here has inspired a feisty local struggle to save this post office in the face of federal disinvestment.

TO LEARN MORE

Andrews, Scott, director. *School Colors*. Alexandria, VA: PBS and the Center for Investigative Reporting, Inc., 1994. (Documentary film)
Noguera, Pedro, and Jean Yonemura Wing. *Unfinished Business: Closing the Racial Achievement Gap in Our Schools*. San Francisco: Jossey-Bass, 2006.

1.5 Black Cultural Zone

2277 International Boulevard, Oakland 94606
In the mid-2010s, the artists and activists connected to the nonprofit East Side Arts Alliance began work on establishing Black Cultural Zones (BCZ), conceived as a series of "safe Black spaces" at points served by new transit lines along International Boulevard, as well as the MacArthur and Bancroft neighborhoods. This effort was a response to the ongoing outmigration of Black people from Oakland. The International Boulevard corridor is the commercial and cultural heart of the racially and ethnically hetero-

geneous neighborhoods of East Oakland, stretching from Lake Merritt to the southern border of Oakland (the street continues, under other names, through several cities). More broadly, East Oakland, often overshadowed by the dynamics of downtown and West Oakland, has become known for creative approaches to urban change, including a much-lauded program of transit-oriented development that specifically guarded against displacement around the Fruitvale BART station. The Black Cultural Zone is another such effort, an example of proactive grassroots planning to prevent further displacement of residents and what are now commonly known as "legacy businesses."

The effort grew out of cultural work that dates back to 2000, when four arts organizations in this area organized the first Malcolm X Jazz Arts Festival, an annual May event in San Antonio Park (1701 E. 19th Street), featuring local and visiting musicians alongside graffiti battles, dance performances, and booths representing local crafts and community organizations. The East Side Arts Alliance (ESAA, 2277 International Blvd.) was born from that first festival, positioning itself as a voice in local politics, advocating for "development without displacement" in city government meetings, and securing properties in East Oakland through nonprofit and grassroots partnerships. The organization bought its own building, offering a counterpoint to gentrification in the area by incorporating affordable housing into its art-and-politics organizational structure. When the city developed a new bus rapid transit route along International Boulevard, ESAA secured foundation grants and city support to help align the transit corridor with the values and experiences of longtime residents. Building on these efforts, the Black Cultural Zone project envisions a shift in Oakland's land use that highlights the economic and cultural resources of longtime residents as a platform for equitable development. Working with neighborhood partners, the BCZ will be integrated into new public plazas that will partner with existing businesses, nonprofits, and religious institutions as well as new mixed-use developments with below-market housing. At this writing, the large historic building that once served as the headquarters for Safeway, at the intersection of International Boulevard and 57th Avenue, had been proposed as the BCZ's geographic hub. (Diana Negrín da Silva)

NEARBY SITES OF INTEREST

San Antonio Park
1701 E. 19th Street, Oakland 94606
Since the early 1970s, every last weekend of August has been commemorated as Xicana Moratorium Day, although the celebration has not always been held here. This park is a symbol of preconquest California for many locals.

Estuary Park
115 Embarcadero, Oakland 94607
Situated at the point where Lake Merritt meets the bay, this park offers unique views of the estuary. It was also the site of the first (soon to be annual) daylong Bay Area festival "Hip-Hop on the Green" in 1993. In an era when music venues, the police, and many radio stations were actively stifling live hip-hop shows, this annual

event throughout the '90s was a unique opportunity for the rising stars of the Bay Area scene to perform to larger audiences. Nearly thirty artists performed at the first event, including Vallejo's E-40 and the politically radical hip-hop group the Coup (with Boots Riley as lead vocalist and chief lyricist).

See Eric Arnold's *Hip-Hop Atlas of the Bay* (Oakland Museum of California, 2018) for forty sites important to rap, hip-hop, and related music forms.

1.6 "Black Panther Park" (Dover Park)

Dover Street, between 57th and 58th Streets, Oakland 94609

Tucked behind the former Merritt College site on Martin Luther King Jr. Way, this is one of many places associated with the creation of the Black Panther Party (BPP) in 1966. BPP founders Bobby Seale and Huey Newton lived and studied together in this neighborhood before forging, with many others, the vision for Black liberation codified in the party's Ten Point Program. Their political message, a response to the conditions of this neighborhood and others like it at the time, spoke of transforming power relations with the police, uplifting Black people, and providing for the basic needs of everyday Oaklanders.

Serving as a framework for the party as it expanded from its Oakland roots, the program articulated a set of baseline beliefs that shaped the politics of the organization while inspiring others around the world. "We want freedom. We want power to determine the destiny of our Black Community," they wrote. "We want land, bread, housing, education, clothing, justice and peace." Under

this banner, they created free breakfast programs for kids, and international solidarity with other working-class people, across racial lines. The community college where they polished these ideas, and where they anchored some of their early community-organizing efforts, was relocated in 1960; the building on that site is now a senior center.

By the fiftieth anniversary of the BPP's founding in 2016, things had changed significantly in the Bushrod, which is one of a few names for the neighborhood surrounding Dover Park. By then the real estate website Redfin had labeled it the hottest neighborhood for housing sales in the country. This shift in the neighborhood's fortunes came not long after officials created a gang-injunction zone in the area, which Restorative Justice (RJ) activists used to show the connections between policing and real estate speculation. They showed, for example, that the decreased visibility of young men of color on local streets and the increased police presence (both of which were produced by the gang injunction) fed into the intensified marketing of the neighborhood as "safe" to new home buyers.

Traces of the political history of the area remain in the landscape, and Dover Park continues to maintain and reinvigorate the message of Black Panther activism. Since 2010, Dover Park has served as host to the Phat Beets food justice collective, which merges urban agriculture with social justice organizing, maintaining an edible public garden here. The garden circles the park with fruit trees, vegetables, herbs, and native

Through these gates, Dover Park's edible perimeter is lush with fruit trees, a bee sanctuary, and a vegetable garden maintained by the organization Phat Beets.

plants, labeled to serve as tools of beautification, education, and public engagement. The food grown here has at times gone to support Aunti Frances's Love Mission Self Help Hunger Program, a local group that cooks free meals in nearby Driver Plaza at the intersection of Adeline, Stanford, and 61st Streets. Aunti Frances's program is one of many organizations around Oakland that was explicitly inspired by the BPP's call for self-help on a community scale. Frances has said that she learned the value of community care and organizing as a child, when she personally benefited from the BPP's free breakfast programs.

NEARBY SITES OF INTEREST

It's All Good Bakery
5622 Martin Luther King Jr. Way, Oakland 94609
This building once served the BPP's newspaper operation. Check out the vibrant poster display of art and newspaper clippings in the lobby.

"Black Panther Stoplight"
55th and Market Streets, Oakland 94609
Former members of the BPP and students at the California College of the Arts marked this corner with a sign that commemorates the impact of the Panthers on everyday urban basics. In this case, the BPP used direct-action political tactics to persuade the city to install a traffic light at a dangerous intersection that their children needed to cross on the way to school.

TO LEARN MORE

Cadji, Josh, and Alison Hope Alkon. "'One Day, the White People Are Going to Want These Houses Again': Understanding Gentrification through the North Oakland Farmers Market." In *Incomplete Streets: Processes, Practices, and Possibilities,* edited by Stephen Zavestoski and Julian Agyeman, 154–75. London and New York: Routledge, 2014.

Murch, Donna Jean. *Living for the City: Migration, Education, and the Rise of the Black Panther Party in Oakland, California.* Chapel Hill: University of North Carolina Press, 2010.

Melissa Crosby, Zachary Norris, and Tiara Jackson on the Bay Bridge demonstrating with Black.Seed in a 2016 action that blocked westbound car traffic. (Brooke Anderson photo)

1.7 Black.Seed Demonstration, one expression of #BlackLives Matter

San Francisco Bay Bridge, just east of Yerba Buena Island

210 Burma Road, Oakland 94607

(This is the parking lot with closest access to the bike/walk trail on the bridge.)

On Martin Luther King Jr. Day in 2016, westbound traffic on the San Francisco–Oakland Bay Bridge came to a halt. Activists—chained together to block the road—raised their fists and displayed a banner declaring "Black Health Matters." To see this site, you should not stop in a vehicle on the car lanes of the Bay Bridge. But you can get close to it via the bike and pedestrian path that runs from Oakland's industrial waterfront

along the bridge to Yerba Buena Island. You may want to bike, bus, or drive all the way onto the island, where you can look back at the eastern span of the bridge from Forest Road. From there you can get a sense of the impact that a takeover of the bridge would have, with all six westbound lanes blocked in the middle of the afternoon.

The 2016 demonstration was led largely by gender-queer African American activists and their allies affiliated with Black.Seed, one of many groups that formed in the first few years of the Black Lives Matter movement. The group coordinated their entry to the bridge through the East Bay car tollgates. Once they stopped, they chained their bodies to each other through the cars to create a true barrier across every lane. Posing with their sign about Black health, they sought media attention to shift the public dialogue.

The name of the larger struggle—Black Lives Matter—was born from a social media post coauthored by Bay Area activist Alicia Garza, who cofounded that movement in 2013 in the wake of the acquittal of the killer of young Trayvon Martin in Florida. Soon after, transit and transportation disruptions across the nation sought to draw public attention to the problems of overpolicing, mass incarceration, police killings, and health disparities in the Black community. Drawing from the civil rights playbook, activists employed the strategy of reaching the public as they engaged in everyday activities; with their urgent message about the value of African American life, activists blocked highways from Minnesota to Dallas. In Oakland a shutdown of the West Oakland BART station in 2014 stymied trans-bay trains for four and a half hours to remind the public of the police killing of Michael Brown in Ferguson, Missouri, after which police left Brown's corpse on the street for more than four hours. Others took speeches and poetry on Sundays to restaurants around the bay in predominantly white neighborhoods as part of a "Black Brunch" action.

The Black.Seed bridge takeover brought together many of these concerns. The group issued a set of demands, including "the immediate divestment of city funds for policing and investment in sustainable, affordable housing so Black, Brown and Indigenous people can remain in their hometowns of Oakland and San Francisco." They also called for the firing of officers involved in police killings locally—including that of Mario Woods, Richard Perkins, Yuvette Henderson, Amilcar Lopez, Alex Nieto, Demouriah Hogg, Richard Linyard, and O'Shaine Evans—and for the resignation of mayors and police chiefs who failed to hold officers accountable for shooting residents. They weren't the only ones calling for this, and San Francisco's police chief resigned under pressure a few months later.

While you're here, we'll note that the views on this four-and-a-half-mile bridge are incredible, but they come at significant financial and social cost. The state rebuilt the eastern span of the bridge in the 2010s to replace a 1936 structure that had been a source of concern since its dramatic partial collapse during the 1989 Loma Prieta earthquake. Completed in 2015, the eastern span went far over budget, costing $6.5 billion to date. The new span has its own structural problems, however, and more spending has been required for repairs and adjustments to ensure the stability of the span when we face the next big earthquake.

NEARBY SITE OF INTEREST

Treasure Island

This artificial island has served as the site of a world's fair, a naval base, a site for transitional and affordable housing, a site for a popular music festival, and an interim-use artists' zone. There are plans for mega-development here, but developers will have to grapple with building on ground that could liquefy in an earthquake, which is still toxic from the legacy of military use, and which is deeply vulnerable to sea-level rise.

TO LEARN MORE

Anti-Police Terror Project, www.antipolice
terrorproject.org

Nondabula, Nolizwe. "'We Are the Ones We've
Been Waiting For': Exploring the Rise of Black
Feminism in Black Liberation Movements."
Master's thesis, Urban Affairs, University of San
Francisco, 2017.

1.8 Emeryville Shellmound Memorial

4597 Shellmound Street, Emeryville 94608

If you head to the Bay Street Mall on the day after Thanksgiving—known widely as Black Friday and as the start of the Christmas shopping season—you may find Native people and their allies gathering here at the Emeryville Shellmound Memorial. They'll be encouraging shoppers to take their money to other places, where businesses are not built on the bones of Ohlone ancestors. They don't mean this metaphorically, but quite literally: this mall was developed on top of an Ohlone shellmound, one of the ritual burial sites that once thickly dotted the East Bay landscape.

Shellmound refers to ceremonial burial grounds made of layers of shells, human remains, and other materials. Non-Native settlers, if they acknowledged the shellmounds at all, have largely viewed them as archaeological novelties, rather than recognizing that they are sites of spiritual or religious importance. Some 425 such burial sites were documented in the region in 1909, but nearly all have been bulldozed or buried in a century of urban development. The region's largest once stood about sixty feet high, right here at the mouth of Temescal Creek. It was excavated in sections over the years, first covered by an amusement park and then a factory. In the 1990s the local redevelopment agency repurposed the area to build the Bay Street Mall. As the mall's construction moved forward, community members demanded that the city of Emeryville engage in careful preservation and recognition of the shellmound site and its remains.

Emeryville's leaders voted against shellmound preservation, however, and instead agreed to develop this memorial, in recognition of the approximate location of the shellmound. Native people widely view it as a site of desecration. Even though the memorial's presence means that the Ohlone's long presence is recognized here, the memorial suggests that their experience is largely historical—perhaps an ancient story that cannot be retraced. This erases the contemporary Ohlone presence and their request to respect ancestors buried there. So, although some form of memorial is probably better than none, it remains part of the pattern of ignoring the contemporary presence of Native people.

There has been another important contemporary shellmound struggle underway a few miles north in Berkeley, where a proposed development in the Fourth Street shopping district has long threatened to unearth burial grounds and other remains. Early phases of construction at 1900 Fourth Street disturbed human remains, giving force to a campaign to pressure the Berkeley Planning Commission to protect the site—which was already designated as a historic landmark.

This controversial representation of an Ohlone shellmound (sacred burial site) is tucked into a corner of the Bay Street Mall.

Ohlone communities and their allies developed this mandala to represent the ongoing struggle to save the historical site that is buried by this parking lot at the West Berkeley Shellmound site. (Scott Braley photo)

These campaigns to acknowledge, preserve, and access shellmounds are connected to the ongoing struggle for tribal recognition from the US government and to the essential element that recognition can bring: access to land and resources. Forging another path toward resources, the group Indian People Organizing for Change has worked to develop a different legal tool for access and control of land. Using the name Sogorea Te', after a sacred place in nearby Vallejo that was paved for parking in 2011, they have been developing a nonprofit community land trust. The land trust is a land-management tool through which organizations acquire property and place it in a democratically controlled trust, removing it from the real estate market. Sogorea Te' members had not yet acquired property at this writing, but they were working to establish housing and ceremonial space while also working to bring the languages, songs, and food of their people back into the contemporary urban vernacular.

RELATED SITE OF INTEREST

West Berkeley Shellmound and Village Site
1900 Fourth Street, Berkeley

Believed to be the first location of human settlement on the bay, some five thousand years ago, a shellmound and village have been largely obliterated by urban development here at the mouth of Strawberry Creek. One section has no structures, and has only been developed as a parking lot; given this, Ohlone communities and their allies argue that much remains of archaeological significance below the 2.2-acre site. The fight to stop a proposed development here has been used to educate the public about the contemporary presence of Native people in the Bay Area. See shellmound .org for updates (also see photo, p. 37).

TO LEARN MORE

Bean, Lowell John, ed. *The Ohlone Past and Present: Native Americans of the San Francisco Bay Region.* Socorro, NM: Ballena Press, 1994.

Lunine, Seth Roger. "Iron, Oil, and Emeryville: Resource Industrialization and Metropolitan Expansion in the San Francisco Bay Area, 1850–1900." PhD diss., University of California, Berkeley, 2013.

Miranda, Deborah A. *Bad Indians: A Tribal Memoir.* Berkeley, CA: Heyday Books, 2012.

Steinberg, Michelle Grace, director. *Beyond Recognition.* Watertown, MA: Documentary Educational Resources, 2015. (Documentary film)

1.9 "Fossil Fuel" Corridor

Lone Tree Point Park
413 San Pablo Avenue, Rodeo 94572 (for a view of whole corridor)

Conoco–Phillips 66 San Francisco Refinery
1290 San Pablo Avenue, Rodeo 94572

Chevron Refinery
525 Castro Street, Richmond 94801

Kinder Morgan
1140 Canal Boulevard, Richmond 94804

Located in the small city of Rodeo, Lone Tree Point Park gives visitors a close-up view of the flow between the Suisun and San Pablo Bays. It's also a key place from which to study the toxic oil refinery landscape of the East Bay. At the edge of the bay, bird and plant species point to a complex ecosystem that persists despite a century and a half of heavy industry and continuous urban development. The natural scenery of this location is punctuated by periodic commuter and cargo trains that run alongside the delta and, later, the San Pablo and San Francisco Bays. But the tranquility of the landscape and the small-town feel of the community of Rodeo contrast with the constant discernible humming of machinery at the Conoco–Phillips 66 San Francisco Refinery located just one mile from the park.

Built in 1896, the Conoco-Phillips oil refinery links to a two-hundred-mile pipeline that stretches from Rodeo to the Santa María Phillips 66 facility in Arroyo Grande, in California's Central Coast. The processed oil is distributed by pipeline, rail, and barge to various retail outlets in California and beyond. As of 2017, the facility was seeking to expand its deep-water port here in order

(Left) The Chevron oil refinery in Richmond in 2017.

(Below) The oil refinery landscape of the East Bay was established a long time ago. This is John D. Rockefeller's Standard Oil refinery, 1905. (Photographer unknown)

to more than double the traffic of ships bringing in crude oil to 130,000 barrels a day. Environmental justice groups like Communities for a Better Environment and downwind communities in Vallejo and Benicia are concerned that this traffic will increase air pollution and the risk of serious oil spills, like the one that occurred in September 2016. Phillips 66 is just one of several massive refineries along the northeastern edges of the Bay Area, stretching to the Sacramento Delta. The most notable is Chevron's 2,900-acre facility in the city of Richmond. Chevron's plant, with its hill of shell-like oil storage tanks, is hard to miss as you cross the Richmond–San Rafael Bridge. Adjacent to the refinery, Chevron houses its Richmond Technology Center, where chemists and engineers develop a range of projects, from fuel additives to fracking technology, industrial solvents to plastics, agricultural fertilizers, and pesticides.

The presence of oil research and refining has a long history in this corner of the bay. John D. Rockefeller's Standard Oil refinery was established at this site in 1902; it grew and gained prestige as a leading center for the innovation of petroleum as national demand grew through the twentieth century. For Richmond residents, the Chevron Refinery has played an omnipresent role as the city's single-largest employer and with its direct work shaping the local political, economic, and environmental landscape. Chevron actively works to steer legislation, and the company plays a local philanthropic role to generate goodwill by funding education, arts, and culture initiatives.

The sour smells emanating from the refinery and the long list of accidents at the plant, however, have led to chronic illness for many who live and work downwind from Chevron. Between 1989 and 1995, for example, there were more than three hundred reported accidents, which include leaks, explosions, fires, flares, and toxic gas releases. On August 6, 2012, an explosion and serious fire, labeled critical by the corporation's own criteria, prompted a government order that residents "shelter in place," while some fifteen thousand people sought emergency medical attention. Five years after this incident, oversight agencies like the Division of Occupational Safety and Health (Cal/OSHA) and environmental organizations continue to accuse Chevron of falling behind on important repairs that ensure greater worker and environmental safety.

Meanwhile, organizations like the Richmond Progressive Alliance (RPA) offer a different vision for the city, one grounded in principles of social and environmental justice. The RPA has sought to limit Chevron's influence on local regulations and develop human-scale solutions to entrenched local problems like toxicity and violence. In the aftermath of the 2012 explosions, the city sued Chevron, and locals have participated in international climate-change negotiations while allying themselves with Indigenous leaders who oppose the continued growth of the fossil fuel industry. Idle No More SF Bay, for example, organized a series of public walks, as long as thirteen miles each, to bring attention to this "fossil fuel corridor" over a period of four years (2014–2017). The Refinery Corridor Healing Walks linked labor and environmental issues, calling for "a just transition toward a safe and clean renewable energy future, a transition to healthy jobs for people who work in the fossil fuel industry and an immediate transition off of fossil fuels." The walks shed light on the fossil fuel industry's legacy of environmental racism. This includes corporations, such as Kinder Morgan, that build oil infrastructure, including the long-distance pipelines that have been sites of protest in the 2000s at places like the Standing Rock Sioux Reservation in the Dakotas. (Diana Negrín da Silva)

TO LEARN MORE

Early, Steve. *Refinery Town: Big Oil, Big Money, and the Remaking of an American City.* Boston: Beacon Press, 2017.

Refinery Healing Walks. 350.org video: https://www.youtube.com/watch?v=PFqtU6ubRNo

1.10 Frances Albrier Community Center

2800 Park Street, Berkeley 94702

San Pablo Park's Community Center commemorates the life of African American activist Frances Albrier as part of the long and rich history of cross-class multi-ethnic culture, community, and social struggle in South Berkeley. Albrier's life story sheds light on the character of her neighbors, who fostered a strong sense of community that was often forged in the sports fields of San Pablo Park.

(Left) The art deco lettering is partially hidden by two shade trees at the Frances Albrier Community Center in San Pablo Park.

(Below Left) A flyer from 1940 outlines the goals of an antidiscrimination campaign: "Don't Buy Where You Can't Work." (Below Right) Frances Albrier photographed in a successful 1940 demonstration against workplace discrimination in South Berkeley. (Presley Winfield photos)

Born in 1898, Albrier grew up in Alabama with her grandmother, a former enslaved woman and midwife who cared deeply about education. Albrier's grandmother was a founding supporter of the Tuskegee Institute, the prominent Black school where Frances studied before joining her father in Berkeley in 1920. She received further training as a nurse, married, and settled into a house nearby at 1621 Oregon Street to raise her three children. Racial discrimination prevented Albrier from securing work as a nurse, but she later found employment with the Pullman train company and became active in a labor union. Having been refused a job as a welder at the Kaiser shipyards in Richmond (although she had twice the hours of training needed), Albrier leveraged her knowledge of a new federal antidiscrimination law to pressure Kaiser. She won and began work as the first Black woman welder in 1942. Her persistence helped pave the way for thousands of African American and women workers to get better-paying jobs in the shipyards (see Rosie the Riveter Monument and National Park, p. 65).

Outside of her own workplaces, Albrier engaged in a series of campaigns to challenge discrimination and social injustice. She organized a women's club that pressured the Berkeley schools to hire the first Black teacher at nearby Longfellow School. She initiated a "Don't Buy Where You Can't Work Campaign" at Sacramento and Ashby—just a few blocks from San Pablo Park—that pushed local shopkeepers to hire Black employees. She was the first African American to run for Berkeley City Council in 1939. She didn't win, but she went on to hold prominent positions in the local and statewide Democratic Party and served on Berkeley's Model Cities program, which brought federal community-development dollars to South Berkeley.

Albrier was a powerful person and leader, but she was also a product of a remarkable community. Byron Rumford lived nearby at Acton and Russell. His Sacramento Street pharmacy became a neighborhood institution, and in 1948 Rumford became Northern California's first Black elected official when he won a seat in the state assembly through the work of an alliance of African Americans, progressive labor unions, and liberals of all ethnicities. He leveraged these coalitions to pass landmark state legislation for fair employment in 1959 and fair housing in 1963. A statue of Rumford by sculptor Dana King stands in the median on Sacramento Avenue, near his former pharmacy.

Berkeley's Japanese American community was centered just east of this area in a thriving community with dozens of organizations, churches, and cultural groups. During WWII the federal government incarcerated more than thirteen hundred Japanese American Berkeley residents. Under Albrier's and Rumford's leadership, Berkeley's Interracial Committee protested wartime treatment of Japanese Americans, and some entrusted the deeds to their homes to Albrier while they lived behind barbed wire. (Donna Graves)

NEARBY SITES OF INTEREST

Former home of Sargent Johnson
2779 Park Street, private residence
Johnson was the first African American artist from the western US to receive national prominence. His award-winning work, some of which was supported by the New Deal's Works Progress Administration, included portraits of South Berkeley children; one is in the permanent collection of SFMOMA.

Nearby, at **2725 Dohr Street**, a Greek immigrant family ran a grocery store. One of the children in that family was Johnny Veliotes, who began his musical career in 1939 as a drummer with Count Otis Matthews and His West Oakland Houserockers and later headed to the Rock and Roll Hall of Fame under the stage name Johnny Otis.

A 2006 mural outside the Intertribal Friendship House. Artist Jason Dobbs; restored 2018 by the Community Rejuvenation Project.

1.11 Intertribal Friendship House

523 International Boulevard (previously East 14th Street), Oakland 94604

The Bay Area has long been an important center for urban American Indian community building. Enduring institutions like the Intertribal Friendship House (IFH), established in 1955, speak to ongoing efforts to maintain and expand cultural identities and practices. Affectionately referred to by community members as Oakland's "urban rez" (as in reservation), the IFH remains a dynamic cultural and organizational space for the area's intertribal residents, many of whom are the children and grandchildren of family members who arrived here through the federal government's relocation program that ran from 1956 to 1972. Though the relocation program—which moved people from across the country off reservations and into cities—sought to forcibly assimilate Indigenous peoples into broader US culture, the persistence of places like the IFH shows how communities refused that federal narrative, reconnected with their own roots and their links to other tribes, and wrote their own urban story.

While the region is home to its own rich Indigenous history, with multiple tribes represented here, cycles of migration built the contemporary Bay Area American Indian community. In the early 1920s, just a few miles north in Richmond, Native Laguna Pueblo railroad laborers established the "Santa Fe Indian Village," having come from New Mexico to work on the Atchison, Topeka, and Santa Fe railroads. Tribal councils and activities were organized in this "worker village," which established ties with other newly arrived American Indians. These first generations and their efforts to reterritorialize their traditions set the stage for the formation of an organized intertribal community; Oakland later became a center of intertribal kinship. During the 1930s and 1940s, others found home here after being sent to boarding schools on the edges of the

Bay Area, and still more came for work in WWII industries. The largest wave of arrivals came via the Federal Relocation Program of 1956, which used the pretext of acculturating young American Indians to offer meagerly resourced job training and a one-way bus ticket from rural reservations to cities across the country. Los Angeles and the San Francisco Bay Area were two primary destinations.

The relocation program may have inspired young people to leave their tribal territories, but many rejected the pressure to assimilate and abandon their cultures; they found each other in Oakland and formed new *inter*tribal communities. Prior to the establishment of the IFH, American Indians would gather at the downtown Oakland YMCA on Broadway for the weekly Thursday Four Winds Club, which had been established in 1924. The club brought together people in the armed forces, young domestic workers placed with local elites, and those attending trade school after graduating from the Bureau of Indian Affairs boarding schools. Later the IFH provided a space for continuous programming like regular Wednesday night dinners, the organization of sports leagues, and powwows throughout the region.

Ultimately the continued arrival of American Indians to the Bay Area through the 1960s created an unprecedented opportunity for political and cultural work. The fourteen-month-long occupation of Alcatraz Island (see p. 196) represents the most widely politicized result of the intertribal organizing that emerged from these spaces. As of 2018, California was the state with the largest and most heterogeneous American

---

EXCERPT OF "BLUES-ING ON THE BROWN VIBE," BY ESTHER G. BELIN (DINÉ), FROM *URBAN VOICES*, SUSAN LOBO, ED.

And Coyote struts down East 14th
feeling good
looking good
feeling the brown
melting into the brown that loiters
rapping with the brown in front of the
    Native American Health Center
talking that talk
of relocation from tribal nation
of recent immigration to the place some
    call the United States
home to many dislocated funky brown

ironic immigration

more accurate tribal nation to tribal nation

and Coyote sprinkles corn pollen in the
    four directions
to thank the tribal people
        indigenous to what some call the state
        of California
        the city of Oakland
for allowing use of their land.

Indian and Indigenous population. The IFH has remained a central point for political debate and organization, while providing space for educational and cultural activities that also welcome the area's indigenous residents from Mexico and Central America. (Diana Negrín da Silva)

NEARBY SITE OF INTEREST

Native American Health Center
3124 International Boulevard, Oakland 94601
Established in 1971 by American Indian and Alaska Natives to provide holistic and culturally and linguistically respectful intertribal health services,

the center first opened at 160 Capp Street in San Francisco before moving to Oakland in 1983. Later NAHC opened locations in Richmond (2566 Mac-Donald Avenue) and Alameda (1151 Harbor Way) and provides on-site health services at area schools.

TO LEARN MORE

Lobo, Susan, ed. *Urban Voices: The Bay Area American Indian Community, Community History Project, Intertribal Friendship House, Oakland, California.* Tucson: University of Arizona Press, 2002.

1.12 Jingletown

Mary Help of Christians Catholic Church
2611 E. 9th Street, Oakland 94606

Union Point Park
2311 Embarcadero Street, Oakland 94606

Bay Area working-class history, typically told through narratives about San Francisco–based struggles, has important roots in Oakland's Jingletown, which is now a burgeoning arts district. Local lore attributes the name *Jingletown* to the coins that would jingle in local workers' pockets on payday, beginning in the late nineteenth century. The first major working-class community in the area included Azorean and Portuguese immigrants at that time, and their children helped drive the rise in labor unionism in the city. With the advent of World War II, Jingletown and its adjacent neighborhoods witnessed an influx of working-class Mexican Americans and African Americans and became, like so many Bay Area neighborhoods at that time, an arm of the war production machine. These workers later formed the nexus of a rare cross-cultural social justice organizing effort, centered on a century's development of working-class spaces.

Jingletown's Union Point Park features this statue titled *Sígame/Follow Me* (Scott Donahue, 2001), depicting a woman whose traits and dress represent a fusion of female historical figures from Oakland—beginning with Huichin and Jalquin tribal members and ending with writer Amy Tan.

Also known as the North Kennedy Tract, the Jingletown neighborhood is located along the Oakland Estuary. Prior to the arrival of Spanish expeditions in the late 1700s, the Huichin-speaking peoples (called *Costanoan* by the Spanish and later grouped as Ohlone) established shellmounds here, one of which is memorialized at Union Point Park. After the Spanish claimed what became known as Alta California, this area became part of the Rancho San Antonio land grant in 1820. Between US conquest and the turn of the twentieth century, the district boomed into a center of industrial activity, drawing workers from southern Europe to work in canneries and mills.

45

From the late 1960s through the 1970s, Jingletown became a center of Chicano organizing, just as industry accelerated its exodus. Mary Help of Christians Catholic Church (2611 E. 9th Street), founded in 1915 by Portuguese immigrants, hosted the Chicano Revolutionary Party's first Breakfast Program here in 1969 (aided by the Black Panthers). The church played a central role in community organizing after that—for example, as the meeting point for the July 1970 Chicano Moratorium Committee March, which protested the Vietnam War while calling for justice at home as well. (Diana Negrín da Silva)

NEARBY SITE OF INTEREST

California Cotton Mills

1091 Calcot Place, Oakland 94606

Part of an early wave of industrial loft conversions, this is one of the few remaining mill buildings from an industry that dominated the area from 1883 to 1954.

RELATED SITE OF INTEREST

Dorothea Lange's home photography studio

1163 Euclid Avenue, Berkeley 94708 (private residence)

Lange's iconic black-and-white images of workers and everyday people during the Great Depression, funded by FDR's New Deal Farm Security Administration, still reverberate around the world. The rustic wood-shingled home, where she developed photos in a basement studio, is around the corner from the Berkeley Rose Garden, itself a New Deal project, funded by the Works Progress Administration.

TO LEARN MORE

Walker, Richard. "Industry Builds Out the City: Industrial Decentralization in the San Francisco Bay Area, 1850–1950." In *Manufacturing Suburbs: Building Work and Home on the Metropolitan Fringe*, edited by Robert D. Lewis. Philadelphia: Temple University Press, 2004.

1.13 Kaiser Convention Center

10 10th Street, Oakland 94607

Originally known as the Oakland Civic Auditorium, the Kaiser building has a long and storied history as a site for public events and concerts. Oaklanders proudly remember it as a site where Dr. Martin Luther King Jr. spoke to a crowd of over seven thousand in 1962, and where the Black Panther Party distributed free breakfasts. A 1914 Beaux Arts building and historic landmark, it is a regular feature on architectural tours. Less likely to come up is that in 1925, a local order of the Knights of the Ku Klux Klan (KKK) held a mass rally here, inducting new members and publicly flexing its racist muscle.

More than a terrifying or embarrassing blip in East Bay history, the presence of the KKK at Oakland's civic auditorium should be understood as part of an ongoing, violent, white-supremacist project that stretches back to initial conquest and forward to the rise of the alt.right in the 2010s. Indeed, formally organized white-supremacist activity in the Bay Area goes back to the slaughter of Native groups across the US West, and to the call to repopulate the West as part of Manifest Destiny, which has persisted in anti-immigrant movements. By the 1920s, what historians describe as the second Ku Klux

Henry J. Kaiser Convention Center, 2019.

Klan established beachheads in many cities outside of the US South, where whites who declared that they were "native-born" were already primed to hate Black people, Jews, Catholics, and nearly all immigrants. This "second KKK" has been characterized as the largest right-wing movement in US history, a movement that saw national KKK membership swell to between four million and six million. Locally, KKK members ran for public office and sought positions throughout government, leaving an ideological legacy that no doubt remains in some quarters, even as Oakland has shifted toward multiculturalism in many ways.

In 1925 the KKK brought a show of force here to the center of Oakland when eighty-five hundred members and supporters from across the country filled the Oakland Civic Auditorium for a swearing-in ceremony, which was said to include cross burnings inside the huge civic space. While this moment was stunning, Klan events of the 1920s mark many East Bay geographies. Sociologist Chris Rhomberg writes about a ritual rally that took place in the Oakland hills in 1922, during which the organization brought some five hundred new members into its ranks. Soon, three thousand members marched through the city of Richmond to an initiation ceremony in the El Cerrito Hills. By 1924 Oakland had at least two thousand men enrolled in the Klan. Downtown, Klan office No. 9 provided a centralized presence.

The growth of the KKK intersected with the expansion of explicitly racially restricted new suburban housing opportunities in East Oakland and the Oakland Hills. With deed covenants calling for racial homogeneity, these areas became core strongholds for the organization and provided opportunities for it to expand its reach into civic activities, like taxes and city services. Although Klan No. 9 dissolved in 1925 amid internal disputes, the KKK was still active in Oakland through the end of the 1920s, having a wide support base and several political, civic, and fraternal leaders within its membership. Elected Klansmen, however, turned out to be (unsurprisingly) unscrupulous, and their poor performance and occasional violence may have done more to undo their organization than any broader objection to overt racism. Two Oakland Klan-affiliated officials were both indicted, convicted, and sent to prison following a grand jury investigation into graft. The KKK faded from formal politics but, according to Rhomberg, conservative downtown-business elites continued with more subtle promises to maintain a stable social order of white control of land, jobs, and wealth.

Oakland still struggles with this legacy of long-held beliefs in white racial supremacy, right up to debates over how the empty Kaiser center should be redeveloped, who is responsible for its decline, and who "deserves" to have such a storied building at the heart of their city. (With research by David Woo)

NEARBY SITE OF INTEREST

Oakland Museum of California
1000 Oak Street, Oakland 94607
This local gem bridges the old story of California with the new one. You'll find exhibits on gold and the clashes between cultures during California's pre-urban era. But you'll also find deeply researched exhibits that center on the array of ethnicities and cultures that have long shaped the state but have not often appeared in museums in the past. Notable exhibits in the 2010s included *Queer California: Untold Stories*, one on the local roots of hip-hop, and ongoing work on the complicated histories of migration and immigration that make the state what it is.

TO LEARN MORE

Chris Rhomberg. *No There There: Race, Class, and Political Community in Oakland*. Berkeley: University of California Press, 2004.

1.14 Lake Merritt

The Pergola at Lake Merritt
599 El Embarcadero, Oakland 94610
Oakland's Lake Merritt serves multiple purposes. It offers recreation, as a place for exercise and social life, from multi-ethnic barbecue picnics to Dragon Boat races that require fleets of paddlers to propel forty-foot boats. It anchors Oakland's place in history as the nation's first officially recognized wildlife refuge back in the 1870s. The park offers sweeping views—and raises the real estate values—for the tall residential towers that surround it. It also provides a place of refuge for city residents, including people struggling to make it in a harsh urban reality. Meanwhile, the 155-acre park (this includes the lake itself, an island, and the open space that rings it) serves as a barometer of how Oakland is doing, particularly in terms of race and class conflicts. Where the lake has a long history of serving the multiracial community that makes up Oakland, its location at the intersection of changing neighborhoods means that when places gentrify all

A 2019 demonstration supporting the Sudanese Revolution joins a drum circle at the Pergola, at the northeast point of Lake Merritt.

around it, the social world of the park also gentrifies.

In 2018 a series of conflicts drew national attention to this pattern, with a white woman calling the police to report a group of Black people for "illegal grilling" and a white jogger angrily throwing the belongings of a houseless man into the lake. These incidents were caught on video and became part of the national conversation on who has the right to be in a city, in a park, or on a street. In many ways, these were not new kinds of events but the latest expression of historical tensions. Other struggles over music at the lake, where a longstanding drum circle was suddenly viewed by new residents as too loud and potentially not legal, highlighted similar tensions echoing

similar situations across the country, where public culture becomes the flash point for urban change.

NEARBY SITE OF INTEREST

Grand Lake Theater
3200 Grand Avenue, Oakland 94610
Although public movie houses are all but gone from the urban fabric, there are a few left. The Grand Lake is one example of programming that reaches beyond the basics. You can catch the latest superhero blockbuster here, and you can also see lesser-known or local films, events with local filmmakers, and more. The place may be best known for the political views that appear regularly on the marquee, for example: "Dissent is the highest form of patriotism. Read the First Amendment."

A contemporary view of Latham Square, where Broadway and Telegraph Ave. intersect around a sunny pedestrian park. This is where the streetcars once converged, enabling strategic protest that froze transit in multiple directions.

1.15 Latham Square

Latham Square Plaza, intersection
of Broadway and Telegraph Avenue,
Oakland 94612

After months of struggle, in the early dawn hours of December 1, 1946, retail workers began gathering in the general area of what is now Latham Square Plaza to block a shipment of supplies to two major department stores. The Retail Merchants Association (RMA)—an employer's group that bitterly opposed unionization among the largely female workforce—was fighting union organizing efforts in Oakland's downtown retail sector. The department stores at the center of the struggle were Hastings (1530 Broadway) and Kahn's (1501 Broadway). Retail clerks had picketed through the fall of 1946, angling for better pay and working conditions. The clerks, a majority of whom were female, were vulnerable; the winding-down of the WWII home front meant that many firms were pushing women workers out of

their jobs to make way for male GIs as they returned home.

As the workers demonstrated here in the street, Oakland police stepped in to support the merchants. The struggle grew, with unionized streetcar drivers allying with the retail clerks and refusing to cross the picket lines, which were coincidentally here at the epicenter of Oakland's streetcar system. The standstill blocked much of the city's north-south streetcar and bus traffic and rippled across the entire transportation system and the economy, most essentially stopping deliveries of goods to targeted employers.

The police worked to break the strike by forcing a path for the shipment, and in the chaos at least one worker was hit by a police vehicle. The involvement of police sparked fierce debate among rank-and-file workers, labor organizers, and allies about not only how to prevent police from strikebreaking, but also about the broader strategy of collective action in the postwar climate. After a

Demonstrators in front of Kahn's department store in 1946, when a struggle for the rights of largely female retail clerks sparked the Oakland general strike. (Photographer unknown)

long day of discussion within a group large enough to warrant the use of Oakland's Municipal Auditorium (later named Kaiser Convention Center, p. 46), a strategically titled "worker's holiday" was announced for December 3. A broad array of businesses across Oakland ground to a halt as workers, from newspaper printers to transit operators to the retail clerks themselves, abandoned their jobs and gathered downtown. Labor allies filled the streets with marches, meetings, dancing, and the occasional fight.

The strike was part of a larger shift going on across the country at that time. Changing working conditions, along with new support coming from FDR's New Deal, meant workers felt empowered to claim a piece of the nation's growing prosperity that they were producing—some 4,985 strikes, involving 4.6 million workers, were called nationwide. Ultimately all of this activity led to the most significant rise in organized-labor power the nation had seen, with union representation growing sharply and remaining relatively high for about thirty years.

Back in Oakland, union leaders called off the general strike after two days, with a settlement in which city officials agreed to keep the police out of labor struggles. But retail picketing at the department stores continued for another six months with additional demands. Although very few seemed pleased with the settlement on its own terms, the event revived electoral energy for social change in Oakland. A community-labor coalition called the Oakland Voters League emerged with broad claims that went far beyond labor rights, calling for public health and education reform, rent control, public housing, and publicly controlled transit. Candidates supporting this slate won several seats on the city council the next fall, with support from the Negro Labor Committee.

This struggle was long invisible in contemporary downtown, but in 2016 the city regraded the streets at the intersection of Broadway and Telegraph and created Latham Square Park, with a brief description of the strike on a plaque. The square is an excellent place from which to understand a changing contemporary Oakland. To the north and west, along the branching lattice streets that still follow the paths of the pre-1950s streetcars, you'll find evidence of former mayor Jerry Brown's "Uptown" rebranding of the central city. To the southeast, you'll see the elegant Tribune Tower, a twenty-story clock tower office building that has represented the *Oakland Tribune* since 1923. Although the newspaper operation left the building in 2007, the tower itself remains a touchstone in the urban landscape, telegraphing a message that the business class is watching over the city from its elevated perch.

NEARBY SITE OF INTEREST

Oakland Chinatown

Between Broadway and Oak, and 12th to 6th Streets, Oakland, 94607

As with many Chinatowns, Oakland's is home to residents and businesses representing the larger Asian diaspora—from Vietnam, Japan, Thailand, and more. Relocated five times in the nineteenth century, the neighborhood expanded after the 1906 quake and fire produced thousands of San Francisco refugees, and then grew beyond the borders of "Chinatown" with the onset of 1960s immigration laws that opened up immigration quotas from many countries. For wonderful first-person accounts, see the Oakland Chinatown Oral History Project, http://memorymap.oacc.cc.

TO LEARN MORE

Rhomberg, Chris. *No There There: Race, Class, and Political Community in Oakland*. Berkeley: University of California Press, 2004.

Wolman, Philip J. "The Oakland General Strike of 1946," *Southern California Quarterly* 57, 2 (1975): 147–78.

1.16 Mandela Grocery Cooperative

1430 7th Street, Oakland 94607

Defying a history of grocers abandoning Oakland flatlanders, leaving them in neighborhoods without access to fresh food ("food deserts"), this worker-owned cooperative represents decades of organizing for "food justice" in West Oakland. On a business corridor devastated by 1960s urban renewal and then again by disinvestment following the 1989 Loma Prieta earthquake, the 2009 opening of a grocery cooperatively owned largely by people of color marked a sea change toward community empowerment. The co-op's founding followed a decade of organizing and fundraising by Mandela MarketPlace, a food-justice nonprofit and incubator. The co-op's formation builds on legacies formed by a broad network of East Bay institutions addressing the scarcity of healthy food in certain neighborhoods, as part of broader economic justice efforts.

Mandela's cooperative stands in a decades-old tradition of alternative business development in the Bay Area, which was a key place for the revival of co-ops—whether worker owned, consumer owned, or collectives with alternative management structures—particularly in the 1970s. Nearly fifty years

Mandela Grocery Cooperative in 2019, just before plans were announced for a major expansion.

Employee Ownership (1629 Telegraph Avenue, Oakland). In 2015 the Oakland City Council began to listen to community pressure about establishing low-interest loans to help convert traditional businesses into worker co-ops, granting preferential status to co-ops as they engage with city contracts and local taxes and fees. At the state level, some lawmakers also sought to clear hurdles, removing some legal barriers to co-op formation and expansion. The legal and political landscape that can enable or undermine such organizations remains in flux; meantime, the Mandela market offers an example to learn from.

later, in the face of pressure to let free-market forces gentrify the neighborhood, the Mandela Co-op's worker-owner model offers one possible route to sustaining the neighborhood's working class by generating local jobs with a social and economic stake in the community. The food-justice vision guides the co-op toward buying from local farms and producers within a few hours' drive of the store, and is implemented through its work with other institutions that serve the community, including corner stores that need support in offering fresh produce. The co-op hosts monthly events with live music and a soul food restaurant.

Many of the Bay Area's famous radical businesses from the 1970s are now shuttered, but local organizations strive to pave the way for worker co-ops like Mandela: for example, the US Federation of Worker Cooperatives (1904 Franklin Street), the Sustainable Economies Law Center (1428 Franklin Street), and the National Center for

NEARBY SITES OF INTEREST

Esther's Orbit Room
1724 7th Street (historical)
This was one of the best-known blues and jazz clubs in the neighborhood, opened by Esther Mabry and her husband, William, in 1963. The iconic club, which hosted luminaries like Etta James and BB King, closed in 2011.

RELATED SITE OF INTEREST

Arizmendi Bakery
4301 San Pablo Avenue, Emeryville 94608
One of the worker-owned co-op stalwarts in the Bay Area is Arizmendi Bakery, which has developed a local chain of bakeries and pizza shops in

several cities. The nearest bakery is about three miles north of the Mandela co-op.

TO LEARN MORE

Mandela Grocery Cooperative, https://www .mandelafoods.com/

Nembhard, Jessica Gordon. *Collective Courage: A History of African American Cooperative Economic Thought and Practice*. University Park: Pennsylvania State University Press, 2014.

1.17 Marcus Books

3900 Martin Luther King Jr. Way, Oakland 94609

The East Bay offers a strong counter to the notion that the age of independent booksellers is over. Between Oakland and Berkeley alone, an array of independently owned and operated stores and small local chains serve niche audiences and the broader community alike. Marcus Books holds a special place on this list as the oldest continuously operating Black-owned and -operated bookstore in the United States. Marcus was founded in 1960 by Julian and Raye Richardson as the Success Book Company in San Francisco. The institution was part of a wave of Black bookstores that opened in the 1960s and 1970s, offering access to books by and about people of the African diaspora, including information absent or scarce in other bookstores, public libraries, and schools. The spread of books by W. E. B. DuBois, Toni Morrison, Frantz Fanon, and many others provided intellectual foundations for transformations in Black community consciousness.

The Richardsons opened the original Success Book Company in the front of their independent San Francisco printing shop, where they published writers who were shut out of the white-dominated publishing industry or whose work was difficult to find. Julian Richardson published Marcus Garvey's *Philosophy and Opinions* in 1966 after discovering that it had been out of print for forty years. He also printed two influential literary magazines of the Black Arts movement, *Black Dialogue* and the *Journal of Black Poetry*, and published a number of books of poetry under his own imprint. The bookstore–print shop was a hub for Black artistic and cultural activity in San Francisco, hosting events and political meetings, playing an active role in local political struggles.

In 1970 the Richardsons opened a second location in Berkeley and changed the name to Marcus Books, after Garvey. The East Bay expansion allowed Marcus Books to conduct business with schools and other large institutions in Alameda County, such as prisons and social service facilities, according to a 1978 interview with Julian Richardson. They moved the East Bay store from Berkeley to its current site in Oakland in 1976. The new location was around the corner from the recently opened MacArthur BART station and close to the first storefront location of the East Bay Negro Historical Society (the earliest predecessor of the African American Museum and Library of Oakland). This new location was central to political activity in the neighborhoods of North and West Oakland as well as downtown.

Meanwhile, the San Francisco location moved to the heart of the Fillmore district in 1980, to Victorian Square, a small cluster of buildings that had been rescued from the

The outer wall of Marcus Books, painted with titles by Zora Neale Hurston, Carter Woodson, Elaine Brown, and others. Malcolm X (left) and Marcus Garvey (right) stand watch. Mural coordinated by Community Rejuvenation Project.

redevelopment bulldozers some years earlier. In 2014, after a long community struggle to save it, the San Francisco location at 1712 Fillmore shuttered. The Oakland location remains and stocks a catalog of Black books in all genres and hosts events on-site and in partnership with other organizations. Even amid the Black outmigration of the 1990s and 2000s that has changed Oakland's demography dramatically, and after financial troubles that plagued the store for some time, Marcus Books remains rooted here on MLK Way. (Simon Abramowitsch)

RELATED SITE OF INTEREST

African American Museum and Library of Oakland (AAMLO)
659 14th Street, Oakland
There are at least a dozen sites of historical importance to the Black community along the Martin Luther King Jr. Way corridor. AAMLO is a couple of miles south; see Dover Park entry, p. 32, for more.

TO LEARN MORE

Davis, Joshua Clark. *From Head Shops to Whole Foods: The Rise and Fall of Activist Entrepreneurs.* New York: Columbia University Press, 2017.
Marvin X. *Somethin' Proper: The Life and Times of a North American African Poet.* Castro Valley, CA: Black Bird Press, 1998.
Smethurst, James. *The Black Arts Movement: Literary Nationalism in the 1960s and '70s.* Chapel Hill: University of North Carolina Press, 2005.

1.18 Middle Harbor Shoreline Park
2777 Middle Harbor Road, Oakland 94607
In addition to an unusual and interesting view of San Francisco, from here you can watch the work of the Oakland Port unfold:

Find a unique view of San Francisco, looking west from Middle Harbor Shoreleline Park from the viewing tower or the beach.

Climb the viewing towers at the south end or simply look through the fence that separates the park from the port on the east side. As you watch massive shipping containers shuffle, you'll be witnessing labors that connect back to the origins of the Bay Region. San Francisco expanded beyond gold-rush fever largely because of its potential as a port city, and port labor has been central in global supply chains, and in political organizing (see "An Injury to One . . .," p. 131). For example, during the Occupy Wall Street movement, on November 2, 2011, tens of thousands of people marched here from the Occupy Oakland camp downtown. The Oakland Port, which was the fifth most productive in the nation at that time, came to a halt. Protestors had arrived in time to block workers from their shifts, which froze port operations without asking workers to participate in what would have been an il-

legal work stoppage. While port employees sat in idled cars and trucks outside the gates, protesters filed through the long fingers of the port complex out to the dozens of shipping berths.

The historical rise of the Oakland Port, at the receiving end of the transcontinental railroad, provided the competition and labor pool to fuel the rise of regional industry—eventually surpassing the San Francisco Port. For workers this meant exploitation, but it also brought power: The Bay Area is known for labor successes in part because waterfront workers have leveraged their location in the global production system. Shutting down the port, or even challenging port-management policies here, has thus historically helped improve working conditions more broadly. Occupy Oakland built on this legacy, stalling this behemoth to materially and symbolically draw atten-

Looking east from Middle Harbor Shoreline Park, you can watch the operations of the Port of Oakland from a safe distance.

tion to increasing economic inequality here and around the world. Some protestors walked along rail ties and marched to the very end of the west arm of the port, which extends out about a mile. Others held Occupy assemblies to discuss what would be next for the Occupy movement using the sound-carrying practice of the "people's mic," in which declarations are repeated by the crowd multiple times in concentric circles, so that people on the outer ring of the crowd can hear what's said. Still others climbed up and danced on the immobilized shipping containers, waving signs condemning capitalism. The march was the culmination of what organizers called the Oakland General Strike, and although the strike did not mobilize a true general strike, which would have meant that multiple labor sectors ceased work in solidarity, Oakland's downtown was nevertheless filled with marches and political theater all day long, until demonstrators flooded out to the port in coordinated waves.

It is not typically possible to get access to the port itself to explore the berths; given the traffic of global goods, port security is high, and the work of moving multi-ton shipping containers from ship to shore is dangerous for workers and visitors alike. You can, however, observe the port from the Middle Harbor Park, which is an interesting place in its own right, with nearly three miles of walking and biking trails and Oakland's only real beach. The park is a short drive from the West Oakland BART station. Because of traffic and the absence of sidewalks, walking to this park is discouraged; cycling is possible, but requires navigating major freeway intersections with heavy truck traffic. Get there before dusk to access the whole park.

TO LEARN MORE

Selvin, David F. *A Terrible Anger: The 1934 Waterfront and General Strikes in San Francisco.* Detroit: Wayne State University Press, 1996.

Waterfront Action, www.waterfrontaction.org/learn/parks/mhp.htm

1.19 Ogawa/Grant Plaza

1 Frank H. Ogawa Plaza, Oakland 94612

Urban civic centers—though they tend toward formality, filled with symbolism and monuments that lend an air of finality—are always spaces under contestation. Oakland's Civic Center offers a telling example of how social and political tensions at any given moment are revealed and what happens when a governing regime claims a place while a broad public also claims it. How a civic area is used, who has the right to use it, and what it is called are all more uncertain than official signs might suggest.

Oakland's City Hall, with its office-like tall tower, nods in its architectural design to the business leaders who supported its development in 1914 while also, in its stoic façade, promising an era of corruption-free government to Oakland's taxpayers. It is bordered by some of the city's finest examples of well-preserved Beaux Arts architecture, host to government

offices, private law firms, art galleries, and retail. At its front door is the heart of the civic center, the park historically known as Memorial Plaza, in recognition of Oaklanders who died fighting in WWI, renamed in 1998 for Frank Ogawa. Ogawa was Oakland's first Japanese American city councilman and was active in California politics for three decades. Prior to his political career, Ogawa survived incarceration in the Topaz War Relocation Center during WWII. For a city with a long history of white-supremacist influences in local politics (see Kaiser, p. 46), but helmed at that point by a Black mayor, renaming the plaza was an important move. Recognizing the son of immigrants who had been severely wronged by the government was an opportunity to officially acknowledge unpleasant truths about the past while suggesting that Oakland was becoming a more open and welcoming place.

In 2011 Occupy Oakland activists took over the plaza over the course of about a month. They set up a collective kitchen, and

The Occupy Oakland camp filled Ogawa/Grant Plaza in 2011 for months. (Myles Boisen photo)

bookstore, and offered medical services, like similar camps around the country. Before it was cleared by police, the camp was home base for political conversations about economic inequality, and it also became a de facto home for many of the region's houseless. At one point camp residents voted to rename the space after Oscar Grant, who had been killed by BART police on New Year's Eve 2009. Grant's story was documented in the film *Fruitvale Station*; the title refers to the name of the BART train station where Grant died. The grassroots vote to rename the place for Grant likely wasn't a rejection specifically of Ogawa, but an attempt to remake the image of Oakland's civic core based on the urgent issues of the moment.

The plaza here remains an important place for culture and protest alike, where Oaklanders bring their grievances, hold rallies, and simply gather. It's also a creative cultural space, with homegrown events like the Oakland Book Festival, which brought free book readings and literary panels to the meeting rooms of City Hall for several years.

TO LEARN MORE

King, Mike. *When Riot Cops Are Not Enough: The Policing and Repression of Occupy Oakland*. New Brunswick, NJ: Rutgers University Press, 2017.

1.20 Pacific Center, Front Steps

2712 Telegraph Avenue, Berkeley 94705

Though it's far from the tourist-heavy Castro District in San Francisco, Berkeley's Pacific Center is the Bay Area's oldest LGBTQ

The Pacific Center is a meeting ground for many communities, including the Berkeley South Asian Radical History Walking Tour, photographed in 2012 by Sharat G. Lin.

center. Founded in 1973, the center offers sliding-scale mental health services and a unique array of support groups focused on LGBTQ life. There are important stories to be told about the center and the ways that it has impacted queer communities from its perch here in the East Bay. We focus here on just one event that took place on the steps of the center, which was researched by Barnali Ghosh and Anirvan Chatterjee, the story-scholars at the Berkeley South Asian Radical History Walking Tour.

It was here on these steps in 1986 that Bangladeshi American Berkeley resident "Tinku" Ali Ishtiaq stumbled upon a simple black-and-white flyer that posed a simple question, something like, "Are you South Asian and Gay? Call Arvind." Ishtiaq had recently moved to the area from Bangladesh via Boston, where he had studied computer engineering at MIT. He called the number and later went to San Jose to meet Arvind Kumar. At a time when coming out as gay could be deeply stigmatized and personally risky, the two gay South Asian techies had a lot to discuss. Ishtiaq would go on to be one of the earliest members of Trikon, later Trikone, which is believed to be the first formal South Asian, or Desi, LGBT-identified organization in the world.

Trikone "came out" organizationally that same year by marching in the San Francisco Pride parade (then called the International Lesbian and Gay Freedom Day Parade). While Trikone maintained its base in the Bay Area, its newsletter and network—echoing the Ghadar movement of the 1910s (see Ghadar Memorial, p. 148)—became an organizing tool across the US and internationally, connecting LGBTQ+ people across the South Asian diaspora; this includes people who trace their ancestry to places like India, Pakistan, Bangladesh, Sri Lanka, Nepal, Bhutan, and the Maldives. Trikone's work builds on a long history of LGBTQ+ South Asian presence and resistance in Northern California, starting with early South Asian immigrants imprisoned for sodomy at San Quentin State Prison in the 1910s. (Thanks to Ghosh and Chatterjee for editorial input.)

TO LEARN MORE

Berkeley South Asian Radical History Walking Tour, www.berkeleysouthasian.org

Shah, Nayan. *Stranger Intimacy: Contesting Race, Sexuality, and the Law in the North American West.* Berkeley: University of California Press, 2012.

NEARBY SITE OF INTEREST

White Horse Inn
6551 Telegraph Avenue, Oakland 94609
Follow the rainbow crosswalks at 66th Street to this bar with an unassuming white and blue facade, operational as a gay and lesbian bar—far from the storied LGBT venues of San Francisco—since at least 1933.

1.21 Parchester Village

Parchester Park
900 Williams Drive, Richmond 94806
While there are many stories of segregation and exclusion in Bay Area housing, Parchester Village represents an attempt at an alternative. Situated between two railroad tracks along the northern limits of what eventually became part of Richmond, the village was established as a master-planned project in 1949, imagined as a racially integrated suburban community that could respond to the twin problems of postwar housing shortages and widespread housing discrimination against African Americans. The village is tucked into a landscape marked by the striking paradox of heavy industry, the West Contra Costa County landfill, and marshlands that are protected as regional parks. This landscape shifts slightly as one turns from Richmond Parkway onto Giant Highway, leading to the Richmond Country Club and its adjacent large suburban homes, before descending toward the San Pablo Bay.

The Reverend Guthrie John Williams, founding pastor of the Mount Carmel Mis-

The welcome sign for Parchester Village.

after African American clergymen who were founding members of the community. The Community Center holds a colorful 1999 mural of children at play that reads "Parchester Village Touches the World."

Distinguishing it from the history of exclusionary, white-led neighborhood associations in the Bay Area, Parchester Village's homeowners created a neighborhood association that fought for broader inclusion of African Americans into city life and for an active say regarding planned developments that could devalue their homes. Residents successfully organized for transportation improvements, the right for their children to attend Richmond's public schools, and access to the previously all-white Richmond Country Club. In the 1990s, Richmond experienced significant growth in its Latinx population, some of whom have since made the village their new home. The village has also played an important role in Richmond's environmental justice movement, particularly around the fate of the 238-acre marsh at the edge of the property. When Parr sold the land in the 1970s, the Reverend Richard Dotson—one of the founding African American residents of the community—fought to keep the marshland undeveloped. Despite proposals to convert the land into an industrial park, a new hous-

sionary Baptist Church and an ardent promoter of desegregation, lobbied Richmond's politicians for housing for African American residents, many of whom had moved to the area to support the WWII shipbuilding effort. Williams eventually met developer Fred Parr, who agreed to donate his shoreline property for the project. Parchester Village is named after Parr and his son Chester, whose vision included access and views to the bay for residents who had lived and continued to work in and around Richmond's otherwise industrial landscape. In a 2010 interview with *Richmond Confidential*, lifelong resident Mary "Peace" Head remembered noting the beauty of the natural landscape surrounding the lots and asking, "Are you sure this is for Black folks?" The village of four hundred homes is enclosed within a perimeter wall that slightly conceals the charming rows of one-story homes, each with a distinct aesthetic, and front yards that show signs of a thriving family-oriented community. Many of its streets are named

ing development, and even an airport, the Dotsons and other local residents successfully preserved the marshland. In 2008 Dotson's son Whitney was elected to the East Bay Regional Park District Board, where he helped lead the public acquisition of the land through eminent domain. The Dotson Family Marsh restoration brought environmental improvements to the local habitat, a one-and-a-half-mile extension of the San Francisco Bay Trail, and preparations for sea-level rise. (Diana Negrín da Silva)

NEARBY SITES OF INTEREST

Point Pinole Regional Shoreline
5551 Giant Highway

This 2,315-acre public East Bay Regional Park just north of Parchester Village was once home to the Giant Powder Company, the first US maker of dynamite, which relocated its nitroglycerin plant here to Point Pinole after a series of deadly explosions at its plants in San Francisco's Glen Canyon and West Berkeley. The company established the area around its new plant as a "company town" called Nitro, later renamed Giant.

The West County Detention Center
5555 Giant Highway

Built in 1991, this "medium-security" coeducational prison also served as a detention center for undocumented immigrants for the Department of Homeland Security's Immigration Customs Enforcement. In 2018 West Country tried to ban public demonstrations but later halted contracting with ICE under public pressure.

1.22 Peralta Hacienda Historical Park

2465 34th Avenue, Oakland 94601

From collectively managed Indigenous space, to privately held ranch land, to de-velopment real estate and finally a publicly managed park, the Peralta Hacienda Historical Park embodies the complex processes through which histories are layered into a sense of place. The contemporary experience of the park, with diverse multigenerational residents enjoying Peralta Creek and tending vegetable gardens, represents a turn from the park's historical place at the center of cycles of dispossession and changing property regimes.

For millennia, this land was shaped by the Ohlone and Coastal Miwok, who lived in extended settlements and villages here and took advantage of the diverse habitats and weather patterns from the hills down to the tidal marshes. But after 1776, Spanish invaders brutally displaced indigenous peoples and reconceptualized the land as private property, taking much of it for the newly established mission system, where indigenous people were forced into labor. The Spanish granted some of their newly claimed land to men like Luis Peralta, whose surname appears in a variety of contexts across the East Bay. Peralta, a son of the first Spanish settlers, received the land as payment for his military service in which he rounded up and detained Native peoples on behalf of the missions. His 44,800 acres of land would become Rancho San Antonio, the original boundaries of which now cut across seven cities. The Peraltas oversaw one of the largest Spanish land grants in California and had extensive herds of cattle, horses, and goats. The Peraltas' success in the hide and tallow trade continued after Mexico's independence from Spain in 1821; the Per-

Just behind this garden, a creek flows through the edge of Peralta Park; the house holds a small museum.

altas, along with the Vallejo family, have long served as examples of Californio prosperity. However, in the wake of US conquest, most of what had been Rancho San Antonio was lost or sold off—by unscrupulous lawyers on the one hand, and through the enforcement of the new Anglo-American legal system that rejected Spanish and Mexican property regimes on the other. The last remaining eighteen acres of the Peraltas' land grant were sold off by his granddaughter to a developer in 1897.

The remaining Peralta house, completed in 1870 just as Oakland began to emerge as an industrial city, anchors the contemporary park. A visit there can begin at the Native Plant Garden, which includes medicinal plants like wormwood and soaproot. The community garden has flourished under the stewardship of Mien women who immi-grated to the neighborhood after being displaced by wars in Southeast Asia during the 1960s and 1970s. A lone pine stands as a reminder of the ways in which Native peoples used fire to clear the land of chaparral and other bushes in order to provide space for the cultivation of grasses and trees with edible seeds and nuts. Over the years the park has added sculptures that seek to high-light the area's ecology and its multiracial and multiethnic past and present. A ramp on the southern end of the park leads down to the tree-lined Peralta Creek with picnic tables. The house hosts a small museum with permanent exhibits that seek to illus-trate the Peraltas' history while remaining inclusive of other communities that have lived in the neighborhood over the last 150 years. The park also hosts a variety of exhib-

its, performances, and festivities throughout
the year, and a summer program for youth.
The Center for Community and History is
a small multipurpose facility located on the
park's property that is available for events
and workshops for the public. The park is
open every day, but the museum has limited
hours. (Diana Negrín da Silva)

TO LEARN MORE

Almaguer, Tomás. *Racial Fault Lines: The
Historical Origins of White Supremacy in
California.* Berkeley: University of California
Press, 2008.
Orsi, Richard. *Summary of Environmental Change
in California through 2000: The Oakland-East Bay
Area as a Case Study.*
Peralta Hacienda, www.peraltahacienda.org

1.23 Piedmont-Oakland Border

Grand Avenue and Wildwood, Piedmont
94610

Surrounded on all sides by the economically
and racially diverse city of Oakland, the
independent city of Piedmont negotiates a
complex mix of connection and separation
with its much larger neighbor. The border
here is marked by an invisible fence: the
license-plate readers installed to deter property crime and identify motorists with criminal records (see map, p. 65). These surveillance cameras appeared in 2013, soon after
a campaign by two Oakland teenagers to
"Liberate Piedmont" by annexing it earned
some media coverage. At that time, Piedmont Mayor John Chiang was quoted in the
press declaring that he would be "tarred and
feathered" if he proposed merging the two
cities, which are distant neighbors in socioeconomic status and public-school rankings
despite their tight functional and geographic
integration. Instead of a merger, Piedmont
shored up its borders with more than thirty
automated license-plate readers (purchased
from a 3M subsidiary for around $600,000),
quietly reinforcing the long-sought isolation
of this elite community. While the technology doesn't stop motorists from entering the
city, it tracks each entry and exit, collected in
a massive regional law enforcement database
and stored for at least a year.

Piedmont incorporated as an independent city in 1907 to escape annexation by a
rapidly growing Oakland that was swelling
with refugees from the 1906 San Francisco
earthquake and fire. After fruitless efforts

License plate cameras track movement in and out of Piedmont, including here at the intersection of Linda and Kingston Ave.

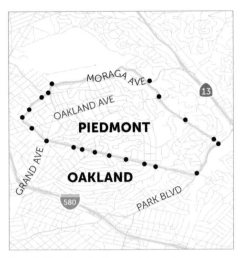

Potential locations for license plate reader cameras in Piedmont. Twenty were approved for locations like these.

to farm Australian eucalyptus and produce silk, city leaders turned to a more reliable turn-of-the-century crop: real estate. By the 1920s, Piedmont was a "city of millionaires" through the efforts of tycoons like Frank Havens, a partner in the Realty Syndicate, which developed thirteen thousand acres of the East Bay along the firm's electric Key System trolley lines. Havens hired architect Bernard Maybeck, designer Louis Comfort Tiffany, and a team of East Asian artisans to build his mansion, Wildwood, which included an opium den for entertaining Bay Area bohemians.

Today Piedmont remains protected as an elite enclave overlooking Oakland, one with both transoceanic and regional entanglements. Wildwood's more recent owner, attorney Norman Givant, for example, made his fortune in 1980s Shanghai helping Western corporations navigate Chinese law as Deng Xiaoping opened China to foreign investment. On the local level, Piedmont's eleven thousand occupants (about 74 percent white and 18 percent Asian, per the 2010 US census) have maintained tight control over zoning decisions, property tax revenues, and who comes and goes through city borders. (Will Payne)

TO LEARN MORE

Brechin, Gray. "An Evening on the Edge of the Western World: A Talk Given at Piedmont's 'Wildwood,' an Estate Designed by Bernard Maybeck for Frank C. Havens, March 3, 2007." https://graybrechin.net/articles/2000s/wildwood.html

1.24 Rosie the Riveter Monument and National Park

Marina Park, Regatta Boulevard, Richmond (monument)
1414 Harbour Way South, Richmond 94804 (national park)

Visitors to Richmond's waterfront would be forgiven for not immediately seeing the legacy of female empowerment in the landscape around them. At one point the city of Richmond had nearly erased the fact

The massive building here is just one element of the "home front" park that recognizes the social changes brought by the people who worked in the WWII industrial landscape.

The distinctive roof line to the left belongs to the Craneway Pavilion, once a Ford factory. To the right you can see the offices of the Rosie the Riveter National Park, under the distinctive national park shield.

that from 1941 to 1945, the Kaiser shipyards here buzzed with tens of thousands of women and men. The development of the largest and most productive shipbuilding facility in the world dramatically changed Richmond—it went from a small city to a twenty-four-hour boomtown in just a few years, and its ballooning population reflected the diversity of migrants who poured into the Bay Area for defense jobs. Almost fifty years later, grassroots pressure created public documentation of that time.

It started with the Rosie the Riveter Memorial monument, a public-art project on women's contributions to the war effort. The design by Susan Schwartzenberg and Cheryl Barton uses abstracted forms of Liberty ships, evoking the labor of assembling the prefabricated ships. Meant to draw parallels between the acts of constructing ships and reconstructing memories, the form suggests a vessel under construction. The Richmond Redevelopment Agency sponsored the memorial project as part of the reimagined waterfront known as Marina Bay, where street names like Schooner, Spinnaker, and Regatta bring to mind images of a moneyed, leisure class—rather than the welders, pipefitters, and other blue-collar workers who built ships here. In its drive to woo middle-income residents to the neighborhood, Marina Bay was deliberately disconnected from the central portion of the city, primarily African American and Latino. The 580 freeway further reinforces this sense of urban fortress; completed in the early 1990s, the freeway drives straight through Richmond, with eight highway lanes dividing low-income neighborhoods from Marina Bay.

The Rosie memorial drew the attention of the National Park Service, which had no sites commemorating the WWII home front. Although Richmond's contributions had been largely overlooked in the decades after the war, few US towns or cities can claim a home-front story as dramatic as this town, which was dubbed the Purple Heart City in 1944. A small community of 23,000 when war began, it exploded to over 100,000 with wartime migration. While many newcomers faced racial discrimination, the shipyards were eventually pushed to the forefront of wartime endeavors in crossing racial, ethnic, and gender lines at workplaces.

Despite the nearly wholesale erasure of the waterfront shipyards themselves, the park service interprets the remnants of one shipyard and other sites conveying Richmond's rich history, including housing for defense workers, childcare centers and schools, and Kaiser's medical facilities (a birthplace of the Kaiser Permanente health system). Many of these structures were built in a hurry, but they still stand, in part because the city suffered from a postwar economic slide driven by suburbanization and disinvestment in the historic downtown, much like urban centers across the US. Congress authorized creation of Rosie the Riveter/World War II Home Front National Historical Park in 2000.

Walking along the Richmond segments of the Bay Trail, visitors now find multiple markers conveying aspects of this history, from the local effects of wartime "internment" of Japanese Americans, to fights for housing rights, to the blues clubs, dance halls, and all-night movie theaters that once entertained weary workers. The National Park Visitor Education Center offers events, exhibits, and self-guided tours of other WWII sites. In its complexity, the park reflects tensions between historical interpretation, aesthetics, politics, and the requirements of commerce and tourism. (Donna Graves)

NEARBY SITES OF INTEREST

Ford Assembly Plant (now the Craneway Pavilion)
1414 Harbour Way South, Richmond 94804
Built in 1930, this plant was already one of Richmond's major employers and then continued under military contract during the war.

Shipyard No. 3

Canal Boulevard, Richmond 94804 (parking lot)

Although most of the shipyard structures are gone in Richmond's only surviving wartime yard, the area retains historic buildings and the last surviving ship built in Richmond, the *SS Red Oak Victory*, as well as a Whirley crane, used to move the ship components within the shipyard.

TO LEARN MORE

Richmond Museum of History, https://richmondmuseum.org

Rosie the Riveter/World War II Home Front National Historical Park, www.nps.gov/rori/index.htm

Wollenberg, Charles. *Marinship at War: Shipbuilding and Social Change in Wartime Sausalito.* Berkeley, CA: Western Heritage, 1990. (For the larger narrative about wartime shipyard labor.)

1.25 South Berkeley Social Justice Corridor

3000 Block of Shattuck Avenue, Berkeley 94705

Three murals in view, on La Peña and the Starry Plough, blending music and politics.

While all cities contain noticeable retail blocks, with clusters of certain kinds of stores—what economists call an *agglomeration*—the East Bay also contains what might be described as agglomerations of social justice activity. Whether through nonprofits that focus on a range of causes, activist publishing, or groups that blend culture with politics, these are corridors of political activity that create a sense of community identity and promote the desire to create a world that is not focused only on sales and profit.

The block of Shattuck Avenue between Woolsey and Prince is one such place-mark in Berkeley's legacy of grassroots work. The brick-and-mortar businesses and organizations on this block represent the spirit of resilience that has laced South Berkeley's mixed racial and socioeconomic demographics. On the east side of Shattuck, the Starry Plough Irish Pub is a legendary arts and progressive politics venue founded in 1973, hosting poetry slams and music, along with weekly political-Left events. Across the street, the Long Haul is an anarchist resource center and community space. In 1988 the Long Haul established *The Slingshot*, an independent radical newspaper; the group also produces a widely distributed calendar, now published by worker-owned anarchist publishing house AK Press. Next door is the Homeless Action Center, which has provided free legal and other services for homeless and low-income people since 1990.

Also on the east side of Shattuck is La Peña Cultural Center, founded by Latin American exiles and North American allies in the aftermath of the 1973 US-supported overthrow of Salvador Allende in Chile. A nonprofit cultural center, it serves as a space for intercultural and intergenerational dialogue and social justice organizing, emphasizing the performing and visual arts. *Song of Unity*, the 1978 mural at the entrance, underwent a remodel in 2012, so the version you can see now is different from the original, but its emphasis on global connections persists, with Latin American arts and politics at the center. With a long history of building solidarity with the people of Central America, Cuba, Puerto Rico, and the Southern Cone, La Peña hosts events that engage topics ranging from US military intervention and environmental justice struggles across the hemisphere, to local housing and food security matters. (Diana Negrín da Silva)

NEARBY SITES OF INTEREST

Ashby Flea Market
BART parking lot at Ashby Avenue, Berkeley 94705
The Lorin District, to the west of Shattuck, is home to a variety of local nonchain businesses and institutions that have persisted in the face of urban change. The largest East Bay Juneteenth Festival takes place here every June, on Adeline Street. As we completed this book, however, the flea market itself was threatened with closure.

TO LEARN MORE

Kinzer, Stephen. *Overthrow: America's Century of Regime Change from Hawaii to Iraq.* New York: Times Books, 2007.
Neruda, Pablo, and Oswaldo Guayasamín. *America, My Brother, My Blood/América, Mi Hermano, Mi Sangre: A Latin American Song of Suffering and Resistance.* Melbourne: Ocean Press, 2006.

1.26 Sproul Plaza, UC Berkeley

From the intersection of Bancroft and Telegraph Avenues to Sather Gate, University of California, Berkeley 94720

UC Berkeley is internationally famous for radical politics, in no small part because of the iconic images of student demonstrations in this plaza. It is not necessarily the institution, the city, or the state that are radical, however. It is the students, activists, and allies who have used this space for decades to demand their rights to free speech, community space, peace, and public education. The government's violent repression of those demands—with police and the National Guard, with batons, rubber bullets, and tear gas—has kept Sproul in the limelight and brought generation after generation back to the same spot to demand their rights.

Sproul's best-known images come out of the mid-1960s Free Speech movement protests. The plaza opened in 1962 as part of the UC's physical expansion to accommodate massive post-WWII campus growth. Though this was designed as a public space, university administrators banned tabling in 1964 to appease Berkeley business owners

The Free Speech Movement era was just one of several cycles of student and community protests that have filled the plaza. Sproul Hall's regal columns are peeking out of the trees on the left in this 1964 photo by Steven Marcus.

wary about growing student involvement in civil rights activism. Defiant students set up political information tables to challenge the ban, and when the university sent police to cite them, students continuously rotated through seats to keep the police busy and flustered. The tabling citations sparked a mass rally that galvanized a unified front of students, from the socialists to the Goldwater defenders (in other words, from the Left to the Right wing), all defending the right to table as "free speech." The media captured the iconic image of Free Speech movement leader Mario Savio atop a police car surrounded by hundreds of protesting students unwilling to let the police haul him away. A few months later, from the steps of Sproul, he would deliver what would become per-

haps his most-quoted call to protest: "There is a time when the operation of the machine becomes so odious, makes you so sick at heart, that you can't take part, you can't even passively take part, and you've got to put your bodies upon the gears and upon the wheels, upon the levers, upon all the apparatus, and you've got to make it stop. And you've got to indicate to the people who run it, to the people who own it, that unless you're free, the machine will be prevented from working at all."

Over the years, with Savio's words reverberating among students, the plaza filled to overflowing time and time again as students at this flagship public institution became radicalized and learned firsthand about the top-down power of the state. The experience of mass protest on this plaza brought thousands together, and soon those vast numbers turned to focus on the many heated issues of the day threatening their communities and lives. The war in Vietnam escalated, and students organized with the growing peace movement to create mass marches through Oakland to protest the military draft—seeking to physically block draftees from enrolling. Some formed alliances with the Black Panther Party, and others went on to participate in the other major movements that coalesced at that time: second-wave feminism, the burgeoning LGBT movement, and a broad range of organizations founded around ethnic race-class struggles, like the American Indian Movement and the Third World Liberation Front.

Students continue to return to Sproul with creative protest, often centered around making the campus and its education accessible to more people. In the 2000s, students protesting fee hikes and financial austerity set up tents in the plaza, while teaching assistants graded papers to make their work visible. When police confiscated their tents, students returned with new tents attached to balloons so they would hover over the plaza. Campus administrators again called

in the police. Echoing the 1960s, cops in riot gear marched on peaceful protesters, who wanted to attend classes in rooms with sufficient chairs and who sought tuition that they could afford without working three jobs.

NEARBY SITE OF INTEREST

People's Park
Between Haste, Bowditch, Dwight, and Regent Streets, Berkeley 94704

Just a few blocks away from Sproul, the site of People's Park stands as another symbol of struggle. In 1969 students and others turned a campus parking lot here into a public open space to materially represent their work toward an egalitarian world. Their greening efforts were met with the crush of bayonet-wielding National Guard troops, whose chilling use of violence included shooting dozens of people and killing one. Later, then-Governor Ronald Reagan dismissed the violence as necessary, infamously stating, "If it takes a bloodbath, let's get it over with." Periodically the university discusses renewed development plans for the site.

TO LEARN MORE

Dalzell, Tom. *The Battle for People's Park, Berkeley 1969*. Berkeley: Heyday Books, 2019.
Kitchell, Mark (producer and director). *Berkeley in the Sixties*. California Newsreel, 1990.

2

The South Bay and Penin- sula

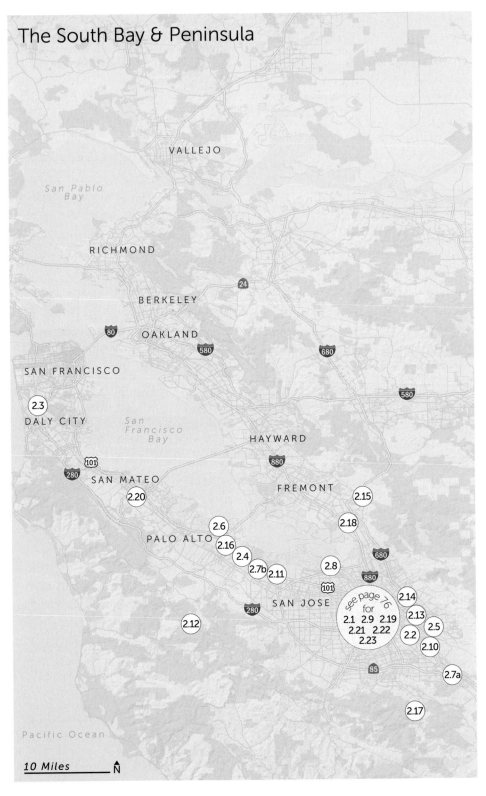

The South Bay & Peninsula

VALLEJO

San Pablo Bay

RICHMOND

BERKELEY

OAKLAND

SAN FRANCISCO

2.3

DALY CITY

San Francisco Bay

HAYWARD

FREMONT

2.15

SAN MATEO

2.20

2.18

2.6

PALO ALTO

2.16

2.4

2.7b 2.11

2.8

2.14

SAN JOSE

see page 76 for
2.1 2.9 2.19
2.21 2.22
2.23

2.13

2.5

2.2

2.12

2.10

2.7a

2.17

Pacific Ocean

10 Miles   N

Introduction

Today the South Bay is synonymous with Silicon Valley, but this tech-centered name belies a geography with a far more diverse history than the name suggests. First, the region's dominance in silicon-based electronics manufacturing lasted only a few decades. Still, the *silicon* of Silicon Valley has thus largely become a metaphor for a complicated technology sector that entwines everyone—from service workers to highly paid software engineers at corporate campuses, from the titans of venture capital speculation and real estate development to myriad families running small businesses, shops, and restaurants serving multicultural communities. The valley is tucked around the southern marshes of the San Francisco Bay, between the Diablo Range to the east and the Santa Cruz Mountains to the west. At its heart is San Jose, the largest city of the valley, which turns out to be the only city in the entire Bay Area with more than one mil-

lion residents. But the valley has become, in both the popular imagination and the built environment, a much less clearly bound place. As the sites that we've included in this chapter suggest, Silicon Valley now stretches far up the San Francisco Peninsula on the west side and pays no mind to the Alameda County border to the east, with newly built housing and tech campuses in places like Redwood City and Fremont. Silicon Valley is more of a regional identity than one specific place.

If there is an iconic landscape element that calls out Silicon Valley, it's the Googleplex. You cannot see much of Google's storied headquarters campus from afar, but you may glimpse its neighbor, the hulking skeleton of the former airship hangar at Moffett Field, where Google executives park private jets. This and the other well-photographed tech campuses tend to be tucked behind grassy berms, ever present

THE SOUTH BAY & PENINSULA

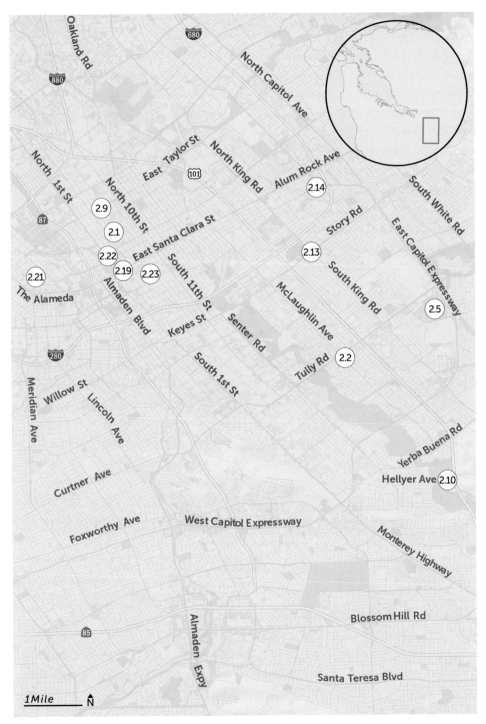

DETAIL FROM PAGE 74

but inaccessible. With no widely recognized skyline or iconic bridges, then, the Silicon Valley landscape may be characterized more by sprawl than any other feature. In the end, this means that your sense of the place may depend on how you approach it. For those finding Silicon Valley from the south, via the 101, the view is downright pastoral; from the north, it emerges as a nearly uninterrupted stretch of suburban office parks, strip malls, and cul-de-sac developments. Devoid of the more obvious cosmopolitanism of San Francisco or Oakland, the low-slung, sprawling landscape rarely sparks emotion beyond frustration over traffic or the inadequacy of the transit system.

It is our hope, however, that this chapter will encourage you to look closer and find that the banality of this—or any other—suburban landscape works to hide fascinating histories and a dynamic present. While strip malls and office parks may suggest that nothing was there before and nothing will ever come after, in truth the built environment and people of the valley have been through remarkable revolutions with each wave of new inhabitants. And the landscape itself continues to transform.

An Ever-Changing Place

Like most of the bay's marshy coastline, the south end of the bay is a diverse ecosystem supported by creeks and rivers that flow from the mountains. Long before urbanization, the fish and shellfish, mammals, birds, and plants provided significant resources for Ohlone-speaking indigenous communities

that coexisted along the valley floor. The sprawl of development devastated the ecology of the bay, and industrial and corporate uses now dominate the shoreline. Even so, environmental restoration efforts in recent years continue to remake the place in ways that remind us that the tech era is only one phase in a much longer history.

When eighteenth-century Spanish soldiers first established outposts in what would become San Francisco, they found limited water and arable land on the peninsula. By contrast, the ranches and farms they established later, here in the Santa Clara Valley, provided the first glimpse of California's now-legendary fecundity. After the gold rush, predominantly Anglo (eventually called white) immigrants wrested control of the region's agricultural land, which had access to water, ideal year-round temperatures, and rich topsoil. In a matter of decades, they transformed this valley into a new kind of agricultural landscape. This was not the fabled small family farm of Jeffersonian lore, but a vast patchwork of agricultural empires organized through industrial logics. Firms dedicated acres upon acres to growing high-value agricultural commodities to supply massive canning operations and global shipping at the core of San Jose's early industrial growth. By the twentieth century, Santa Clara boosters who were encouraged by the sale of its peaches and pears had christened it the Valley of the Heart's Delight. As with the agricultural empires of the San Joaquin and Southern California valleys, fields and factories alike became profitable through the wholesale exploitation of immigrant workers.

Depression-era San Jose was already home to migrants from China, Japan, India, Portugal, Sweden, England, and the Philippines, as well as Black and white US migrants, and Native American communities that remained in the Bay Area. Some had come with the Spanish colonial mission system as early as the eighteenth century; others had come to work on railroads and mining in the nineteenth century; others joined waves of agricultural labor recruitment. By the mid-twentieth century, residents of San Jose and the Santa Clara Valley already lived in a remarkably racially and ethnically diverse place. The diversity of the region would only increase in the post-WWII era, as the US lifted some of its most restrictive immigration policies. Some new migrants were refugees from US-backed wars in Southeast Asia and Central America, others drawn by universities and the booming tech sector. As was true across California, diversity did not necessarily mean inclusion; elites maintained racial barriers in housing and labor across the South Bay.

In the postwar era, houses, shopping centers, and factories came to dominate the landscape. A central driver for sprawl was the mass construction of electronics research and manufacturing facilities. Primed by Cold War funding from the Department of Defense, a new tech industry exploded across the South Bay. Many of the developments that still dot the region were born from a dose of Cold War paranoia:

Suburban boosters thought dispersed settlements would fare better in a nuclear attack than a dense city. This mixed with the need for flat, wide spaces for mass production and a newfound corporate interest in "university style" corporate campuses. As landscape historian Louise Mozingo has put it, the valley was built by and for engineers. Meanwhile, the city of San Jose gobbled up new developments and smaller towns in every direction, growing in size from 11 to 137 square miles between 1940 and 1970.

The rapid development of the tech sector meant a change in the composition, if not the conditions, of work in the valley. Where workers once faced toxic exposure from pesticides in fields and mercury from mines, they now dealt with space-age compounds in electronic assembly lines. At one point, the industrial facilities of Silicon Valley were dumping so much heavy-metal runoff from manufacturing into the sewers that the city of Palo Alto built a new waste treatment plant to extract precious metals out of the waste stream. By the end of the 1980s, Silicon Valley lost much of its manufacturing capacity to the Global South, leaving behind a legacy of toxic landscapes, inefficient suburbanization, and an increasingly precarious workforce, while keeping its reputation as the global center of innovation and "disruption."

The dispersal of work and shopping through suburbanization meant that downtown San Jose lost its economic core, like many US cities, creating a hollowed city—ripe for poorly conceived urban renewal projects and freeway building. Palo Alto, with its ties to Stanford University, financial firms, and a growing number of tech headquarters, became the de facto financial and intellectual capital of the region, despite being outside the physical boundaries of the valley. Even as San Jose officials continue to redesign and rebuild their central business district in efforts to lure corporate tenants back, the city's name no longer evokes the same technological awe as Palo Alto, Mountain View, or San Francisco.

As we write, neither the cataclysmic dot-com crash of the early 2000s nor the global financial crisis of the mid-2000s seems to have significantly slowed Silicon Valley's growth. Rather, its tendrils seem to be wrapping around not just San Jose and Santa Clara, but San Francisco, Oakland, and all points between, with satellites in places as far flung as Nevada. The vast pools of capital that once flowed through electronics companies into the mass suburbanization of the valley now slosh through tech-worker wages into the pockets of real estate developers as seemingly ceaseless gentrification unfolds alongside the building of yet more suburban tracts and "new urbanist" condos at the urban fringe.

None of this landscape was inevitable, and never did it go uncontested. As this chapter shows, people have always struggled against all forms of injustice in the valley and fought to carve out spaces for themselves and their communities. From indigenous peoples rebelling at the missions to striking cannery workers to contemporary environmental justice activists, people have

always challenged power, and in many cases they have thrived. Finding these stories in the landscape makes this region fascinating and inspiring.

To visitors and students of the South Bay, the sprawling suburban landscape offers several challenges. We'll focus on three here: navigation, the erasure of history in the landscape, and our own mental roadblocks when it comes to understanding suburbs. First, unlike parts of the East Bay and San Francisco, it is more difficult to walk or bike your way through this chapter. You may indeed take advantage of the extensive bus network, downtown trolleys, and flat bikeable streets. But the absence of bike lanes in many places and exceedingly slow bus timetables throughout can prove challenging. Second, in contrast with dense cities with longer histories, as development unfolded here it became more difficult to see traces of each supplanted space in the landscape. Therefore, the sites in this chapter have been chosen to reveal where slivers of sedimented cultural landscapes still show through and how our "naturalized" suburban landscape serves to obscure both the past and alternative futures.

Finally, the South Bay challenges what we might consider a "progressive" or "people's" agenda. Today the imagined "good" city is composed of mixed-income, diverse, and dense urban spaces with good public transportation connecting walkable neighborhoods. This narrative casts suburban sprawl, with its presumed zealous consumerism, antiurban whiteness, and environmental destruction as the quintessential problem for the future. As you wander across the South Bay, you will indeed find these tropes. But you'll also find vibrant single-family housing tracts occupied by first-, second-, and even seventh-generation immigrants representing dozens of languages. You will find strip malls with signs in Hindi, Chinese, Vietnamese, Tagalog, Spanish, English, and Portuguese, sometimes all in a row, representing a remarkably diverse set of communities. The commuting patterns and class dynamics of these communities form their own subgeographies that may challenge our sense of the way suburbs work.

■ ■ ■

2.1 Boyer Home

446 N. 5th Street, San Jose 95112

This Victorian house persists as part of the legacy of Black San Jose, a community with roots stretching back to the mid-nineteenth century, and with a legacy that includes civil rights work long before the civil rights movement of the postwar era. The history of Black communities in the Bay Area is often told via the WWII-era migrations, primarily to San Francisco and Oakland. But there were important earlier migrations to the entire region, including San Jose, where newly arrived Black workers, business owners, and community leaders helped establish the core of a rapidly urbanizing California. The Boyer family, for example, owned businesses and served as community leaders, organizing important local institutions that forged networks and support for other newcomers and for African Americans in the South Bay more generally.

The Boyer Home, photographed in 2017, is now a private residence.

By 1906, the Boyers owned this home on North 5th Street near the center of downtown. Dr. D. W. Boyer ran a medical office in the Porter-Stock Building at 85 South 1st Street (that building is no longer there), which specialized in the health benefits of the newly popular Swedish massage. Sometime between 1906 and 1908, his wife, Elizabeth Boyer, hosted the first meeting of the Garden City Women's Club at their home. The group was one of many such clubs organized across the US, building on the success of the Convention of Colored Women (the first one in Boston in 1895 included Harriett Tubman, Margaret Murray Washington, and Anna Sprague, the daughter of Frederick Douglass). By 1911, there were nearly thirty such clubs across California.

For working Black women—especially those employed in service work in predominantly white areas—the club represented one of the few spaces outside of the church to socialize and organize. In official documents the club stated that its explicit purpose was "to strengthen community services and aid in the promotion of racial understanding." In this regard, the clubs worked like many immigrant social-aid organizations in the days before larger government-run programs came along. The clubs formalized social and economic networks for new arrivals and furthered an explicitly antiracist agenda.

That agenda would become increasingly important as the Second Great Migration brought more African Americans to San Jose in the WWII years, and as whites solidified racial segregation in response. New Black migrants to the city faced severe limitations on where they could rent, and even highly skilled workers were excluded from employment. The Garden City Women's Club served as an important incubator for community organizers who resisted de facto racism in the city. By the 1950s and 1960s, the club was engaged in activities ranging from organizing health days and Black history weeks to boycotts of department stores in solidarity with sit-ins across the country. Much of the historical record about these clubs was preserved by club member Inez Jackson, who also joined the local NAACP chapter. Through a long career of teaching and community organizing, she fought to preserve the history of the Black community, and specifically Black women, and their contributions to San Jose.

TO LEARN MORE

Garden City Women's Club, ed. *History of Black Americans in Santa Clara Valley*. Sunnyvale, CA: Lockheed Missiles and Space Co., 1978.
For more on the history of Black conventions, see the Colored Conventions Digital Archive: http://coloredconventions.org.

2.2 Chùa Đức Viên

2420 McLaughlin Avenue, San Jose 95121

This temple and its unique facade offer a physical manifestation of three key aspects of the Vietnamese immigrant experience: navigating the forces of assimilation in multi-ethnic San Jose, dealing with exclusion from networks of white-dominated power brokers, and balancing cultural preservation with building a Vietnamese American cultural identity. Chùa Đức Viên, with its gleaming white-pillared gate and ornate facade, is nestled between blocks of typical suburban homes. Situated near a major intersection with gas stations on every corner, the temple reveals key aspects of the post-1975 experience of Vietnamese American San Jose.

The temple was founded by Dam Luu, a refugee, social worker, and community advocate who was one of the first ordained Buddhist nuns in Vietnam. After nearly a decade of saving toward building the temple, collecting recyclables for refunds, and receiving small donations from the emergent Vietnamese community, Dam Luu

Dam Luu's Chùa Đức Viên temple.

was able to finance the $400,000 temple. It took three years to build, and when it opened in 1998 as a religious center, it was the first home to Buddhist nuns in the US. At the time, it became an education and cultural center aimed at bridging cultural gaps between Vietnamese immigrants of different generations. Dam Luu organized English language instruction for adults, Vietnamese language instruction for younger generations, and annual festivals and celebrations to provide grassroots education to a Vietnamese American community mostly unfamiliar with Vietnamese culture outside of the context of war and refugees.

Following the long decade of US war in Vietnam, tens of thousands of Vietnamese immigrants and refugees had been pushed and pulled to the US in search of safety. In defiance of US policies aimed at dispersing them across the country, they formed tight new urban and suburban communities across California. In San Jose, signs announcing that you've entered "Little Saigon" only hint at the geography of the Vietnamese American community here. The spatial reach of the community has shifted—sometimes as people pursued opportunities, and other times as they were pushed out for new development—and organized itself around multiple centers, commercial developments run by and for Southeast Asians, and temples like Chùa Đức Viên. Tensions over legacies of the war in Vietnam and refugees' relationship to the current Communist government linger. In the mid-1990s when Vietnamese monks were invited to visit the temple, anti-Communist Vietnamese protestors showed up at the gates to denounce their presence.

Dam Luu's own story within this context reveals both a common trajectory and a unique path. As a young nun, she was jailed in 1963 for protesting the South Vietnam government. She later earned a master's in social work in Germany in the late 1960s and returned to Vietnam to run an orphan-

age in Saigon until its fall in 1975. After she refused to denounce fellow Buddhists to the new regime, Dam Luu fled the country on a small fishing boat, becoming a refugee first in Malaysia and eventually in the United States. She established a temple in a rented home in East San Jose and began to translate, publish, and use chant books in Vietnamese, departing from the usual practice of Chinese-language prayers, which were sung but not understood by lay members. As the temple's membership grew, she was able to build Chùa Đức Viên, a space more reflective of the Vietnamese Buddhist tradition, but still in the context of a new US landscape. Dam Luu died in 1999.

NEARBY SITE OF INTEREST

Lee's Sandwiches
260 E. Santa Clara Street, San Jose 95113
This corner is where Lê Văn Bá and Nguyễn Thị Hạnh began selling *bánh mì* sandwiches from the food truck they borrowed from their sons in the early 1980s. The now-ubiquitous blending of French-style bread stuffed with Vietnamese ingredients was largely unknown in the US prior to the arrival of Vietnamese refugees in the 1970s, including the Lê family (which they anglicized as Lee), who made these sandwiches famous.

TO LEARN MORE

Lorentzen, Lois Ann, Joaquin Jay Gonzalez, Kevin M. Chun, and Hien Duc Do, eds. *Religion at the Corner of Bliss and Nirvana: Politics, Identity, and Faith in New Migrant Communities*. Durham: NC: Duke University Press, 2009.

2.3 Daly City Teen Center

1901 Junipero Serra Boulevard, Daly City
94014 (historic site)

San Mateo is a vast county that eats up much of the peninsula, stretching from San Francisco all the way down to Stanford University on the east side and to Año Nuevo State Park, just shy of Santa Cruz, on the west side. Its cities, several of which are just across the San Francisco border, are not often mentioned in stories of political organizing in the Bay Area. But in the late 1990s, Daly City briefly came to the fore as an important node in region-wide youth organizing. If you visit this site today, you'll be greeted by a movie megaplex. But before redevelopment transformed the area, this was home to the Daly City Teen Center, which opened in 1997 as the first drop-in youth center in the county under the name Neutral Territory.

The teen center was created as a result of youth advocacy, including a school walkout in 1994 that connected to youth actions across the Bay Area. Throughout 1993 and 1994, Latinx students joined the region-wide Student Empowerment Program (StEP), which organized a series of student walkouts throughout the area. These actions were largely composed of high school youth and college undergraduates protesting policies that criminalized Latinx youth and their families, including the statewide Proposition 187—which barred undocumented immigrants from services like education and non-emergency health care—as well as gang injunctions that justified increased policing of youth of

PERSONAL REFLECTION FROM SERGIO ARROYO, TEACHER AND COMMUNITY ORGANIZER

The Peninsula had a distinct experience. In the sense that . . . in the East Bay you all were lucky, you had the family out here that had politics or exposure of some kind, you know what I mean? And there were folks in Frisco who were organizing Frisco, and you know San Francisco just has always been a magnet for Chicano movement type stuff since the '60s and '70s. But when it came down to Daly City, ain't nobody wanted to go down to Daly City. It wasn't cool, it wasn't sexy. So it really made us become the mentors, at like sixteen years old, to people who were also sixteen years old. So it was hella pressure like that, but hella beautiful in the sense that it gave me, at least, a sense of purpose at a really young age, and a sense of belonging.

color and attacks on bilingual and bicultural education.

These actions also included confronting school districts and local boards of education. Drawing on their lived experiences, students became a visible and outspoken force whose demands helped lay the groundwork for the eventual reversal of many of these policies. Proposition 187 was found unconstitutional in 1997 and, along with other bills that had aimed to deny immigrants access to services, has been removed from California law.

Coming out of this activist milieu, the center sponsored youth programs such as tutoring and summer activities and became an organizing home base for the grassroots youth group Voices of Struggle (including youth in Daly City, South San Francisco, Pacifica, and San Bruno). Here young people organized trainings, workshops, and parent education meetings. At least three direct-action protests were organized from the Teen Center, as well as the first Ethnic Studies Conference for High Schoolers. The center was closed in 2001 as part of the area's commercial redevelopment, and its programming dispersed and grew through other organizations. Voices of Struggle moved to South San Francisco High School, and Ben Franklin Middle School in Daly City hosted a short-lived Raza club for Latinx youth. (Diana Negrín da Silva)

2.4 Drew Center Pharmacy

2111 University Avenue, East Palo Alto 94303

The Drew Center Pharmacy in 2019.

The last visible evidence of a late-1960s effort to bring health care to the low-income Black and immigrant neighborhoods of East Palo Alto lives on, for now, in an unassuming building in East Palo Alto. The area is a study in contrasts. University Avenue stretches across just over four miles from the marshy edge of the San Francisco Bay to the old Southern Pacific rail lines that are now used by the commuter-rail CalTrain. At one

end is Facebook's headquarters campus in Menlo Park; at the other is Stanford University. In between, the town of East Palo Alto endures as a working-class Black and Brown enclave in the increasingly superwealthy peninsula.

In East Palo Alto, as is the case in many communities of color throughout the US, one of the forms racism takes is in limited access to basic medical care. In the late 1950s, what would become East Palo Alto was still an unincorporated and underdeveloped community (at the time it was still called Ravenswood). Private medical practices were sparse, and since the community lacked an organized municipal government, San Mateo County failed to provide much in the way of services. Because of this, families had to travel long distances to access care from clinicians who were not particularly attuned to the experiences or conditions of East Palo Alto residents. The result for many was poor health and premature death.

East Palo Alto residents, in connection with radical political movements and the expansion of Great Society programs, organized the East Palo Alto–Menlo Park Neighborhood Health Center in 1967. The center provided community-focused access to doctors and health advice—for example, counseling on sickle cell anemia—and a pharmacy. The clinic and information center opened on Bay Road. Within two years it had incorporated as a nonprofit, tapped into federal funding, and moved to its current location on University. Eventually the center established a foundation to oversee its multiple services and was renamed in honor of Black surgeon Charles Drew. In 1983 the pharmacy was split off as an independent entity; the Drew Health Foundation lost federal funding in the early 2000s and could no longer provide health-care services. And at the time of this writing, the land under the facility was slated to be redeveloped into (yet more) class-A office buildings to house the unabated expansion of Silicon Valley. (Ofelia Bello)

TO LEARN MORE

Loyd, Jenna M. *Health Rights Are Civil Rights: Peace and Justice Activism in Los Angeles, 1963–1978.* Minneapolis: University of Minnesota Press, 2014. Although this book is about Los Angeles, it offers a great history of political organizing for health care in postwar California.

2.5 Eastridge Shopping Center

2200 Eastridge Loop, San Jose 95122

One can't visit the suburbs without thinking about malls and the way they forever altered the economic life of nearby urban downtowns. San Jose's Eastridge Shopping Center emerged in the age of "white flight," opening to great fanfare in 1968 with dozens of city and business leaders in attendance. Speaking to the press in a place where orchards had stood only a few years before, they proclaimed a new age in modern shopping, for those with the cars and disposable income to enjoy the massive structure on the outskirts of East San Jose. The cultural promise of the project seemed proven seven years later when the San Jose Symphony Orchestra played on the Eastridge lawn to an audience of, it was reported, five thousand,

the largest in the history of the symphony to date.

At the time, the mall was the largest shopping center on the West Coast, boasting 160 shops, eight banks, four anchor department stores, and fourteen restaurants. It was undeniably also a cultural center for the then largely white suburbs—hosting weddings, homeowner-association meetings, fairs, and concerts. Meanwhile, the success of malls like Eastridge was eviscerating traditional city centers, where the working poor and people of color who had been largely excluded from suburban home ownership now found themselves living without a diverse business base as mom-and-pop stores suffered or disappeared. Perhaps most importantly, urban dwellers found themselves without a sufficient tax base to fund basic city maintenance and social services.

Though the mall was once a testament to white working-class upward mobility in the suburbs, a 2004 fight over the mall's redevelopment not only revealed the limits on who could access that mobility but it also emphasized that investor profits would not be sacrificed for idealism. Despite ordinances that mandate hiring a certain percentage of locals, Eastridge's Chicago-based owners brought temporary laborers from Arkansas, Texas, and Iowa to do the physical work of the much-needed remodel. In response, the Santa Clara and San Benito Counties Building Trades Council (SCBTC) ran a public campaign showing how the company was getting away with paying well below San Jose's prevailing wages while providing no health insurance to workers. This was more

The sprawling Eastridge Mall was once the epitome of the modern ideal.

than a wage fight, though. The campaign demonstrated the growing inequality of the valley as SCBTC workers tried in earnest to organize a boycott of the mall by explaining to mall shoppers that their own families would not be able to afford the much-touted new shops, and that low wages and skyrocketing housing costs were pricing them out of San Jose. In 2016 the mall was purchased for an estimated $200 million by a Goldman-Sachs-backed investor, promising to maintain a landscape of extravagant consumption.

2.6 Facebook HQ

One Hacker Way, Menlo Park 94025

A larger-than-life welcome sign with Facebook's thumbs-up icon marks the entrance to Facebook headquarters, one of many such campuses that, through the 2000s, largely replaced skyscrapers as the flagship buildings of powerful corporations in the new economy. Meant to evoke the collaborative and innovative space of a university, the place functions a lot like a company town where employees never stop working. They work, eat, recreate, nap, and work again—all in the endless pursuit of keeping billions of eyes focused on their platform, so that the data collected can be sold for billions in profits. Facebook allows visitors with an escort only, but if you are nearby you can stop in at the parking lot for a glimpse, if only to more accurately visualize the deep divide between such South Bay campuses and towns like East Palo Alto, just across the highway.

Along with Google and Twitter, Facebook has redefined the purpose and function of the Internet. Critiques of their impact on global culture, economics, and democratic elections abound. But companies like these are not just virtual entities with ethereal global reach. They are essentially tech factories, with real employees who significantly impact the geography of the region. Where the famed robber baron Leland Stanford once made nearby Palo Alto into the home of his eponymous institution, billionaire CEOs like Mark Zuckerberg wield unprecedented power with increasing infamy as they meddle in local and national politics, make demands of city planners, and buy naming rights to hospitals and other institutions. At the same time, the army of engineers, managers, and marketing professionals at these companies take home six-figure salaries that get sucked into the steeply rising rents that are driving out many longtime residents and businesses across the region.

Big Tech still likes to imagine itself aligned with a scrappy, innovative, or (the more recent buzzword) disruptive ethos. They continue to cast themselves as the rebels operating as hackers that disrupt outdated social and economic systems rather than as mass-production stalwarts like General Electric or General Motors. Yet they are as wealthy, powerful, and exploitative as any of the famed industrial giants of prior centuries. Despite placing itself quaintly on One Hacker Way, the Harvard-founded, venture-capital-fueled Facebook is not actually at the forefront of tech innovation. Rather, like most of the Internet, Facebook runs the majority of its software on open-source code and software. This is technology that is shared freely between programmers; no entity holds legal ownership of the code. Open source, developed over the last sev-

eral decades by people for free, has been used by corporations—from Microsoft to Apple and more—as the foundation for their profit-making operations. Meanwhile, the codes and algorithms that Facebook keeps exclusive are protected by draconian intellectual property laws and fiercely guarded by the company; of course, they claim to own your photos too. Their true innovation has been mastering the psycho-social tools that keep users' eyes glued to screens, providing near-infinite personal data that the company alchemizes into profitable ads and surveillance information.

NEARBY SITE OF INTEREST

Stanford University

450 Serra Mall, Stanford 94305

Though Stanford is most famous now as the training ground for Silicon Valley entrepreneurs and workers, the sprawling estate campus is also home to the Dr. Martin Luther King Jr. Papers project and an agro-ecological experimental farm with the latest in sustainable food practices.

TO LEARN MORE

Mozingo, Louise A. *Pastoral Capitalism: A History of Suburban Corporate Landscapes*. Cambridge, MA: MIT Press, 2016.

Saxenian, AnnaLee. *Regional Advantage: Culture and Competition in Silicon Valley and Route 128*. Cambridge, MA: Harvard University Press, 1996.

Tufekci, Zeynep. "Yes, Big Platforms Could Change Their Business Models." *Wired*, December 17, 2018.

2.7 Fairchild Semiconductor

101 Bernal Road, San Jose 95119 (site of former fabrication facility)

844 E. Charleston Road, Palo Alto 94303 (site of first integrated circuit)

Suburban landscapes like this one hide the unsettling origins of the digital devices that enable our postindustrial lives. Once home to tech manufacturing firms like Fairchild Semiconductor, this area was poisoned when a purportedly safe storage process for toxic waste began to leak. In 1981 some 58,000 gallons of chemicals from a Fairchild factory were discovered in the water supply that served 16,500 homes in the Los Paseos neighborhood. Over the course of forty years the high-tech industry of semiconductor and microprocessor fabrication had transformed the region from the agricultural "Valley of the Heart's Delight" to "Silicon Valley." In its new form, the valley was free of smoke-belching factories. Instead, companies quietly buried hundreds of tons of toxic runoff in underground storage tanks at their facilities. This kept the industrial fallout of the new era of manufacturing out of sight——until the tanks began to leak. Today a shopping center covers the history of the twenty-two-acre Fairchild Semiconductor facility that was here, leaving no visible clues of the site's former use or of the contaminated soil below.

The fact that chip manufacturing was toxic came as no surprise to the predominantly female, Asian, and Latinx employees who worked in Silicon Valley facilities in the 1970s and 1980s. For decades they had complained of headaches and nausea from activities ranging from soldering to washing components with noxious solvents. But with no labor union and only minimal federal oversight, workers had little recourse to force companies into cleaner or safer production methods. At the one plant where workers managed to organize a union, largely around health and safety concerns, their efforts crashed as the company declared bankruptcy the very afternoon that the National Labor Relations Board ordered it to recognize the union. So it was not until toxic chemicals appeared outside of the facilities—impacting communities near the plant in addition to workers—that advocates formed organizations like the Silicon Valley Toxics Coalition (SVTC) to organize for greater regulation, transparency, and the cleanup of toxic chemicals.

Fairchild was not the only culprit or perhaps even the worst. One IBM facility, for example, had been releasing toxins since the mid-1950s. Organizations like the SVTC, eventually with support from the Environmental Protection Agency (EPA), discovered dozens more leaks and toxic sites. Public actions, lobbying, and lawsuits forced Fairchild and its parent company, the oil giant Slumberger, to pay tens of millions of dollars for decades-long cleanups. The federal government, however, remains on the hook for much of the cleanup, and no amount of remediation and monitoring will undo the historical damage to people's health and lives.

Today Silicon Valley contains the greatest concentration of EPA superfund sites in the country, but toxic landscapes are hard to see.

There is rarely bubbling green goo or purple smoke coming out of the ground. Chemicals like the trichloroethylene and benzene that Fairchild leaked are invisible to the eye in groundwater, measured at the micro scale of parts per billion. Neither the polluters seeking to avoid further liability nor city officials and developers looking to expand the South Bay are especially keen to announce toxic landscapes. As writer Ingrid Burrington has pointed out, there are plaques (at the second address above) dedicated to Fairchild's significant contributions to the development of electronics manufacturing and the birth of Silicon Valley. But there is no public plaque indicating that many of Silicon Valley's new high-tech software companies were built directly on top of huge fields of contaminated soil and groundwater. This includes the Google headquarters, built at a site poisoned by another former Fairchild plant. Google and others—including residential neighborhoods—sit atop underground toxic plumes that make up the Middlefield-Ellis-Whisman Study Site, a grouping of several federal superfund sites in Mountain View produced by waste left by eleven entities, including Raytheon, Intel, and the US Navy in its operations at Moffett Field.

NEARBY SITES OF INTEREST

Bay Trail, access near Crittenden Lane and Stevens Creek Trail, Mountain View 94304

The Stevens Creek Trail points toward a particularly well-developed stretch of the Bay Trail, which is planned to become a five-hundred-mile loop around the bay for cycling and walking. This part is great for seeing the results of decades of wetland restoration and can take you all the way to San Jose. You can also access the trail through the surprisingly open Googleplex campus if you'd like to see the bustling heart of the Internet's most powerful corporation. See http://baytrail.org/

Stanford Research Park
3160 Porter Drive, Palo Alto 94304

Tech giant Hewlett-Packard occupies one side of the street, and military contractor Lockheed-Martin maintains a facility on the other. This is the center of a seven-hundred-acre research park owned in perpetuity by Stanford University, established in 1951 to build relationships with tech companies flush with military funding and to generate revenue through leasing land. Many of the research scientists who developed the modern transistor, integrated circuit, personal computer, and the business model that makes billionaires out of engineers got their start here.

TO LEARN MORE

Burrington, Ingrid. "Light Industry: Toxic Waste and Pastoral Capitalism." *E-Flux Journal* 74 (June 2016).

Pellow, David N., and Lisa Sun-Hee Park. *The Silicon Valley of Dreams: Environmental Injustice, Immigrant Workers, and the High-Tech Global Economy.* New York: NYU Press, 2002.

2.8 Gold Street Bridge
Gold Street at Guadalupe River,
San Jose 95002

Once a symbol of community power, the Gold Street Bridge has long linked a world of gleaming glass offices and hotels with an underinvested community of shuttered boat builders, canneries, and junkyards in Alviso. Things are changing now as tech companies and luxury apartment buildings spill over the bridge. But there was a time

(Above) The simple Gold Street Bridge is a lovely place to visit, with trails, ample bird sightings, and public restrooms.

(Left) Chicano activists used a self-built toll booth to stop traffic on the Gold Street Bridge in 1973 to draw attention to the socio-economic conditions of Alviso. (Al Magazu photo)

in which Chicano residents used this bridge to demand support from local government. The unassuming bridge itself is a great, undervalued place to visit, with bathrooms and a public park that includes the Guadalupe River estuary.

On March 24, 1973, activists from Alviso blocked the Gold Street Bridge and set up their own tollbooth to disrupt the flow of cars, charging twenty-five cents per crossing. The direct action was intended not to raise significant funds but to draw attention to the underdevelopment of the predominantly Chicanx neighborhood. At issue most immediately in 1973 was the absence of paved streets in the neighborhood, despite its being one of the oldest communities in Santa Clara County. The lack of progress would have come as a surprise to the city's founders, who in the 1840s imagined the small town as the major port connecting the South Bay to the world. For several years it indeed was, and the town boomed around its long piers, used to move the bounty of Santa Clara's agriculture and quicksilver from the New Almaden Mine (see p. 106) to markets around the world. But the 1864 completion of a railroad connecting San Jose to San Francisco's deeper port abruptly halted Alviso's boom. In a pattern repeated around Santa Clara County in the late nineteenth century, first Chinese and then Japanese families found homes and work in the area's fruit orchards. As those communities declined here, Mexican, Puerto Rican, and Portuguese migrants moved to Alviso, where many worked first in agriculture and later as low-wage temporary workers building Santa Clara's electronics manufacturing industry.

By the 1960s, Alviso was a predominantly Chicanx community, and very little had been done to expand the town's footprint from its 1840s origins. In 1968 the town voted to be annexed by San Jose—lured by promises from San Jose officials and developers that joining the larger city would bring development. Instead, Alvisians found themselves in a position with even less political power and autonomy, and the promised new development failed to arrive. Activists, working with prominent organizer and author Ernesto Galarza, had formed an ad hoc committee to build political power. After the annexation vote, the committee temporarily took control of the town's largest employer—a health clinic—but they ran into problems, and meanwhile many of Alviso's more fundamental problems of poor housing, lack of jobs, and crumbling services persisted.

Meanwhile, Alviso faces another challenge: Due to overdrawing of groundwater for agricultural and industrial uses, the land itself has sunk below sea level. Surrounded by water on two sides, much of Alviso is now a bowl waiting to be filled with water. Coyote Creek to the north is prone to jumping its banks in heavy rains and has done exactly that several times. A 1983 flood left some areas with water as high as six feet, displacing dozens from their homes. The neighborhood flooded again in 2014, symbolically and materially reinforcing pressures for low-income communities to abandon their homes and, ultimately, make way for redevelopment in the image of Silicon Valley, which city officials and developers have been dreaming of for fifty years.

TO LEARN MORE

Galarza, E., G. Flores, G. R. Muñoz, R. M. Barrera, and M. G. Vialpando, eds. *Action Research in Defense of the Barrio: Interviews with Ernesto Galarza, Guillermo Flores and Rosalio Muñoz.* Los Angeles: Aztlán, 1974.

2.9 Heinlenville (San-Doy-Say Tong Yun Fow)

6th Street between Jackson and Taylor Streets, San Jose 95112

For every story of attacks on California's Chinatowns, there are important stories of resistance and resilience. Across 1880s California, whites excluded Chinese from the spoils of gold mining and land ownership and ultimately developed a culture of anti-Chinese violence that included burning whole Chinese towns and neighborhoods all over

In 1974 the *San Jose Mercury News* printed this photo of the public burning of Chinatown on May 4, 1887. (Photographer unknown)

the state. Here in 1887 arsonists burned the second of San Jose's Chinatowns, but residents refused to leave. Forging interethnic bonds, they worked to ensure their survival in the face of white supremacy. Though the area was later cleared again for modern development, the site nevertheless contains an important story of strategic community resilience.

After the San Jose arson, the Chinese business class found an ally in local farmer and businessman John Heinlen. As a German immigrant, Heinlen did not fit well into the dominant Anglo culture in San Jose, but as a white man, he could own property—and he owned quite a bit. Over significant objections from other San Jose whites, Heinlen and the Quen Hing Tong (a Chinese immigrant organization) collaborated on a plan to construct a new six-square-block Chinatown on his property, which he would rent to Chinese businesses. The new neigh-

borhood, known as Heinlenville to English speakers, was built from brick, with water and sewers developed in part to deter further attempts at arson, and a gated fence to limit access. Heinlen and the Quen Hing Tong hired the same architect that the city had recently used to build its elaborate city hall, which conveyed the intended permanence of the new Chinatown as part of San Jose.

This third Chinatown, anglicized as San-Doy-Say Tong Yun Fow, functioned as an important economic center in San Jose for the local and regional Chinese community. It was here that Chinese district associations housed offices from which they coordinated immigrant labor. Grocery stores, semilegal gambling halls, and other small businesses occupied the first floors of buildings, while owners and their families, as well as migrant tenants, found housing on the upper floors and back rooms. The Ng Shing Gung Temple—now replicated at the San

Jose History Park—served as the main religious and cultural hub for Chinese people, especially those working in Santa Clara's agricultural economy without access to the temples and centers in the larger San Francisco Chinatown.

Despite the relative safety of the neighborhood and the early success of businesses, the Heinlenville Chinatown declined relatively rapidly, particularly after the federal Chinese Exclusion Act of 1882 limited immigration, slowing the community's growth. Meanwhile some residents moved farther afield to less confined spaces. Heinlen's heirs, who still owned the buildings, declared bankruptcy during the Great Depression, and Chinatown was effectively emptied. In 1949 the city tore down the Ng Shing Gung temple and converted Chinatown's six blocks into a corporate yard for the city of San Jose. Now an empty lot, the site has been slated for redevelopment for years but remains vacant.

NEARBY SITES OF INTEREST

Japantown
Jackson Street between 5th and 7th Streets, San Jose

San Jose's historic Japantown stretches several blocks south and west from here. Plaques along both Jackson and 6th Streets provide some history of the neighborhood. At Jackson and 5th Street is a striking memorial to the Japanese families who were forced into internment camps by the federal government in 1942.

TO LEARN MORE

Gong-Guy, Lillian, and Gerrye Wong (Chinese Historical Project). *Chinese in San Jose and the*

Santa Clara Valley. Mount Pleasant, SC: Arcadia Publishing, 2007.

2.10 Hellyer Park
Hellyer Avenue at Palisades Drive, San Jose 95111

Tucked next to the 101 freeway toward the south end of San Jose, Hellyer Park is one of few large, public open spaces in this city. In the 1970s a predominantly Mexican-American community faced off against law enforcement here as part of a larger movement to hold police accountable for killings. For several generations, the park has served as a site for family gatherings with strong usage by San Jose's Latinx population and as a general social space for the multiethnic communities of San Jose. When San Jose police shot and killed Manuel Lopez in the spring of 1970, the killing fanned a smoldering tension that exploded here at Hellyer Park.

The Latinx community took to the streets to protest the killing of fourteen-year-old Lopez, calling for police reform and a grand jury investigation. Tired of the hopelessness of reacting to the police only after such acts of violence, activists and students formed the Community Alert Patrol (CAP) to proactively prevent police violence. Equipping themselves with walkie-talkies, tape recorders, cameras, and their own cars, the mostly Mexican American volunteers took to following the police across the city to hold them accountable. The police department and district attorney agreed that CAP was well within its legal rights, but police did not take kindly to being watched

On the far side of Hellyer Park's pond, groups of people picnic and play. The red and white piñata here is a typical sight at this park.

and recorded. CAP claimed credit for a decline in incidents of police brutality and harassment, while also noting that the police regularly stopped CAP patrols and harassed their volunteers. Indeed, the police went so far as to pressure and intimidate the entire organization: The Police Officers Association cut its donation to the Santa Clara United Fund (now United Way) citing its support for the Mexican American Community Services Agency, which provided space for CAP's radio dispatch.

Hellyer Park had long served as an important space for Latinx communities to socialize, and it was also a regular patrol site for CAP. On May 23, 1971, a fight broke out at the park. A park ranger and members of the CAP patrol attempted to break up the fight; the ranger called for police assistance. In the chaos, a man was shot and killed, and reports of who he was and how it happened spun out of control.

A general call went out over police channels that an officer was "hit and down." At the same time, word spread to community members that the police had shot and killed another Chicanx youth. Neither story was true, but as police and sheriff deputies poured into the park believing an officer had been shot, they were met with an angry crowd that believed yet another act of police brutality had taken place in the park that day. The crowd threw rocks and bottles at the police, who made several arrests. Two CAP patrols remained on the scene, recording and photographing. Investigators later asked whether the CAP activists had intentionally disregarded a police dispersal order, never heard it, or whether police had consciously prevented CAP from leaving the park. Whatever the case, by the end of the afternoon police ruined CAP's film before it could be developed, smashed their audio tapes, and arrested members of

95

the CAP patrol, confiscating their vehicles and remaining equipment.

In the subsequent trial, the police maintained that CAP incited the riot and refused police orders to disperse. Four of the CAP patrol members were acquitted, while two were given expensive fines and probation of several years. The two convicted of criminal charges were young Chicanx mothers who were profiled by the jury as irresponsible for engaging in activism rather than parenting. CAP, for its part, worked with other Chicanx organizers to demand a grand jury investigation of the illegal arrests and destruction of CAP property. CAP's efforts met with some symbolic success when several police officers were suspended for three weeks without pay. CAP continued to monitor the police until 1974, when they were supplanted by a similar group, the Monitors, who took up the work until 1978.

TO LEARN MORE

Geilhufe, Nancy. "Chicanos and the Police: A Study of the Politics of Ethnicity in San Jose, California." Society for Applied Anthropology, monograph no. 13, 1979.

NEARBY SITE OF INTEREST

Hellyer County Velodrome and Coyote Creek Cycling Trail
Coyote Creek Trail, San Jose 95111
The trail offers an excellent car-free opportunity to see San Jose. The Hellyer County Velodrome is a closed-circuit, banked bike track where you can watch competitive races and take lessons for a small fee. For a longer scenic bike ride, pick up the Coyote Creek Bike Trail in the middle of the park. By 2019 the trail extended 17.8 miles south,

and there were plans to connect to trails north, all the way to the bay.

2.11 Keyhole

1100A La Avenida, Mountain View, 94043 (former location)

The proliferation of marquee tech campuses like the Googleplex and Apple Park has so defined media coverage of Silicon Valley that it can be hard to remember that low-slung, nondescript suburban office buildings have long been much more typical for start-ups in the valley. In the early 2000s, this unadorned one-story beige box could have been home to any one of hundreds of tech companies scratching their way back from the dot-com bust. Start-up company Keyhole, the tenant of Building A, thrived in that ecosystem, thanks to investment from In-Q-Tel, the "not-for-profit strategic investor" company funded by the United States Central Intelligence Agency (CIA) to connect venture capital and start-ups with the "intelligence community." In 2003 In-Q-Tel funded Keyhole to support geospatial intelligence in the just-launched US war in Iraq. In 2005 the six-year-old Google, Inc., flush with $23 billion in market valuation after its IPO, bought Keyhole and two other companies, which provided new tools to move unprecedented amounts of geographic data into the Internet, as well as ways to search, sort, and visualize it in 3D.

The military-industrial complex has powered Silicon Valley from the start, first through massive defense grants that funded transistor, microprocessor, and aerospace development for military applications, and later through investing in start-ups that extend the valley's impact in US intelligence and cyberwarfare. For its part, Keyhole developed the technology to transmit and visualize satellite imagery via the Internet, supplementing the expensive and cumbersome systems the government and industry relied on. Indeed, Keyhole's very name is a nod to the US's first spy satellite systems, code-named Keyhole, started as part of the Corona program in 1956. The CIA developed, tested, and manufactured these systems and related rocketry at a helicopter plant in Palo Alto before moving to Lockheed facilities down the road in Sunnyvale in 1969. The name lingers. To this day, if you download data from Google Maps or Google Earth, it comes stored in the Keyhole Markup Language (KML) file format. Despite Google's public motto at the time, "Don't Be Evil," buying a CIA-funded company fit its other stated goal, to "organize the world's information." More broadly, geolocated user data continues to be highly valued information that tech companies, advertisers, insurance and health-care companies, and the surveillance state continue to work tirelessly to produce, collect, and monetize.

Companies like Keyhole have long benefited from the confluence of defense funding, Silicon Valley entrepreneurship, and the blurred lines between military and corporate applications as pioneered at Stanford University. Stanford's role in shaping the valley stretches back to 1885, when railroad magnate, onetime California governor, and US senator Leland Stanford established the university with his wife, Jane Lathrop Stanford. Future university trustees established the Stanford Research Institute (1946) and the Stanford Research Park (1951) as nonprofit entities explicitly meant to connect research at Stanford University with military and commercial applications and spur regional economic development. Student protests over its role in supporting the US war in Vietnam forced the Stanford Research Institute to break off as an independent institution in 1970, but it would continue a close relationship with the CIA.

TO LEARN MORE

Mozingo, Louise A. *Pastoral Capitalism: A History of Suburban Corporate Landscapes*. Cambridge, MA: MIT Press, 2016.

Powers, Shawn M., and Michael Jablonski. *The Real Cyber War: The Political Economy of Internet Freedom*. Urbana: University of Illinois Press, 2015.

NEARBY SITES OF INTEREST

Moffett Field and 1309 Moffett Park Drive
Sunnyvale 94089
First a naval station and now run by NASA, Moffett Field has been central to relationships between Silicon Valley and the federal government since its founding in 1933. At its far end on Moffett Park Drive is the former site of a Lockheed plant, where the company employed roughly twenty thousand people and secretly built spy satellite and rocket technology.

Computer History Museum
1401 N. Shoreline Boulevard, Mountain View, 94043
This nonprofit museum will take you back to the days of the Macintosh and well before—when the military's ARPANET laid the pathways for the many ways that we work and live now. Check the website for hours.

2.12 Lawrence Tract

Lawrence Lane at Greer Road, Palo Alto 94303

An experiment in carefully cultivated racial integration—one that included Asian, Black, and white people—marks the Lawrence Tract as a unique suburban development in a vast sea of 1950s subdivisions, many of which were the exact opposite, consciously designed as segregated. Standing at the corner of Greer Road, the bucolic Lawrence Lane looks like so many other cul-de-sacs. But when the Palo Alto Fair Play Council built an integrated neighborhood in 1948, over objections and threats from white developers and home owners, the subversive suburban project thrived. The council aimed to prove that not only could racially integrated communities work, but that the racist circular logic used to justify excluding people of color from neighborhoods—that their very presence in the neighborhood would drive down property values—was wrong.

When it was complete, one third of the households were African American, one third Asian American, and one third white. Home values did not sink; many families used the equity they were able to build at the Lawrence Tract to move into larger homes elsewhere in Palo Alto. Unlike segregated suburbs that enforced racial separation through restricted deed covenants, these homes had no explicit agreements to maintain a heterogeneous community (and they were built the same year that the US Supreme Court ruled against the use of racial restrictions in housing). The tract's original, carefully calculated integration has thus faded with time, but as of 2018 a handful of the original owners remained.

The Fair Play Council formed just after World War II at the Woodside neighborhood house of Gerda Isenberg, human rights activist and (later) nursery owner. Isenberg, a German immigrant herself, was concerned with assisting Japanese American families returning from WWII internment camps to a city openly hostile to anyone perceived to be related to "the other side" during the war. Japanese Americans were doubly dispossessed, having had their land, homes, and property stolen when sent to the camps, and then excluded from purchasing or renting once back in Palo Alto. The council recognized that African American migrants to the city were equally excluded, and decided to fight for fair housing across the city. More than just a program of the 1940s, the council's work responded to decades of explicitly racist development in Palo Alto, where the Chamber of Commerce had tried to formally segregate the city in the 1920s. (The segregation plan failed but most new subdivisions followed the statewide practice of including restrictive housing covenants.)

Isenberg asked Elsa Alsberg, a retired social worker who she had met through efforts to help German Jews with immigration papers, to head the council and run the downtown Palo Alto office. Working with a multiracial board of directors, Alsberg oversaw free counseling on housing discrimination, early efforts to provide culturally appropriate education to Latinx students, and the creation of the Lawrence Tract. Paul Lawrence, a council member and an African

(Left) The white picket fences of the Lawrence Tract are like any other, but this development was built as an explicitly interracial suburban community.

(Below) Early city planning map for the Lawrence Tract, from 1948.

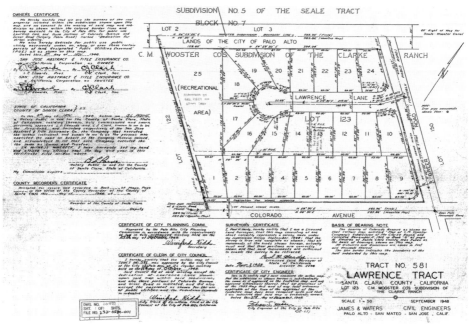

American Stanford student, took on the delicate role of moving the project through the Palo Alto planning board; the development was named after him. The housing development was not an immediate success. Japanese purchasers, for example, hesitated, fearing that Black neighbors would drive down property values. The council worked

with prominent Japanese American community leader Moriyo Nakamura to quell those fears. The Fair Housing Act of 1968 should have eliminated the need for the Fair Play Council's direct advocacy, but banks, realtors, and homeowners continued to perpetuate discriminatory housing practices through more opaque mechanisms. As a result, many other organizations emerged around the same time to push developers and landlords to open up to nonwhite residents.

NEARBY SITE OF INTEREST

Yerba Buena Nursery
12511 San Mateo Road, Half Moon Bay 94019
Isenberg started this nursery in Woodside in 1960 as the first native-plants retailer in Northern California. The nursery has supported statewide efforts to restore historic ecosystems and make them more resilient to drought, fire, and other effects of climate change.

2.13 May Day 2006 March

Story and King Roads, San Jose 95122
On May Day 2006, tens of thousands of undocumented immigrants and their allies stopped work, gathered at the intersection of Story and King, and marched. They walked through low-slung commercial corridors, past the gleaming civic and corporate towers of downtown, and out into Arena Green Park; it was a march to claim the right to live freely in the United States. The immediate impetus for the march was a national grassroots movement against US House Bill HR 4437, the so-called Border Protection, Antiterrorism, and Illegal Immigration Control Act of 2005, which would have introduced draconian laws against undocumented families. But the marches, walkouts, and strikes, which took off without any single national organization coordinating, were fundamentally about immigrants using public space to make themselves collectively visible. The marches showed that they were not living at the margins of society but were central to US culture and economy.

Undocumented immigrants and their allies filled the streets of San Jose in 2006, marking the rise of mass activism focused on the rights on undocumented people. This view from the 18th floor of San Jose City Hall captures the moment. (Sharat G. Lin photo)

San Francisco and Berkeley are more famous for their marches and rallies. And the May Day 2006 marches in New York, Chicago, and Los Angeles—where an estimated million people marched—garnered more national attention than San Jose's estimated 100,000 to 250,000 participants. But for San Jose, the march was unprecedented for a city often imagined to be inhabited solely by apolitical white and South Asian tech workers. Moreover, the actual number of people is not as important as the visual impact of the sea of people of diverse backgrounds who braved terrorizing anti-immigrant politics and claimed the physical spaces they were being denied. May Day brought out and brought together a remarkable array of the Latinx diaspora, with communities from across Central and South America, as well as Mexican and Mexican American communities and allies from across the region.

The impact was enormous and profoundly democratic, in part because the marches appeared spontaneous, although many organizations and social networks had in fact spread the call to action via text messages and social media. Marchers showed that bills like HR 4437 were not only cruel and unnecessary, but could tear apart US cities. The pressure worked, and the legislation stalled. This was a significant victory, and an important one to remember in times when anti-immigrant policies and practices reprise.

NEARBY SITES OF INTEREST

Veggielution at Emma Prusch Farm Park
647 King Road, San Jose 95116
This is one of many community farms and gardens that emerged in the mid-2000s as part of a wave of urban agriculture that built community and economic opportunities. The park is a former dairy that was deeded to the city in the 1960s with the stipulation that it always be used to recount the valley's agricultural past. http://veggielution.org

TO LEARN MORE

Lin, Sharat G. "Undocumented Immigrants in the United States: From Impoverishment to May Day Resurgence." In *Studies in Inequality and Social Justice: Essays in Honor of Ved Prakash Vatuk,* edited by Kira Hall. Meerut, India: Archana Publications, 2009.

2.14 McDonnell Hall
2020 E. San Antonio Street, San Jose

Cesar Chavez, who cofounded the National Farm Worker's Association with famed organizer Dolores Huerta, is most often associated with the Central Valley and the strikes they led there. But this meeting hall and the neighborhood it serves were pivotal in Chavez's formation and training as an organizer. When Our Lady of Guadalupe Mission Chapel was moved here in 1953, it became an important community center for its largely Catholic, Spanish-speaking members. Most of the families in this area worked seasonally on nearby farms and orchards. Well-known labor organizer Fred Ross used the chapel as the base for the Community Service Organization, the Mexican American civil rights organization he cofounded in 1948. He met the young Chavez here, introduced by activist priest Donald McDonnell from the nearby Saint Patrick's Church. Here in San Jose's Mayfair District, at the messy edge between urban San Jose and the agricultural valley, Ross worked with Chavez on strategies for organizing what would become the United Farm Workers (UFW). A National Historic Place landmark plaque commemorates their friendship on the side of the hall.

While the broad story of Chavez and the UFW is fairly well told in California—from the grape boycott to Chavez's globally publicized fasting—the East San Jose neighborhood that helped inspire the work is largely unknown. The Mayfair District, which once stretched from its southern border of San Antonio Street north to Alum Rock Boule-

McDonnell Hall, an essential meeting point for Cesar Chavez, Fred Ross, and other organizers, remains an important community space.

vard, and from the 101 freeway to Jackson Avenue, is the kind of zone at the edge of a city that offers poor people a place to be, but with limited access to the resources of the city center. In the early 1900s, a Puerto Rican migrant community settled here; some lived in tents and others built the first small houses here while working in nearby farms and orchards. The unpaved streets would often flood and become impassible mud. Residents came to call the area *Sal Si Puedes*—"Get Out If You Can."

Over time the colloquial name for the barrio would take on a less literal but more ominous meaning, admonishing those who could to escape the neighborhood for a better life. As the region grew into what regional economic boosters called the "Valley of the Heart's Delight," more Latinx families, mostly of Mexican heritage, settled in the district as part-time agricultural and industrial workers. Houses were, for the most part, small; regular work and functioning infrastructure were scarce. Chavez's family was part of that migration, moving here from Arizona when he was young. He

The Chavez family home, a locally designated historical landmark, is not far from McDonnell Hall at 53 Scharff Ave. in San Jose.

returned as a young adult and connected with Ross and McDonnell as he was forming his ideas about community organizing. Ultimately, from the uncertain conditions of Sal Si Puedes, he would emerge as California's most famous social justice campaigner. There are quite a few references to the Chavez presence here now, including a school and a plaque on the family's historical home, which is inscribed with one of the UFW's core mantras, offering a counterpoint to the old neighborhood name. *Si Se Puede,* it says—"Yes We Can."

TO LEARN MORE

Bardacke, Frank. *Trampling Out the Vintage: Cesar Chavez and the Two Souls of the United Farm Workers.* London: Verso, 2012. (This is just one of many books on Cesar Chavez, Fred Ross, and the UFW.)

Clark, Margaret. *Health in the Mexican-American Culture: A Community Study.* Berkeley: University of California Press, 1970.

National Historic Landmark Nomination Our Lady of Guadalupe Mission Chapel (McDonnell Hall). OMB No. 1024-0018.

2.15 Mission San Jose

43300 Mission Boulevard, Fremont 94539

Established in 1789, Mission San Jose was the fourteenth of twenty-one Franciscan missions in the state. Missions had already been established on the peninsula (San Francisco's Mission Dolores, 1776) and at the southern edge of the bay (Mission Santa Clara, 1777).

But the Franciscans wanted greater access to the land and labor of the Ohlone- and Miwok-speaking peoples within the sphere of protection provided by the San Francisco Presidio. The founding of Mission San Jose prompted the escalation of the Spanish military's role in forcing Native people into the mission system, and soldiers became the friars' allies in using violence to keep captives working. The conditions were deadly: Within forty years of the mission's founding, 72 percent of those baptized there had died, according to one estimate, many from measles and smallpox.

Despite this violence, and despite nearly two hundred years of white narratives that paint Native Californians as both hapless and helpless, there is documentation that both neophytes (newly converted) and nonconverts regularly resisted both Spanish and Catholic rule. The best-documented act of resistance came in 1821, when a Yokut-speaking Native—who was named Cucunuchi before his mission baptism as Estanislao—escaped and subsequently led several hun-

Mission San Jose is one of many places where the mission system left its mark on the California landscape.

dred others away from Mission San Jose and Mission Santa Clara. He gathered some one thousand Indians in open revolt. They raided Mission San Jose and other Mexican settlements stretching from the East Bay to the California interior, taking horses and supplies and liberating Indians.

In the wake of the raids, the mission's padres requested support from military troops stationed in the Presidio. Estanislao's people defeated the Mexican forces twice. A third, much larger expedition was led by a young Mariano Vallejo, who would go on to be a major landowner and powerful player in California's early statehood. The number and extent of the atrocities committed by Vallejo and his men as they pursued Estanislao vary by account, but with some combination of weapons and tactics that included setting the woods on fire and employing a cannon, they managed to break through defenses set up by Estanislao and his fellow resisters. Facing defeat, the free groups of Miwok and Yokut had to choose between rejoining the missions, fleeing further inland, or being murdered by Vallejo's men. Many returned to Mission San Jose.

After the mission secularized, Estanislao also returned; he died there in 1839, not yet fifty years old, of a disease that was probably smallpox.

The era of the missions was coming to a close. Over the next decade, the secular mission administrators proceeded to neglect, abuse, and ultimately force Indians to depart the mission. While some were able to find paid work, autonomous groups of California Indians found less and less space to

exist in the rapidly anglicizing California. However, there are reports through 1915 of Costanoans, Yukuts, and Miwok operating ranchos in the Pleasanton area; others went underground, passing as Mexican for generations. Under Mexican and then American rule, the Mission San Jose buildings were left to rot, and the property was sold in 1845 to a private owner. Most of it collapsed in an 1868 earthquake. It was not until the twentieth century that white Californians (who called themselves "native sons" of California) sought to reconstruct what remained of the former mission and to convert it into the museum and whitewashed attraction that is today.

TO LEARN MORE

Shoup, Laurence H. *Rulers and Rebels: A People's History of Early California, 1769–1901*. New York, IN: iUniverse, 2010.
Stokle, John Gerald. "Mission San Jose and the Livermore Valley, 1789–1842: Demography and Ecology of a Mission Hinterland." MA thesis, University of California, Berkeley, 1968.

2.16 Nairobi School System

805 Runnymede Street, East Palo Alto 94303 (historic site)

In the late 1960s, during the rise of the Black Power movement, residents of East Palo Alto developed a uniquely Afrocentric educational system that served students from preschool through college. Though the schools are now all closed, the story of the Nairobi School System offers a window into one of three core Bay Area efforts to develop educational institutions that centered Black history and epistemologies (ways of understanding the world). These schools were part of a national movement toward Afrocentric education at that time, but Nairobi was unique in that it was an attempt to develop linked educational institutions from preschool through community college rather than a single school; it lasted about fifteen years, from the founding of the day school in 1966 to the closure of the college in 1981.

During the 1950s, the formerly white, middle-class residential enclave of East Palo Alto saw an influx of African American transplants coming both from other Bay Area cities as well as the US South. A combination of factors helped direct them to East Palo Alto's flat, bayside landscape through the 1960s, where many were able to buy homes. Following the demographic shift from majority white to predominantly Black, however, the town faced economic decline and commercial disinvestment and experienced its own round of urban renewal's bulldozers as the 101 freeway tore through the east side. Some members of the community responded to these changing circumstances with creative and restorative activism, developing "self-help initiatives including youth patrols, a neighborhood health center, and a special civilian court endowed with the power to sentence offenders to perform chores in the homes they had burglarized," according to historian Russell Rickford.

One of those local activists was Gertrude Wilks. Born on a plantation to Louisiana sharecroppers in 1927, Wilks formed the group Mothers for Equal Education to mobilize against the de facto segregation of the local school district. In 1967 a series of Black Power summits and private study sessions with prominent Black nationalists such as Stokely Carmichael of the Student Non-Violent Coordinating Committee (SNCC) influenced Wilks. Although she maintained a commitment to cross-racial organizing, she began to embrace a philosophy of local community control and pursued the formation of independent Black institutions in partnership with others from SNCC. She first opened the Nairobi Day School with just ten students in a single-family home on Runnymede Street; it grew to serve fifty elementary and thirty high school students. With no support from the government or philanthropic foundations, the schools operated out of private homes, churches, and community spaces. To raise funds, Mothers for Equal Education sold meals and quilts while students and faculty organized events, and local clergy rallied congregations to donate. As Rickford notes, Wilks does not fit the stereotype of a Black Power radical from the 1960s, yet she built one of the movement's longest enduring institutions. Wilks assembled a faculty and developed a curriculum and teaching methodology in partnership with people like Bob Hoover, who served as the principal of Nairobi High School and became president of Nairobi College in 1969. Community work was not just stressed as a value but was a daily requirement. The school was not accredited and remained small, but educators there developed partnerships with other local universities to use facilities like libraries and science labs.

As in many urban communities across the country, youth in East Palo Alto were undermined by the compounded struggles of the drug epidemic and trickle-down economics of the 1980s; school enrollment dwindled for a variety of reasons, and ultimately all was closed. Today there are only a few physical remnants of Nairobi's facilities, and the community has turned to face other big challenges, including the encroachment of the world's largest tech corporations across the freeway. The Nairobi legacy lives on in a variety of ways, including in ongoing activist efforts to leverage community benefits from tech development and to develop scholarship programs for young people. Today many of the youth who were educated in one of the Nairobi Schools or Nairobi College are now actively engaged in community change work in cities across the country. (Ofelia Bello)

NEARBY SITE OF INTEREST

Runnymede Colony (historic site)
East end of Weeks Street, East Palo Alto 94303
This open parcel—sometimes home to livestock—that runs from Weeks Street to Runnymede Street is one of the few reminders of the socialist utopian colony founded here by Charles Weeks as the Runnymede Colony in 1916. Weeks subdivided land in the colony, selling residents a small-farm home and the promise of "one acre and independence."

TO LEARN MORE

Levin, Michael, director. *Dreams of a City: Creating East Palo Alto*, 1992. (Documentary film)
Miner, Valerie Jane. "Nairobi College: Education for Relevance; One Interpretation of the Community Service Function," 1969, 1–17. Education 260L. Archival material.
Rickford, Russell. *We Are an African People: Independent Education, Black Power, and the Radical Imagination*. New York: Oxford University Press, 2016.

2.17 New Almaden Mine Area
21350 Almaden Road, San Jose 95120

New Almaden holds the story of a gold-rush era that goes beyond the well-told narrative of grizzled forty-niners panning for gold. Santa Clara did not have the gold deposits of the interior, nor did it experience the economic boom of San Francisco. But just south of the city, significant deposits of mercury (also known as quicksilver) provided the foundation for mines that became globally significant. The first and largest mine was named New Almaden by its British-Mexican developers as a nod and challenge to the famous Almaden Mine in Spain (*Almaden* comes from the Arabic word for "metal"). Once developed, New Almaden's became some of the most profitable mines of the nineteenth century, producing fortunes that rivaled those from the deep gold and silver reserves of the Sierra Nevada. The mercury extracted from New Almaden would also become a major source of pollution; it still lingers in the bay's marine ecosystems.

Ohlone peoples had long known the hills that became New Almaden for its abundance of cinnabar, a red mineral used as a decorative pigment. Europeans preferred to vaporize the mineral to capture its mercury for use in amalgamating gold. Cinnabar mining was known to be dangerous, and

This 1854 mansion (now museum) once served as a residence for mine superintendents and guest house for wealthy investors. Access hiking trails to the left.

the decorative red powder it produced was certainly toxic. But the personal and environmental toll of its creative uses pales in comparison to the impacts of the mass mining and production of mercury brought by the European and Anglo business interests at places like New Almaden.

In 1846 the British merchant house of Barron, Forbes and Company caught wind of the mining potential here. A full two years before the gold rush, they leased the mine from the Mexican government, which controlled the territory at that time. They planned to sell the valuable mercury to Spanish American precious metal miners along the Pacific Coast (who at the time were still reliant on expensive mercury shipped around the world from European mines). With access to investment capital, Barron, Forbes and Company quickly built an industrial-scale facility that by 1851 was producing nearly 50 percent of the world's mercury. In the chaos of the US seizure of California, Barron and Forbes lost control of the mine to East Coast investors at the Quicksilver Mine Company—though the

wily financiers maintained controlled access to the valuable mercury markets.

Industrial-scale nineteenth-century mining required human labor—lots of it. The new US mine owners initially tapped networks of Mexican and Chilean miners who had years of experience blasting and digging for metals across the Spanish-speaking Americas. They also hired Mexican Californians, many of whom were losing their land and livelihoods as North Americans seized territory. Conditions in the mines were brutal, and in the above-ground processing facilities, workers faced hot, toxic work. When conditions worsened under the new US owners, Mexican workers unleashed a series of five strikes in 1864 and 1865. The company responded with the classic strategy of reinforcing an already racially stratified labor environment: They hired Cornish miners (skilled miners from the traditional tin mining area of England) and Swedes for the higher-wage and often safer jobs of the mining and processing operation. Meanwhile, workers of Mexican heritage were given the more dangerous and lowest-paid work. In

These images were used by the University of California's College of Mines to represent "typical" workers at the New Almaden Mine. They are identified as Cornish miner William Doidge and Mexican miner Patricio Avila, photographed between 1885 and 1900. (Photographer unknown)

nearby mines, Chinese workers, who had been excluded from gold mining but were trained in similar labor from building the transcontinental railroads, were handed the lowest and frequently most-lethal jobs. As contemporary scholars of quicksilver mining have shown, this rigidly enforced racial hierarchy of labor strained worker solidarity across racial lines. This, paired with a system of subcontracting employment strategies, kept workers in mercury mines from effectively advocating for improved conditions, whether through strikes or other means.

The raw product from New Almaden sold for extraordinary profits to gold and silver mining operations in the Sierra Nevada Mountains, where hydraulic mining had become the method of choice for ripping precious metals from the mountains. High-pressure water dislodged rocks, and the resulting slurry was mixed with mercury, creating a gold-mercury amalgam that could later be heated to release the gold and form bullion.

The mass profits of New Almaden and nearby mines ground to a halt by the end of the nineteenth century due to a combination of financial crises, changes in production, and the replacement of mercury with synthesized cyanide. Many of the mines operated at a smaller scale for another fifty years or so, as mercury remained useful in thermometers, electronic switches, and industrial uses. The surviving labor force was absorbed into the agro-industrial and urbanizing workforce of the region. In 1976 Santa Clara County took over the mine sites and incorporated them to the Almaden Quicksilver County Park by the end of 1978.

Another legacy remains: The tons of mine tailings, leaching mercury, and other toxins that streamed into the waterways feeding the San Francisco Bay are still found today in the guts of fish and other aquatic organisms. The park now has the peculiar attribute of being both on the National Historic Registry and on the list of federal superfund sites. Its toxic legacy is hard to visualize from the graceful rolling hills sliding out of San Jose's suburban sprawl.

You can enter the park from the parking lot at the south end of Almaden Road. The Almaden Quicksilver Mining Museum is just to the south of the parking lot. The park offers excellent hiking, but very little of the former mines is visible. If you take the English Camp trail, it will lead you to a few ramshackle structures left over from the white mining town at New Almaden.

TO LEARN MORE

Brechin, Grey. *Imperial San Francisco: Urban Power, Earthly Ruin.* Berkeley: University of California Press, 1999.

Johnston, Andrew Scott. *Mercury and the Making of California: Mining, Landscape, and Race, 1840–1890.* Boulder: University Press of Colorado, 2013.

Pitti, Stephen J. *The Devil in Silicon Valley: Northern California, Race, and Mexican Americans.* Princeton, NJ: Princeton University Press, 2004.

2.18 NUMMI Auto Plant

45500 Fremont Boulevard, Fremont 94538

The 5.3-million-square-foot Tesla facility sprawls across the Fremont landscape; you can see the company's looming, futuristic logo from the Nimitz freeway (880). The gleaming white building surrounded by fresh-off-the-line luxury electric cars is said to signal the bright new future that Bay Area tech promises the world, in this case replacing fossil-fuel-guzzling cars with purportedly clean electric ones. Undermining this gleaming promise, however, is the company's failure to offer a stable economic future for workers. The electric car company, with its headquarters in Palo Alto, has occupied the site since 2010 when Tesla began manufacturing its first luxury sedan electric vehicles. The story of the evolution of this site—from its origins as a GM auto plant to the struggling Tesla—offers a window into an important slice of Bay Area labor history.

In 1961 when General Motors first built the GM-Fremont plant at this same location, GM promised a bright new future of a different kind. The major auto manufacturers had been building branch plants for booming West Coast cities, beginning with GM's 1916 factory at the corner of International Boulevard and Durant Street in Oakland. But such a small, ornate urban plant was made obsolete with the construction of a state-of-the-art, sprawling factory in the greenfield suburb of Fremont. (Now at the border of Oakland and San Leandro, the original factory building has been converted into shopping centers, including a vibrant multi-ethnic indoor flea market.)

The vastness of today's Tesla plant is best observed from above, but you can see the factory directly from the highway as well.

Auto workers on the West Coast were organized into the United Auto Workers (UAW) District 5 labor union, which fought to match rising profits and productivity with rising wages and benefits. But not all workers had equal access to these good jobs. For workers who lived in Oakland, especially those who relied on the city's bus and streetcar system, the new jobs in Fremont were nearly impossible to reach, and work in Oakland was rapidly disappearing. At the same time, white workers who were able to buy homes with federal subsidies near the plant (this was the era of white flight) became part of a generation of upwardly mobile, white, middle-class suburbanites.

GM closed the plant in the early 1980s, however, and announced an unprecedented plan in 1984 to reopen the factory as New United Motors Manufacturing Inc. (NUMMI), a joint operation with their erstwhile competitor Toyota. At the time, Japanese car companies were producing higher-quality cars for much lower prices, and GM said it wanted to learn the so-called secrets of the Japanese model. For its part, Toyota would gain increased access to lucrative US markets. In its heyday, NUMMI employed over five thousand people earning union wages, and produced about half a million cars annually. The plant operated differently from most of the industry. In economically lean times, the plant would scale back production rather than lay off workers, instead running fewer shifts and using downtime for worker education and classes. Working at an auto factory was, and will likely always be, hard and dangerous work, often with toxic and hazardous materials, but the plant did provide middle-class incomes to what was becoming an increasingly diverse community in the Fremont area. Then in 2009, citing the global financial crisis and dwindling competitiveness, General Motors declared bankruptcy. The company withdrew from the NUMMI plant partnership, and soon Toyota announced plans to close the factory.

Two months later, Tesla, which had been developing electric cars with Toyota, announced it would buy most of the factory. Under its new ownership, the factory has a lot in common with other modern auto factories despite the company's new tech-economy characteristics. Tesla touted its robotic assembly lines, which replaced human labor, but the plant was less automated than most major auto manufacturing at the time. The roughly ten thousand workers at the Tesla factory are not unionized; workers earn between $17 and $21 an hour, far less than the NUMMI workers they replaced. The plant has struggled with rates of injuries higher than industry standards and also struggles to meet the demand for its cars. Though Tesla sells a vision of the future, the suburban development footprint of the factory remains almost identical, including the parking lot filled with cars. The office across the street from the NUMMI factory once housed UAW organizers. Now it's used not for union work but for Tesla's sales.

TO LEARN MORE

Adler, Paul. "'Democratic Taylorism': The Toyota Production System at NUMMI." In *Lean Work: Empowerment and Exploitation in the Global Auto Industry*, edited by Steve Babson. Detroit, MI: Wayne State University Press, 1995.

Wong, Julia Carrie. "Tesla Workers Were Seriously Hurt More than Twice as Often as Industry Average." *The Guardian*, May 24, 2017.

2.19 San Jose Labor Council

Between 70 and 82 N. 2nd Street,
San Jose 95112

The spatial dislocation of organized labor from a prominent perch here in San Jose's downtown to a barely visible suburban office park south of downtown illustrates the dislocation of many unions from their former place in the popular imagination at the center of working-class and urban power. Thousands of men, and to a lesser degree women, relied on the Labor Temple here as an important center of their working, political, and social lives for four decades. It was from here that strikes for better wages and working conditions were planned and organized, including marches and rallies that took place in adjacent Saint James Park (see p. 116). Tradespeople came here to find work, organizations for mutual support were established, and social events celebrated (the wooden floor was reportedly one of the most popular dance floors in prewar San Jose). Built in the 1890s as a YWCA, the building served organized labor from 1907 until 1948. That's when the Labor Council, which is a coalition of unions that represent workers of all trades, made its

PERSONAL REFLECTION FROM AMY B. DEAN, PRESIDENT AND CEO OF THE SOUTH BAY AFL-CIO LABOR COUNCIL (1993–2004) AND FOUNDING EXECUTIVE DIRECTOR OF WORKING PARTNERSHIPS

Our work sat at the crossroads between work, place-based institutions, and community-based organizations. The Santa Clara County labor movement always had a strong presence in the public sector, in building trades, health care, service, and, to a lesser extent, manufacturing. Most of what labor represented in the valley's manufacturing sector was in the defense industry, and by the early 1990s, with the end of the Cold War, this sector had almost all but disappeared. What started to happen in the '90s boom, however, is that industries restructured and began externalizing any jobs that weren't core to the firm's function. Anything that could be outsourced was outsourced, and working conditions deteriorated. Against this backdrop of eroding employment standards, groups like Joint Venture Silicon Valley, effectively a mega chamber of commerce, began publishing reports celebrating the new economy on the basis that unemployment looked to be at record lows and that median household incomes were up.

But employment was seriously degraded, and more people were living together in crowded conditions. We had to ask if traditional measures of the economy were any longer relevant indicators of community well-being. That was our new work in the emerging regional economy: developing research and communication strategies for shifting the narrative in order to create the conditions to advance organizing and advocacy for more equitable decision making and more broadly shared prosperity.

first jump away from downtown, moving again eighteen years later when the county coerced the council into selling the newer building to make way for a freeway.

All that remains of San Jose's first Labor Temple is a sign noting its former location and the highly unlikely story that Jack London wrote much of *The Call of the Wild* in a labor office here. The disappearance of a core urban base for labor matters in a region where elites and revolutionaries alike have a propensity to romanticize the radicalness of past inhabitants while decrying or isolating the radicals of the present. London himself is a great example. The socialist author, orator, and adventurer gave occasional lectures at the Normal School in San Jose, and so this city, like countless places across the Bay Area, claims a piece of his history. But London was a staunch anticapitalist and probably would have been at odds with the development leaders of today's downtown; pushing him and his ilk out to an office park would be just the thing to keep things quiet in San Jose.

2.20 San Mateo Fairgrounds

2495 S. Delaware Street, San Mateo 94403

Suburban San Mateo rarely gets noticed for its role in the political or cultural development of the Bay Area. The story of Filipinx youth and the counterculture scene they built here begins to show San Mateo in a different light. On April 25, 1987, some three thousand people poured into the largest hall at the San Mateo County Event Center to hear twenty-four mobile DJ crews perform at the seventh Imagine DJ exposition.

There's no doubt that the Imagine 7 Expo was unique among the events held at the fairgrounds in 1987. (Francisco Padorla photo)

Young Filipinx DJs made up the majority of the crews. As Oliver Wang, music writer, scholar, and the primary chronicler of the scene, explains, Imagine 7 was in many ways a high-water mark of a cultural moment where mobile DJ crews defined what it meant to be Filipinx in the Bay Area in the late 1970s and 1980s. At the same time, the event was a major public showcase of crews who had been using suburban garage parties, school dances, and other pop-up venues to perfect the kind of nonstop mixing and turntable techniques that would define much of '90s hip-hop and contemporary dance club DJing—far beyond San Mateo.

The scene, as Wang describes it, emerged from the unique experiences of immigrants from the Philippines after the 1965 Immigration Act, who clustered in the middle-class suburbs more than other Asian and Pacific Island immigrants at that time. Unlike even previous waves of Filipinx immigrants, who

had been confined near established ethnic enclaves like San Francisco's Chinatown (see International Hotel, p. 154), this generation was in a position to buy homes in places like Daly City, just south of San Francisco. In the suburbs, young people hosted their own garage parties, bought records and equipment, and transformed notions that those spaces were exclusively white and generally boring. The size and location of the San Mateo Fairgrounds as a venue speaks to a large and dispersed geography of post-1965 Filipinx communities. With San Mateo relatively equidistant from San Francisco and Daly City, San Jose, and the East Bay suburbs of Fremont and Union City, the Imagine concert drew DJ crews and attendees from communities across the Bay Area. By the early 1990s many of the DJs and party promoters aged into nonmusic careers, and new hobbies like streetcar racing replaced DJing for many in the younger generation. Meanwhile, quite a few people involved in the scene transitioned their mixing skills into the scratch turntable style of the 1990s and became global stars, including DJ Q-Bert and Mix Master Mike (also known for his work with the Beastie Boys).

TO LEARN MORE

Wang, Oliver. *Legions of Boom: Filipino American Mobile DJ Crews in the San Francisco Bay Area.* Durham: Duke University Press, 2015.

2.21 Silicon Valley De-Bug

701 Lenzen Avenue, San Jose 95126

At a time when the media served up largely uncritical hype on the world-changing role of tech, from stories of wily start-ups to gossip about tech giants like Google, Silicon Valley De-Bug emerged as a place for working-class people of color to broadcast their own stories. De-Bug—whose name is a playful reframing of the computer debugging metaphor—creates community-based media, produced and written by young people of color, focused on the real challenges facing their communities, whether that's policing and incarceration, gentrification and housing unaffordability, or access to decent and interesting living-wage jobs.

The people-of-color-led organization, founded in 2001, is tucked onto a street corner in the formerly industrial space between San Jose's train station and airport. These days, the De-Bug central office could almost be mistaken for a tech start-up. Large glass windows reveal an open floor plan with modular furniture and banks of computers. But instead of corporate art, the walls are adorned with social-justice-themed posters and covers of the De-Bug magazine and website, which publishes essays and investigative articles alongside poetry and art from incarcerated and formerly incarcerated San Jose youth. In the 2010s De-Bug headlines touched on the conditions in the Santa Clara County Jail, the debate over California's death penalty, poems for mental health awareness, and a podcast story about an exhibit on the local history of lowriders.

Beyond and because of its media-activism roots, De-Bug has served as an important node in antigentrification organizing in San Jose, bridging connections between youth rights, criminal justice reform, and the right for people to remain in place—in affordable homes and sustainable businesses. San Jose, so defined by subdivision-fueled patterns

The De-Bug offices, 2017.

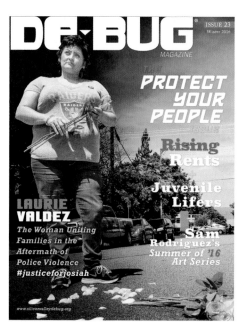

The winter 2016 cover of *De-Bug Magazine* includes a key slogan of the organization: "Protect Your People."

PERSONAL REFLECTION FROM LIZ GONZÁLEZ, ORGANIZER AND WRITER AT SILICON VALLEY DE-BUG

My experience being a part of De-Bug has shaped how I see the world, and on good days, how I move in the world. We were a few young people working on high-tech assembly lines in San Jose, building Silicon Valley's wealth without access to it, at companies that showed very little responsibility toward us. We shared our stories and connected with others to pursue our dreams and support each other. Very early on we organized against police violence because our folks had incidents with police and wanted to do something about it. Our campaign work has started like that—someone wanting to do something about something that happened to them, and we circle up to walk with them. It's what led to the development of the "participatory defense" model, where we work with the families of loved ones facing charges to navigate that system and bring their loved one home from incarceration. It was developed through the experiences of many families drawing on their collective knowledge to make new roads.

It's how we have a unique view of the intersection of the criminal and immigration systems to be able to say local law enforcement should not be entangled with ICE. Because our story began with calling out the myth that is Silicon Valley—and because we still see ourselves as caretakers of San Jose—the resistance to Google and Big Tech's move to buy up San Jose must happen here.

of urban growth, lacks the same history of housing-rights activism that has protected some low-income renters in San Francisco and the East Bay. But activists from De-Bug have been instrumental in strengthening San Jose's rent-control and other tenant protections. Meanwhile, the De-Bug office may be at risk of displacement itself. For some time, Google's physical growth in its home city of Mountain View (about fifteen miles north) has been limited by a city government concerned the mega-corporation could become the only employer in town. In 2019 the corporation was working on plans to build a major new campus about a mile away from De-Bug's space in San Jose, near the Diridon train station. The potential ripple effect from that growth remains uncertain.

TO LEARN MORE

De-Bug San Jose, http://www.debugsanjose.org

Melesaine, Jean, and Raj Jayadev, eds. *De-Bug: Voices for the Underside of Silicon Valley*. Berkeley, CA: Heyday Press, 2017.

95126 On My Block (multipart documentary on De-Bug's surrounding community)https://www.siliconvalleydebug.org/my-block

2.22 Saint James Park

2nd Street at E. Saint John Street, San Jose 95112

San Jose has a reputation as a relatively conservative and apolitical place, but you wouldn't have known that if you were here at Saint James Park in 1931. It was the second year of the Great Depression, with no New Deal economic recovery yet in sight. Santa Clara's cannery workers learned that employers were planning to further reduce their already unlivable wages by between 20 percent and 25 percent. In protest, hundreds of these vulnerable workers walked off their jobs. Communist Party organizers quickly declared the formation of a cannery-workers union and set up pickets at the canneries. Bosses and owners responded in textbook fashion, hiring replacement workers, or "scabs," out of the desperate pool of Depression-era workers and protecting the plants with armed guards. A struggle between guards and strikers resulted in the arrest of eight labor leaders.

The community responded, and several thousand workers packed into Saint James Park with a plan to march to the nearby jail to demand the leaders' release. The park had long been the center of political gatherings in San Jose and was a convenient and accessible central point for workers spread throughout the region's factories, and it was close to the union-labor command center, the Labor Temple on N. 2nd Street. The mass rally was met by more armed police but also by armed citizens. The worst riot in the city's history ensued, and although the violence was sparked by nonunion protestors, twenty organizers were arrested.

Despite contemporary inclinations to imagine the landscapes of agriculture and industry as diametrically opposed, the volatility around the strike illuminates the extent to which both the working and owning classes of California understood the two sectors to be mutually dependent, if not one and the same. As scholar Glenna Matthews has noted, the policing of unions is indicative of just how dependent San Jose was on its largest employer, the fruit canneries. At the same time, the owners of both fields and canneries were dependent on a steady stream of Mexican and Asian immigrants—whom they excluded from factory work in the canneries until after WWII—to harvest field and orchard, and women immigrants from Southern Europe to process products. This racialized and gendered separation of labor would shift significantly as some groups made their way into middle-class whiteness, while other groups were further recruited into low-wage labor.

TO LEARN MORE

Matthews, Glenna. *Silicon Valley, Women, and the California Dream: Gender, Class, and Opportunity*

Saint James Park today offers a respite from the concrete of San Jose, pictured here in 2019 with a mural in progress.

in the Twentieth Century. Palo Alto, CA: Stanford University Press, 2003.

2.23 "Victory Salute" Statue

San Jose State University Campus,
San Jose 95112

The world-shaking moment when two African American medal-winners stood shoeless, fists raised in a Black Power salute during the US national anthem at the 1968 Olympics (which received some revived attention with the media coverage of protests by San Francisco Forty-Niners quarterback Colin Kaepernick) has deep roots at San Jose State University (SJSU). Not only were the Olympians SJSU students, but the statement they made was not a spontaneous action done by just two people. It was the product of collective political organizing that began on this campus.

It is impossible to miss the gleaming, larger-than-life busts of Olympians Tommie Smith and John Carlos, fists proudly held twenty-two feet into the air over the campus's main quad. The sculpture, depicting the stance the two track stars held as they accepted their winning medals at the 1968 Summer Olympics in Mexico City, is an explicit call by students for students to be activists in the present. The SJSU student government voted unanimously in 2002 to raise funds for a sculpture in honor of Smith and Carlos, and for an associated fund to support student activism. The sculpture, designed by artist Rigo 23, was unveiled on campus in 2005.

Smith and Carlos's protest in Mexico City, from taking their shoes off in solidarity with poor people, to their bowed heads and raised fists during the national anthem, often gets cast as a rather spontaneous act of rebellion that shocked the world. But Carlos and Smith headed to the Olympics

117

This sculpture of Tommy Smith and Juan Carlos on the winner's platform of the 1968 Olympics invites you to join the protest.

already activated, as members of the Olympic Project for Human Rights (OPHR), a racial-justice organization that had a list of demands: that apartheid states like South Africa be banned from the games, that teams hire more coaches of color, that the International Olympic Committee fire its overtly racist director. They even called for a boycott by Black athletes. The OPHR was organized by Harry Edwards, a PhD student, former SJSU athlete, and mentor to Smith and Carlos. One year earlier he had organized the SJSU football team to boycott a preseason opening game, making national news as they highlighted the dearth of Black students on campus. By the time Smith and Carlos arrived in Mexico, there was a well-developed theory from San Jose State activists on how athletes could use their platform to call attention to racial injustices through peaceful but disruptive protest.

The sculpture's design aims to bring those protests into the present. The silver medal winner, Australian Peter Norman, declined to be sculpted, but in '68 he had worked with Smith and Carlos to make the moment also a statement of allyship. Standing on the winners' platform, he wore an OPHR patch in solidarity, but kept the focus on Smith and Carlos. The sculpture invites viewers to step into Norman's shoes and consider what actions they can take to call out racism and injustice in the name of shared human dignity. The sculpture is on the lawn between Tower Hall and Clark Hall, a few hundred feet from the intersection of San Fernando Street and E. 6th Street. (Research by Andrew Higgins)

TO LEARN MORE

Carlos, John Wesley, and Dave Zirin. *The John Carlos Story: The Sports Moment That Changed the World*. Chicago: Haymarket Books, 2011.

Edwards, Harry. *The Revolt of the Black Athlete*. Champaign: University of Illinois Press, 2017.

Smith, Tommie, Delois Smith, and David Steele. *Silent Gesture: The Autobiography of Tommie Smith*. Philadelphia: Temple University Press, 2008.

3

San Fran- cisco

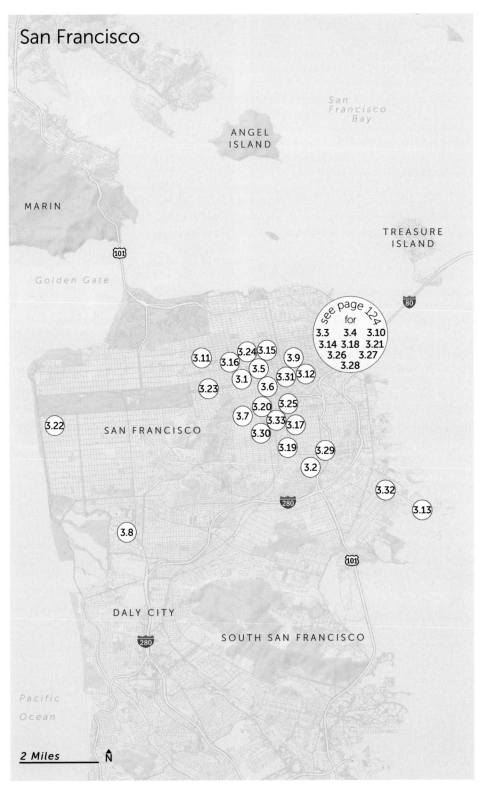

San Francisco

ANGEL
ISLAND

*San
Francisco
Bay*

MARIN

TREASURE
ISLAND

101

Golden Gate

80

see page 124
for
3.3   3.4   3.10
3.14 3.18 3.21
3.26 3.27
3.28

3.11
3.16   3.24 3.15
3.1   3.5   3.9
3.23   3.6   3.31 3.12

3.22   SAN FRANCISCO

3.20   3.25
3.7   3.33 3.17
3.30   3.19   3.29
3.2

3.32

280   3.13

3.8   101

DALY CITY

280   SOUTH SAN FRANCISCO

*Pacific
Ocean*

2 Miles   N

Introduction

To begin to understand San Francisco, stroll through San Francisco's Mission District, where people's history and struggles are evident at every turn. Even amid rapid change, Mission Street still hosts stalwart taquerias and family-owned markets with signs in Spanish and Chinese. Storefront churches and community centers with bright, hand-painted signs are tucked under four stories of rent-controlled apartments—offering home to the immigrant communities that have defined this historically working-class neighborhood for decades, ever since the Irish American–dominated population began to disperse. Blade signs from old movie palaces hint at the contours of an older corridor with a vibrant nightlife as well, where cholos once cruised up and down the boulevard in custom lowrider cars before city officials banned the practice. The neighborhood is full of such cultural-political moments that defined these places but have either faded away or been actively removed over time. Some are easily found, others require scratching beneath the surface.

Two blocks west of Mission Street, on the parallel thoroughfare of Valencia Street, you may pass by a plain door to a staircase that once led to a social club for the deaf, where—in a fleeting moment that captures the radical inclusiveness possible in this space—Bay Area punk bands would play shows loud enough for those without hearing to be able to hold balloons and feel the vibrations of the music. A few blocks in either direction, many of the storefronts

SAN FRANCISCO

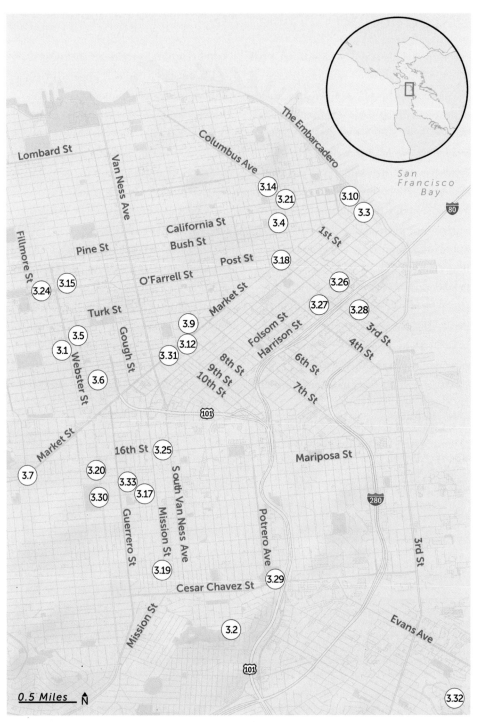

DETAIL FROM PAGE 122

and restaurants that now cater to nouveau riche bohemians were, a generation ago, the epicenter of a queer and feminist movement dedicated to creating safe, creative, supportive, and fun spaces for women in the city. Often socially and economically excluded from the more famous "gay men's" neighborhood of the Castro, because of entwined misogyny and gendered wage disparities, activist and queer women found relatively affordable rents in the Mission and established institutions like the Artemis Café and the Lexington Club. These are now gone, but the murals of the Women's Building and the sex-positive feminism of Good Vibrations remain entrenched in the landscape as a reminder of this historical geographic moment.

Nearby, the short, tree-lined residential street of Albion hosts a bronze plaque that records the site of an Indigenous village and first Spanish settlements. Just to the left of the plaque is a stunning residence with ornate work across the gate and front—no sign tells you that it was once a socialist meeting hall, or that the International Olympic Committee once tried to seize the building in a lawsuit against Tom Waddell for founding the Gay Games, or that his name can be found on an important public health clinic in the Tenderloin. In 2015 this building, once Waddell's four-bedroom house, sold for $6.5 million—a price that stuns, even among San Franciscans dulled to the rising housing market, and a telling example of what has become of the neighborhood over time.

As you move through this area you'll find more present and visible struggles that reflect the Bay Area's many contradictions.

The bike lanes and stoplights timed to facilitate cycling along gentrifying Valencia Street are, on the one hand, an extraordinary victory for people who have fought for decades—in the streets and planning offices—to make the city safer for cyclists and pedestrians, and greener for everyone. On the other hand, the lanes have appeared alongside businesses and people that fuel displacement and gentrification. This tension between the need for urban progress and the ways that progress can crush vulnerable communities is evident all around. On the corner of 16th Street and Mission, at an entrance to the once cutting-edge transit system that is now straining from deferred maintenance, people without homes continue to carve out a social space for themselves. Immigrants, queer youth, and others who simply can no longer afford San Francisco rents continue to occupy the plaza, even as they are pushed from many of the other once-public spaces in the city. At this corner, where decades of history collide with the present—just look to the many different buildings and how they've been repurposed—people who have been here for generations collide with ambitious newcomers. It's a scene that encapsulates the questions of this chapter: Who and what is a city for? How do people make the city through their organized collective struggles and everyday practices?

The Idea of "San Francisco"

The richness of the San Francisco landscape is undeniable. A full-fledged "people's guide" treatment of this city would extend for several volumes and would cover every neighborhood. What we cover in this chapter is a fraction of this larger possibility, both by necessity and by choice. As discussed in the book's introduction, while San Francisco has long been at the center of so much of the region's political and social activity, it lives and breathes in close partnership with the cities around it, as well as the resource-rich expanse of California at large. In the Internet Age, locals often talk about the way that the whirlwind of Silicon Valley flings people, business, and cultural activities to the far edges of the region. Indeed, this dynamic is creating such turmoil that we often wonder how much of the San Francisco we've described will be here by the time you read this book.

At the same time, the places beyond the borders of this city have long been a part of the production of "San Francisco," with its tendency to draw people and resources to it. What would this city be without the long history of industry in Oakland, without the workers—blue- and white-collar alike—who commute to the center each day? What would San Francisco be without the ecosystem of the bay itself, stretching up to the Sierra Nevada, from which our drinking water (and some of our electricity) comes? What would the intellectual life of the city be like without the ring of public and private schools that span the region, from the formidable city colleges and state universities to the flagship research institutions, producing scholarship and quality employment, attracting annual waves of young people with fresh ideas and energy?

These loaded questions are intended to provoke and suggest that the city boundaries are political ones, but the reach of culture, economics, politics—both into and out of San Francisco—is continuous and significant. These connections shape the public and private landscapes of the city in a variety of ways. In selecting sites for this chapter, we thus wanted to identify places that reflect that web of connection. We are drawn to places whose stories reveal how and where communities intersect here. We prefer the sites where those intersections reveal something new and unique. At the same time, we do not turn away from the heartbreaking moments when race, nationality, and other markers of difference have been deployed as excuses for violence and exclusion. Within those contexts, we are particularly interested in the ways that people in San Francisco take care of each other and the land itself. For us, this is one of the defining characteristics of this city's history: that over time, communities have insisted on caring for each other in the face of often brutal economic and social pressures.

Those pressures are important to remember, of course, and they come through in these entries in the form of the harshest dynamics of city life, including the entry on Alex Nieto Park. This is a site that would not exist without the horrific act of police officers killing a young man while he ate a burrito on his way to work; ultimately, in our book the site represents the ways that community members refuse to forget

Nieto while working to prevent more of the same and while also building connections to broader social movements. In another vein, we write here about the Redstone Labor Temple, a building that housed labor union organizing for decades. In and of itself, this is important local history. In our text, its significance is amplified by its long use as a warren for nonprofit organizations and for its role in highlighting the larger struggle between capital and labor that has so defined this city. In this light, a story of grassroots labor organizing is also a story of the top-down ways that capitalists, in their quest for profits and power, created the conditions that compelled workers to band together for survival. This is an old struggle, evident as the Spanish sought to conquer Indigenous communities across California, evident in the mining industry that made this "instant city" back in the 1840s and as the railroads snaked their way to the West Coast, and evident through 180 years of dynamic growth and change.

This chapter, organized alphabetically, starts with a story of tenants' rights organizing, via 829 Fell Street, which is fortuitous because the tenants' movement is one of the most important forces in the city, and housing-rights struggles are threaded throughout the chapter. Another strong theme in this chapter is community planning, where we look at the ways that bottom-up planning has changed places and cemented important histories, often linked to racial justice struggles. The long impact of militarism comes through in several sites. San Francisco's various political cultures are highlighted here, from transit to food, labor to grassroots community development. Surveillance technology makes an appearance, as does the Bay Area's role in creating a more grassroots anticorporate tech culture. Police brutality and community struggles to end it appear throughout. Threading all of these themes together are the political cultures of the city, from tensions centered around urban development, to politicized arts and culture and of course LGBTQ+ history and activism.

■ ■ ■

3.1　829 Fell Street

829 Fell Street, San Francisco 94117
(historic site)

In 1970 the tenants of 829 Fell engaged in an extended strike as part of a wave of tenants refusing to pay all or part of their rent in protest against rent increases. A newsletter produced by strikers in the multi-unit house on Fell quoted international revolutionaries and offered practical advice on legal support and media outreach, alongside sketches and poems that suggested that strikers saw their situation as part of a much larger project of empowerment, far beyond tenants' rights. Fell Street and others inspired many San Francisco tenants to move from what had previously been isolated skirmishes with landlords to unite around a general sense that the city was becoming unaffordable. The strikers were part of a larger do-it-yourself counterculture scene centered in Haight-Ashbury at the time. One of the enduring institutions birthed there was the San Francisco Tenants Union (SFTU), which SF State students opened that same year at 1310

This newsletter was a communication tool of the 1970 rent strike at 829 Fell, which was part of a social-movement escalation of tenant concerns that established the contemporary housing rights movement.

Haight Street (originally as Tenants Action Group, or TAG). One of the key things that the strikes inspired, for the SFTU and others, was a push to create San Francisco's first rent control law at the end of the decade.

The SFTU was founded on a mutual-aid collective model, in which volunteer tenant-counselors help with office duties, a deliberately horizontal leadership structure that allows volunteers and staff to make decisions collectively. Those seeking advice sit together in a room with other tenants to help build the potential for tenant-to-tenant education. Advising tenants on their rights is viewed as a tool for empowerment and a way to build tenant solidarity across economic class. In 1980 the Tenants Union

moved to 558 Capp Street, which it shares with the National Lawyers Guild and where it continues in this organizational model.

During that first decade, the SFTU worked with others across the city to establish rent and eviction controls. The effort received an unlikely boost in 1978, when conservative property owners in California put Proposition 13—an unprecedented plan to roll back and cap property tax increases—on the ballot. Prop. 13 campaigners argued that property owners would pass the savings on to renters through low rents, but even the California Housing Council—which represents corporate landlords and apartment developers—worried that Prop. 13 went too far and that it would all but guarantee the passage of rent control by stirring up tenant activists. Indeed, after Prop. 13 passed, those lower rents failed to materialize, and accumulated frustration sparked a renters revolt in many California cities.

In San Francisco the rent control effort gained steam when landlord Angelo Sangiacomo (later dubbed "the father of rent control") steeply and suddenly raised rents for thousands of middle-class tenants across the city. The Sangiacomo rent hikes motivated additional support for 1979's Proposition R, a citywide ballot measure that would have created eviction protections, limited conversion of rental units to privately owned condominiums, and allowed a relatively powerful form of rent control that, when a unit does become vacant, caps the rent rather than allowing huge jumps to anything-goes "market rates." Weeks before the vote on Prop. R, however, then-Mayor Dianne Feinstein and the Board of Supervisors passed a weaker, sixty-day rent freeze. This placated concerns about out-of-control rents and doomed Prop. R. The rent freeze nevertheless created the foundation for contemporary rent control, which advocates have continually fought to strengthen with some success toward the original goals of Prop. R. (Jennifer Fieber)

3.2 Alex Nieto Park

3450 Folsom Street, San Francisco 94110 (north side parking lot)

Though visitors tend to head to Twin Peaks for a panoramic view of the city, Bernal Heights Park is a locals' favorite, with 360-degree city views and a ring road that connects to a warren of hillside stairways and walkable (if steeply pitched) streets. These days, however, Bernal Hill is also known as Alex Nieto Park, commemorating the life of a young man who was killed here by the San Francisco police in 2014. Nieto's killing became a rallying cry for the antigentrification and anti-police-violence movements, and it also highlighted the tensions present in the contemporary Mission District, in which race and class remain entrenched in the struggle for the very right to exist in the city.

Nieto's death stirred a vocal and energetic response, with activists calling for big changes in the ways that the police interact with Black and Brown communities. That it happened on this hill, which contains many other layers of political and ecological histories, adds poignancy to the park. Particularly during the era of the US war in Vietnam, for

example, the neighborhood surrounding the park was known for the Left-leaning politics of the working-class and antiwar-activist population living on the hill, earning it the name "red hill" in popular lore. The moniker has geologic roots as well, with the hill's red chert rock base, exposed in the mid-twentieth century by quarrying, offering the occasional red dusty glow to the park. In 1974 the passage of Proposition J protected the park boundaries by designating Bernal Heights, along with hilltops across the city, as protected open space while also funding green-space preservation and improvements.

Another layer: the Mission's Latinx roots. Although the 911 call that alerted police to Nieto's presence in the park suggested that he was somehow out of place, his presence there as a Latinx man is part of a long legacy. In the decades prior, the adjacent Mission District had broadly become a haven for Central American and Mexican migrants, with Bernal Heights serving as a hub of the growing Latinx/Chicanx geography of the city. One story places militant members of Nicaragua's Sandinista National Liberation Front on the hill in the 1970s, where they would use the ring road of the park to train for the 1979 revolution in Nicaragua. The presence of Spanish-speaking residents on and around the hill traces to at least the mid-1700s, during the Spanish colonial period in California history. During the period of Mexican control, the government granted a huge swath of this corner of San Francisco as a rancho to José Cornelio Bernal, who left behind his name.

The long Latinx presence around the hill amplifies the significance of Nieto's death.

The community memorial for Nieto, photographed here in March 2016 by Steve Zeltzer. Plans for a permanent memorial designed by Josue Rojas and Armando Vasquez were approved in 2019.

Nieto had worked as a teen youth counselor at a local neighborhood center. On the day he was killed, Nieto was eating a burrito on a bench. The Taser that he was required to carry for his other job, as a nightclub security guard, was at his side. He posed no threat to anyone, yet the police fired at him a terrifying fifty-nine times. When it came out in the news media that the person who called the police on Nieto was both white and a recent arrival to the neighborhood, activists seeking accountability labeled the killing "death by gentrification." This all took place within the rising national awareness about Black and Brown victims of police brutality, from Long Island to Ferguson. Nieto's killing added fire to the movement against police impunity, as friends, family, and community members demonstrated across the city. Community pressure was successful in bringing the case to trial, but there was no conviction.

There were other police killings around the same time that sparked community

action. Within a few months of each other in 2015 and early 2016, San Francisco police killed Amilcar Perez Lopez, Luis Góngora Pat, and Mario Woods. In April 2016 a group calling themselves the Frisco 5 carried out a seventeen-day hunger strike held in front of the Mission police station. They protested the killings as well as ongoing police brutality and sweeps of homeless encampments, and called for the city to fire police chief Greg Suhr, who did indeed resign following another SFPD killing in the Bayview District. The police accountability activism of the Frisco 5 was bolstered by other creative responses around the city, including the work of the Do No Harm Coalition, where doctors and students at the state's flagship medical campus of the University of California San Francisco developed a working group defining police killing as a public health emergency. Back on Bernal Hill, as a reminder of Nieto's life, as well as broader issues of police accountability, the city approved a permanent memorial in 2016. It is planned for the north side of the hill, near the bench where Nieto was killed; this is near where the path slopes down to connect with Folsom Street, just a few hundred yards from the parking lot. (LisaRuth Elliott)

NEARBY SITES OF INTEREST

Alto al Fuego en la Misión mural
24th and Capp Streets

This 2019 mural memorializes and honors Amilcar Perez Lopez, killed by San Francisco police in 2015, and calls for an end to police killings.

Precita Eyes Muralists Association
2981 24th Street

Precita Eyes trains new *muralistas* and has produced many of the Mission District's distinctive murals. See two examples at 346 and 534 Precita Avenue, close to the Bernal Hill Park.

Bernal Heights Neighborhood Center
515 Cortland Avenue

The "red" politics of the hill live on in several institutions, including this one, which has provided services to residents since 1979, with an emphasis on youth work and affordable family housing.

Alemany Farm
700 Alemany Boulevard

Billed as a four-acre "organic farm ecosystem," this is San Francisco's largest urban agriculture site. The onetime dumping site was developed as a working farm for a youth employment program; it later became a site for workshops and organic food production for the general public.

TO LEARN MORE

Do No Harm Coalition,
   www.donoharmcoalition.org

Solnit, Rebecca. "Death by Gentrification: The Killing That Shamed San Francisco." *The Guardian*, March 21, 2016.

3.3 "An Injury to One . . ." Sculpture
Steuart and Mission Streets,
San Francisco 94105

The mural-sculpture here on the corner of Steuart and Mission Streets marks where San Francisco police shot and killed striking workers during the San Francisco Waterfront Strike of 1934. Men responsible for moving commodities on and off ships had already initiated work stoppages all along West Coast ports, shutting down national and international trade. The casualties here drove them to amplify the strike, bringing in workers from far beyond the waterfront. In 1984 a collective of artists created the mural-sculpture here, using the International Workers of the World slogan "An Injury to One Is an Injury to All" as the title, to commemorate the deaths of Howard Sperry and Nick Bordoise and another hundred wounded. The sculpture is a reminder, here in the Financial District, of the eighty-four-day labor action that touched nearly every sector of the city, and which remains a touchstone event for worker activism and union consciousness more than eighty years later.

Going into the Great Depression, waterfront workers had already been struggling with employers around working conditions and access to consistent and safe labor. By 1934, things were bad enough and the employer-controlled union so ineffective that on May 9 of that year, longshore workers began refusing to work at all West Coast ports. The overarching goal was to establish a truly independent union with coastwide representation and power to unite workers

The story of the San Francisco general strike plays across this sculpture, which is named for the IWW slogan "An Injury to One Is an Injury to All."

across cities. The strike hit employers hard. Shipping companies, represented by the Waterfront Employers Association, began losing money from stalled commerce, more and more as the strike wore on. The alliance between the employers and city leaders was tight, and the city called in police to suppress the strike. Among other things, police physically disrupted the picket lines of workers so that trucks of scabs—nonunion workers hired to break the union's strike—could get through to work.

On July 5 physical altercations between striking workers, their allies, and the police escalated as the police rained tear gas, beatings, and eventually bullets on the strikers. "Bloody Thursday" left Sperry and Bordoise dead and scores badly injured, and

laid bare how far antilabor forces would go to stop a strike. It also turned the tide on public solidarity. A mass funeral march filled Market Street for hours, and soon union after union signed on to support a general strike of all workers. For four days, some 150,000 joined the waterfront workers, shutting down much of the city as people walked off their jobs and demanded justice for the longshoremen. The government stepped up its efforts to crush the strike, and police were particularly brutal to those they identified as Communists, or "reds." Police and others raided spaces around the city where workers organized and shared information through workshops, publications, and the like. The California National Guard set up camp at the waterfront, with military tanks aimed across the Embarcadero.

The outcome of the strike was complicated. It demonstrated the power of a general strike, which swept many US cities following WWII, so well that a Republican-controlled US Congress passed the Taft-Hartley Act to seriously curtail legal union activism across the country. Nevertheless, waterfront workers did win a coastwide contract and soon elected much more radical leadership for themselves in the form of one of the strike's key organizers, Harry Bridges. Despite efforts by the federal government to deport him, Bridges helped lead the transformation of what is now the International Longshore Workers Union into one of the more powerful and democratic unions in the US. The ILWU remains a force in West Coast unionism—even amid the rise of mechanization and other major changes on the working waterfront—and continues to flex its power, with workers shutting down ports for national and international causes beyond their own working conditions. (The artists collective that created the sculpture on the corner included Miranda Bergman, Tem Drescher, Nicole Emmanuel, Lari Kiloani, James Morgan, Raymond M. Patlan, Eduardo Pineda, James Prigoff, O'Brian Theile, and Horace Washington, according to artandarchitecture-sf.com)

NEARBY SITE OF INTEREST

Rincon Annex Post Office

180 Steuart Street, San Francisco 94105

The former post office here, an amazing example of New Deal architecture, was partly preserved in the creation of this lobby to the contemporary Rincon Center. The lobby hosts Anton Refregier's twenty-seven-panel mural on the history of California from conquest to WWII. The Rincon murals were federally funded through the New Deal's Treasury Section of Fine Art and were the very last works of art funded by any New Deal agency after more than fifteen years of funding public art. See the Living New Deal Project at livingnewdeal.org for more on this and thousands of other New Deal sites.

3.4 Bank of America Building

555 California Street, San Francisco 94104

This is the fifty-two-story monument that the Bank of America built for itself at the height of its status as one of the most powerful banks in the world. While people tend to equate US financial power with New York's Wall Street, San Francisco has long dominated the flow of capital through the West Coast, from the spoils of mining and agriculture to urban development booms (and busts). Looming over the Financial District, the Bank of America often led the pack, lending out billions that "built California," transforming millions of people's relationships to finance through pioneering branch banking and credit cards, and acquiring dozens of other institutions in and out of the state.

The plaza at the foot of 555 California bears the name of A. P. Giannini, the famed founder of the bank. Born to immigrant parents on a San Jose farm in 1870, Giannini married into one of San Francisco's wealthiest real estate mogul families and by age thirty-one was managing their fortune and acting as director at one of the city's few

Nicknamed "Banker's Heart," given its location, Masayuki Nagare's black granite sculpture here at the foot of the Bank of America building is titled *Transcendence*.

bank's holdings through branches in every city and farm town in California, making loans to whoever he thought could pay back the interest.

In 1930 the Bank of Italy acquired the holdings and name of the LA-based Bank of America, and Giannini's "everyman" bank grew further by backing the nascent wine industry, Hollywood film studios, and the public bonds for the Golden Gate Bridge. At the same time, he pioneered the use of a holding company, the TransAmerica Corporation, to manage financial assets far beyond what the bank could do alone (though federal legislation broke up the firm in 1956). When Giannini died in 1949, the Bank of America was the largest private bank in the world. The new headquarters at 555 California declared the bank's intention to capitalize on that position through interstate and international dealings from the heart of SF's Financial District. The corporation hired three of the top architecture firms to design the tower of iconic bay windows and expensive granite, which opened in 1969. It was briefly the tallest structure on the West Coast before losing the title in 1972 to the Transamerica Building—named for the very holding company that federal legislation had forced the Bank of America out of in 1956.

From its global headquarters, the bank made loans to South American governments, meddled in Mexico's oil company, and joined the ranks of 1980s corporations obsessed with restructuring and consultants. The bank's fortunes plummeted in the 1980s, and in 1987 it sold its flagship building to a San Francisco real estate mogul. In 1998

Italian American banks. According to the legend perpetuated by the Bank of America, Giannini quit in frustration that other banks did not understand there was money to be made from banking for "common people," and founded his own Bank of Italy in 1904. In an oft-exaggerated story, Giannini cemented his legacy in San Francisco following the 1906 quake by smuggling his bank's assets out of the burning city to begin making new loans to rebuild almost immediately, while other banks waited weeks for their fire-cooked vaults to cool enough to recirculate capital. In the following years, he would use the same relentless drive to expand his

NationsBank acquired Bank of America and moved its headquarters to North Carolina, again taking its more famous name and original 1904 charter. It was the largest bank merger in history at the time. The building at 555 California changed ownership several more times, and in 2019 70 percent of it was controlled by real estate trust Vornado and 30 percent by Donald Trump. The building continues to represent a major artery in the global flow of capital, housing branch offices for major financial players like UBS, Morgan Stanley, and McKinsey and Co.

TO LEARN MORE

Bonadio, Felice A. *A. P. Giannini: Banker of America*. Berkeley: University of California Press, 1994.

Mayer, Martin. "The Humbling of BankAmerica." *New York Times*, May 3, 1987.

3.5 Buchanan Mall

Buchanan Street, San Francisco 94115
(between Eddy and Grove Streets)

The story of the Buchanan Mall—a five-block stretch of pedestrian-only walkways in the heart of the historically African American Fillmore District—in many ways is the story of the rise and fall, and then the slow recovery, of a neighborhood that has seen far more than its share of urban anguish. From the bulldozers of redevelopment that decimated the community in the 1950s and 1960s to years of street violence and deep poverty that challenged community reconstruction in the years that followed, the Western Addition/Fillmore has wrestled through half a century of policy failure that

has had deep impact on the neighborhood itself as well as the city at large. At the tail end of that story, the revival and greening of the Buchanan Mall suggest ways that community members are working to remake the place from the ground up.

The Fillmore, once the "united nations" of the city, was home to a range of people by the early 1940s, including a well-established Japanese American community (see Japan Center, p. 156) and newly arrived African Americans coming to work in war industries. This was the Harlem of the West, and Fillmore Street itself is remembered as a lively and rich center for music and culture, with all of the famous musicians of that era passing through—including Ella Fitzgerald, Louis Armstrong, and Billie Holiday, to name just a few. But it was also a time of exclusion. First, the federal government forced all people of Japanese descent into relocation camps during WWII (see Hotel Whitcomb, p. 150). The postwar years brought another kind of federally backed displacement in the form of the "urban renewal" program. The local redevelopment agency declared the area blighted—targeting the dilapidated Victorians that are now so valued in the city—and razed some twenty square blocks, eliminating more than four thousand businesses and displacing some twenty thousand residents.

The community response was multilayered and persistent. Key national laws that aim to protect tenants came out of lawsuits that began right here on these streets, and multiple generations of low-income housing advocates cut their teeth on housing

Historical and contemporary community photos are embedded in the entry gates to the Buchanan Mall at each intersection.

struggles here, taking their knowledge and skills to other neighborhoods. And through the efforts of local advocates, the remaking of the neighborhood included largely government-subsidized affordable housing. But the Brutalist architecture of much of this housing, and the lack of widespread economic development, gave the neighborhood an abandoned feel for outsiders even as for residents it grew dangerous with the onset of the drug war and its attendant overpolicing.

In the midst of all of this history lies the Buchanan Mall (which draws on an older use of the word *mall,* signifying public open walkways rather than shopping centers). The city remade two sections of Buchanan Street through redevelopment as a pedestrian walkway, without car traffic. One short block lies north of the Japantown Mall. Another four blocks are here, south of the

Geary Expressway, abutting nine affordable-housing developments and three major community centers. Though it was constructed as public open space, for decades this part of the Buchanan Mall was regarded as unsafe by many locals. The design contributed to this: The lighting was poor, and there were few places to sit amid the under-tended greenery. Beginning in 2015 the community rallied a group of agencies to reinvest here. A series of public meetings brought community members together to talk about the space, draw maps, and imagine new public uses. The result: new benches, lighting, and a series of artistic plaques that reference the rich histories of the neighborhood, with historical photographs and names of key neighborhood leaders. The process brought people together across generations, and many spoke of how they had been inspired by their mothers or grandmothers who learned community-organizing skills during the redevelopment era. Those women probably would have appreciated this relatively bottom-up urban planning process that was tied not to immediate gentrification, but rather to community self-definition and control.

NEARBY SITES OF INTEREST

Ella Hill Hutch Community Center

1050 McAllister Street, San Francisco 94115
The center offers programming for children and is covered with a multiwall mural representing the faces of dozens of neighborhood heroes.

African American Arts and Culture Complex

762 Fulton Street, San Francisco 94115
The complex hosts theater and has an art gallery on the first floor with rotating exhibits and is home to the African American Historical Society. One of the meeting rooms contains a well-preserved New Deal mural on the neighborhood's earlier history.

TO LEARN MORE

Brahinsky, Rachel. "'Hush Puppies,' Communalist Politics, and Demolition Governance: The Rise and Fall of the Black Fillmore." In *Ten Years That Shook the City: San Francisco 1968–1978*, edited by Chris Carlsson and LisaRuth Elliott, 141–153. San Francisco: City Lights Publishers, 2011.

Pepin, Elizabeth, and Lewis Watts. *Harlem of the West: The San Francisco Fillmore Jazz Era*. San Francisco: Chronicle Books, 2005.

Trust for Public Land. "Buchanan Street Mall Vision Statement." San Francisco, 2017, https://sfrecpark.org/project/buchanan-street -mall-activation-project/

3.6 Buddhist-Oriented Hospice Projects

Zen Hospice Project

273 Page Street, San Francisco 94012 (San Francisco Zen Center, historic site)

Maitri Hospice

401 Duboce Avenue, San Francisco 94117 (Hartford Street Zen Center)

When the HIV/AIDS crisis hit San Francisco in the 1980s, many individuals and institutions turned away from those who contracted the devastating and previously unknown disease. The San Francisco Zen Center (SFZC), by contrast, responded with compassion, seeking to have a positive influence on how people died as well as on how others viewed the dying. Their care of those living with and dying from HIV/AIDS—at a time when those same people were vilified and ignored by the political and medical establishment—also helped to reshape the public narrative around homosexuality. (Although gay men certainly aren't the only victims of HIV/AIDS, they were the public face of the disease for decades.)

Tucked away in a dense but relatively quiet residential district, Zen Hospice Project operated until mid-2018 in a regal Victorian building on Page Street. The Zen Hospice "Guest House" was located downhill from the brick practice center, Beginner's Mind Temple (Hosshin-Ji) at 302 Page, designed by architect Julia Morgan in 1922. Originally a Jewish home for single women, in 1969 it became home to the first Buddhist spiritual center on the West Coast. As members of its own community became ill from HIV/AIDS-related illnesses, the SFZC

The Zen Hospice Project building on Page Street, 2019.

opened up another building it owned at 273 Page Street for people to die with dignity, creating one of the city's first residential hospices. In 1988 Zen Hospice Project began offering care at the hospice ward at San Francisco's Laguna Honda Hospital. The project became a recognized innovator in palliative end-of-life care, and leaders in all faith traditions support the work with trainings and workshops. Although the Guest House closed and was sold in 2018, this program continues to train thousands of caregivers and serves those with all terminal illnesses. In 1981 the Hartford Street Zen Center in the Castro followed suit, operating as a hospice facility for the next decade. The hospice on Hartford Street was named Maitri Hospice in 1987 and today provides long-term residential care at Church and Duboce for people living with AIDS.

Even as these projects evolved, a wide array of HIV/ AIDS services emerged across the city, including the 1987 founding of the AIDS Memorial Quilt, the 1991 creation of the AIDS Memorial Grove in Golden Gate Park, and today's vaccine trials through the San Francisco Department of Health. Projects to house, feed, and support those living with HIV/AIDS abound, with a network of over fifty organizations providing services. Meanwhile, the San Francisco Zen Center has had a strong influence on everyday life, far beyond hospice care, through its affiliated projects that span the greater Bay Area: from bread baking (*Tassajara Bread Book*, published by the Tassajara Zen Mountain Center in the mountains above Big Sur) to organic farming (Green Gulch Farm in Marin) and vegetarian cuisine (Greens Restaurant at Fort Mason in SF).

(LisaRuth Elliott)

TO LEARN MORE

Downing, Michael. *Shoes outside the Door: Desire, Devotion, and Excess at San Francisco Zen Center.* Berkeley, CA: Counterpoint Press, 2001.

Zen Hospice Project History, https://www.zenhospice.org/about/our-history

The Castro Commons serves as a space for formal and informal political activity, a performance venue, and a crossroads for interaction between social groups.

3.7 Castro Commons Parklet

Intersection of 17th, Castro, and
Market Streets, San Francisco 94114

One of the easiest-to-love urban tendencies in San Francisco in the 2000s was the advent of miniparks, in which slices of streets—from awkwardly shaped intersections to parking spaces for cars—were reclaimed as pedestrian public space. The movement took off after the design/art studio Rebar organized the first PARK(ING) Day, an arty annual protest against the car, where people filled parking spaces with imaginative temporary public "parks" with things like couches, tables, and greenery. The city later followed with policy that allows and encourages homeowners and businesses to replace parking spaces with public parklets all over town. Some of the larger parklets were made from the remnants of jigsaw intersections; these are relics of the old streetcar city, like the one here at the triple intersection of 17th, Castro, and Market Streets. Centrally

located in the historic Castro District, the Castro Commons parklet is a great place to ponder the power struggles in the landscape. Across the street is Harvey Milk Plaza, named for the iconic politician who was the first openly gay elected official in California and who was assassinated by political opponent Dan White in 1978. Photos of Milk line the wall of the entryway to the Muni underground station.

The intersection between this parklet and Milk Plaza has been a gathering place for celebration and demonstration, and is itself a site of contested spatial politics. This is where people gathered to protest police violence against gays and lesbians in the 1970s and where Milk and others drew crowds for political rallies. This is also the place where mourners massed before marching to City Hall in collective rage against White's murder of Milk and Mayor George Moscone. People still gather here for a slow candlelit processional down Market Street each

November, in remembrance of Milk and his social justice legacy. This continues to be the place where marches to celebrate LGBTQ victories, and mourn losses, typically begin or end.

The parklet area is also an epicenter for the Castro's various cultural events. In the 2000s some residents complained about naked revelers having sex and getting drunk in the streets, and city supervisors sought to ban the public nudity that had been central to identity formation in the neighborhood. As the nudity fight wore on, a city ballot measure produced new tensions by criminalizing sitting and lying down on city streets and sidewalks. The "Sit-Lie" measure was marketed as a law-enforcement tool that would stanch aggressive panhandling, but it was in fact an attack on houseless people and their existence on the streets. Some Sit-Lie rallies centered in the Castro Commons, often an outdoor home for LGBTQ youth, who form a majority of independent young people without homes in the city.

In many ways, the campaign against Sit-Lie followed the PARK(ING) Day pattern, with clusters of people holding "sitting" parties across the city, some with tea and crumpets, others with guitars and ad hoc chaise longues, and still others sitting in the middle of the Castro Commons, defending their rights as humans who get tired and need to sit down every once in a while. This raised an important contradiction in the way public space is used and policed: A behavior that is defined as criminal by people who appear houseless (sitting) is seen as whimsical and bold when employed by others.

The measure passed, but the activism that challenged the law expanded the circle of San Franciscans willing to make public their support of people who, by dint of the bad luck that landed them on the wrong side of the capitalist equation, have no house keys of their own.

NEARBY SITES OF INTEREST

Harvey Milk Plaza
Castro Street Muni Station, Castro at 17th Street, San Francisco 94114

GLBT History Museum
4127 18th Street, San Francisco 94114 (archives at 989 Market Street, San Francisco)
The museum hosts regular events, has a beautiful array of changing exhibits, and maintains an archive and research center on Market Street.

Harvey Milk Civil Rights Academy
4235 19th Street, San Francisco 94114
This social-justice oriented alternative public elementary school was founded in 1996.

Kite Hill
19th and Yukon Streets, San Francisco 94114
Corona Heights
Roosevelt Way at Museum Way, San Francisco 94114
Corona Heights and Kite Hill are two underappreciated San Francisco hills, with expansive views.

TO LEARN MORE

Shilts, Randy. *The Mayor of Castro Street: The Life and Times of Harvey Milk.* New York: St. Martin's Press, 1982. (Also see the documentary film by the same name or the Hollywood take on Milk's story, titled simply *Milk.*)

Courtyard of the Chavez Center at SFSU; note the upper-balcony bleachers, which offer an interesting view.

3.8 Cesar Chavez Student Center, San Francisco State University

1600 Holloway Avenue, San Francisco 94132 (main entrance at 19th and Holloway)

This building exists because of the movement to bring ethnic studies into university curricula, a cross-cultural political movement that was centered here on this public university campus. The Cesar Chavez Student Center at San Francisco State University (SFSU) is adorned both inside and out with murals depicting decades of these and other activist struggles, and it contains a gallery featuring work by four decades of local artists, all of which offer an education in the history of social justice. The university, founded in 1899 as the San Francisco State Normal School for training teachers, moved in 1953 to its current location near Lake Merced in the city's windswept southwestern corner. In the 1960s it became an epicenter for political organizing, as students spearheaded marches, rallies, teach-ins, and ultimately a strike that resulted in the creation of and institutional support for Black studies and ethnic studies departments and the Chavez Center in 1975.

In the spring of 1966 the Black Student Union (BSU), like others across the country, formed with the goal of recruiting, admitting, and retaining Black students. As gains were made in recruitment, campus discussions turned to political and economic matters beyond the curriculum or student body makeup. Students and faculty challenged the culture of academia to shed its historically Eurocentric framework, in line with

This inset mural at the SFSU Chavez Center reflects the intergenerational and international struggles of Asian and Pacific Islander communities. (Artists: David Cho and Albert Yip, 2004)

Connections between Native American history and contemporary Native life highlight this inset mural at the Chavez Student Center at SFSU: *We Are Still Here* (Artist: Marc Nicely with Larry Sillaway, 2009)

the call by civil rights leader Kwame Toure (formerly Stokely Carmichael) for Black students to learn about their own histories as a form of decolonization and positive identity formation. SFSU hired two of the Black Arts Movement's most noted poets, Amiri Baraka (Leroi Jones) and Sonia Sánchez, as well as the Black Panther Party's minister of education, George Murray. The radicalism of these instructors and their ties to the Black Power Movement led to contentious debates with conservative administrators

and students. Political organizing on campus expanded in 1968 when the BSU, along with the Chicano organization El Renacimiento, the Latin American Students Organization, the Asian American Political Alliance, and the Pilipino American Collegiate Endeavor came together in a coalition they called the Third World Liberation Front (TWLF). The TWLF, in alliance with campus workers and other groups like Students for a Democratic Society, developed a list of demands that included the creation of Black, La Raza (Chi-

PERSONAL REFLECTION BY JASON FERREIRA, ASSOCIATE PROFESSOR OF RACE AND RESISTANCE STUDIES, SFSU

One of the things that made San Francisco State unique as opposed to Berkeley or some other places is that it was a commuter school. The students were older, and it was a working-class school. Among the type of students who went to San Francisco State, not only did many have work experience, but they also had political experience that they brought with them to the campus. . . . What happened at San Francisco State remade the city. I think of it as similar to the famous 1934 strike of longshore workers, and the impact that had on the political terrain of San Francisco. Many of the institutions bettering the city right now have connections to the strike—if not directly, then indirectly. So the strike produced a wave of energy that permeated the city: The I Hotel, Alcatraz, Los Siete, the Panthers—they were all connected to what happened at SF State and propelled forward by the strike, even if the struggles had national and international reverberations. (Edited with Ferreira's permission from an interview in *Socialist Worker*.)

darity from local churches, labor unions, and community organizations, and from parents of student strikers and students from nearby college campuses. California Governor Ronald Reagan backed Hayakawa by sending in state troopers, defining the standoff in the press as "a kind of Vietnam" that was led by a "militant minority." After four and a half months, the longest student strike in US history ended with an agreement to establish robust ethnic studies departments with deep commitments to teaching and scholarship. The fulfillment of this promise has taken a long time, with ups and downs, but with persistent pressure by activists, the university continues to expand ethnic studies programming. While SFSU was at the forefront of this movement, schools throughout the Bay Area followed suit, from San Jose State University to Merritt College, UC Berkeley, and Berkeley High School. The murals that today cover the outside of the Cesar Chavez Student Center represent the people, moments, and visions of these formative years of student activism. (Diana Negrín da Silva)

NEARBY SITE OF INTEREST

Richard Oakes Multicultural Center

1650 Holloway Avenue, San Francisco 94132
The center honors SFSU Mohawk student activist Richard Oakes, who helped lead the occupation of Alcatraz Island.

TO LEARN MORE

Biondi, Martha. *The Black Revolution on Campus.* Berkeley: University of California Press, 2012.

Dawson, Alex, and Abby Ginzberg. *Agents of Change.* San Francisco: California Newsreel, 2016. (Documentary film)

canx/Latinx), American Indian, and Asian American studies departments, with full-time faculty and staff. In response to resistance to these demands and to administrative actions against several faculty members, the TWLF called for a strike on November 6, 1968; the campus was ultimately shut down for four and a half months.

Incoming SFSU president S. I. Hayakawa responded to the strike with heavy police force, which had the countereffect of escalating student militancy and galvanizing soli-

Kendi, Ibram. *The Black Campus Movement: Black Students and the Racial Reconstitution of Higher Education, 1965–1972*. New York: Palgrave Macmillan, 2012.

3.9 Civic Center and United Nations Plazas

Hyde Street at Fulton Street, San Francisco 94102 (Civic Center is bounded by Hyde and Polk Streets, between Grove and McAllister Streets)

Civic centers represent urban power, and the struggles over control of these spaces are defining sociopolitical moments. Here at the intersection of Hyde and Fulton Streets, the power struggles over which public has the right to public space are on display. The people who are typically gathered here on the sidewalks, calling to one another, pushing carts, lugging their personal items—their entire lives often visible—are some of the most marginalized in the city. Many are simply trying to stay active and awake in an environment in which sitting or lying down is punishable by arrest (see Castro Commons, p. 139). The growth of Bay Area houselessness in the dot-com era has pushed even more people to the Civic Center. This has long been a place where people gather, whether seeking refuge or a sense of connection to a broader public. This is, after all, the epitome of the public square, with the open central areas surrounded by public buildings—the library, the courts, other civic buildings. Pair these with museums, the ballet and opera, and these streets are grand monuments to urbanism, announcing, This City Matters. Meanwhile, there has always been a parallel story. This is where groups like Food Not Bombs and Curry Without Worry have offered weekly free meals. Protests incorporating tent cities have popped up here to offer a concentrated visualization of the need for affordable housing—and to offer actual shelter to people who need it. An annual memorial for those that have died on the streets is held by faith leaders here in front of the grand City Hall.

With San Francisco City Hall and food carts in the distance, UN Plaza is a heavily policed area.

The ongoing crisis in the region, in which tens of thousands of people live without permanent housing, is often lost in conversations about the high cost of living in the Bay Area. Across all Bay Area counties, people scrape by day to day under freeways, in cars and beaten-down motor homes, surfing between temporary shelter beds

In the shadow of City Hall, this big gold-gilded marble palace, you have people experiencing complete destitution in the streets, having their very last belongings confiscated by police and thrown into garbage trucks to be destroyed. Civic Center shows this severe disparity that is representative of San Francisco's striking inequality: deep poverty in the shadows of affluence. This is the geographic center of the city's power structure, and the plaza itself is one of the few open spaces in a densely populated neighborhood that is home to the city's most impoverished residents. The library serves as an indoor respite for the many neighbors who have no place to call home, or whose home has no common space in which to spend time with friends and family, while the plaza itself offers respite in the outdoors. It is common to see impoverished neighbors lounging on the grass, or on the cemented corners, or sometimes lying over grates to keep warm. Many of the people who populate the plaza serve as a visible reminder to those in power of the presence of severe poverty. As a result, Civic Center and the adjacent steps of City Hall have been the primary choice for protests on homeless issues. Creative actions, such as organizing a game of musical cots among San Franciscan homeless children, throwing a banner off the mayor's balcony, or building graveyards in the plaza symbolizing the many who have died homeless in the city, offer an important platform to lift the voices of the city's most destitute residents.

70 percent according to recent research, became homeless while already living here. While there are many ways people lose their homes, studies have confirmed that homelessness itself is a root cause of mental and physical health problems and addiction.

Although homelessness is widespread, people without homes are often considered to be "out of place" in the urban landscape. Public officials often call for more policing (rather than the obvious answer: housing), and this area has been used as a test site for draconian laws criminalizing life on the street. In 1987 a group of houseless and housed activists formed the San Francisco Coalition on Homelessness (COH), shaped by the wisdom of people living on the streets themselves. The philosophy of the group is embodied in the work of the *Street Sheet*, the nation's first newspaper produced by homeless people and sold by homeless vendors. In tandem with the Poor News Network and the East Bay's *Street Spirit*, the *Street Sheet* pushes the public to remember the humanity of people on the streets. The publication counters punitive policies that focus on pushing people out of sight rather than dealing with the conditions that create homelessness, such as under- or unemployment, no-fault evictions, domestic violence, and rejection by homophobic parents.

Making these arguments in defense of the humanity of the homeless, advocates have scored many concrete wins, like the Community Housing Project, which was the city's first supportive-housing effort, and which became a national model for housing paired with supportive services. In 2005

and single-room-occupancy hotels. Somewhere between eight thousand and eighteen thousand people are homeless throughout the year in San Francisco alone. Most, about

members of the COH founded the Western Regional Advocacy Project (WRAP), bringing the philosophy of bottom-up organizing to regional political work on homelessness that spans the Western states. Several organizations that work on ending homelessness focus on art as a tool for healing and communication. WRAP's posters, for instance, illustrate the social problem of homelessness with craft and beauty; you can find examples on the group's website and in the *Street Sheet*, and they're regularly available at the Coalition on Homelessness's annual art auction. Creativity, in the hands of these groups, becomes part of the way people connect and express themselves, while also raising money for advocacy under the slogan House Keys, Not Handcuffs.

TO LEARN MORE

Gowan, Teresa. *Hobos, Hustlers, and Backsliders: Homeless in San Francisco.* Minneapolis: University of Minnesota Press, 2010.

San Francisco Coalition on Homelessness, www.cohsf.org

Western Regional Advocacy Project, https://wraphome.org

NEARBY SITES OF INTEREST

Historic Fire Hydrant

Van Ness Avenue and Ellis Street, northwest corner

Local lore says this hydrant was one of just a few that kept on chugging during the 1906 fire, vitally saving lives and structures. Stop here to ponder the role of infrastructure in shaping urban power. For example, San Francisco's public water system is channeled from the Hetch Hetchy Valley in Yosemite National Park, through an incredible gravity-fed system that spans more than 150 miles. This feat of engineering was enabled by land and resource grabs that still shape the city. One lingering aspect of that drama is the privately managed electric power system: Back in the 1920s Pacific Gas and Electric Company maneuvered to establish a monopoly over the power system, circumventing a federal law that required the public Hetch Hetchy dam also to provide public electricity to the city. Officials went along for the ride, and a hundred years later struggles for local control over energy continue. The urban wildfires of the 2010s revived interest in the politics of infrastructure, particularly when PG&E admitted at least some responsibility for one of the deadliest fires, in the town of Paradise (with a death toll of eighty-five people, and fourteen thousand homes gone).

San Francisco City Hall

1 Dr. Carleton B. Goodlett Place, San Francisco 94102

This building and the plaza around it has seen so much history that a terrific book could be written based simply on events that took place within its sphere, from the everyday work of governance to countless demonstrations and rallies. Some moments were particularly dramatic: In the 1960s a hearing of the House Un-American Activities Committee (HUAC) inspired mass protest, in which demonstrators were pushed and dragged down the iconic cascading steps in the central atrium. Meanwhile just across the plaza from City Hall, the modern disability rights movement made headlines with a sit-in and takeover of the Federal Building (located at 50 Fulton at the time), which lasted more than three weeks in 1977. Other moments were tragic and still shape the city: In 1978, for example, disgruntled Supervisor Dan White snuck a gun through a basement window to murder progressive and gay Supervisor Harvey Milk and his ally Mayor George Moscone in their offices on the second floor.

Cyclists ride southeast on Market Street in a September 2008 Critical Mass. (Dave Snyder photo)

3.10 Critical Mass

Market Street, starting at the Embarcadero,
San Francisco 94105

There are a variety of mega events by which contemporary San Franciscans can set their clocks. There are the near-empty streets occasioned by the Burning Man Festival in late August, and the colorful Pride celebrations of the third weekend in June. And then there's the cluster of bicycles snaking through city streets on the fourth Friday of each month, when the Critical Mass ride wends its way from the Embarcadero Plaza out to all parts of the city. Since 1992, when a small group gathered, to later years when hundreds rode together, Critical Mass has played a key role in the political and cultural landscape of the city. Here's how it works: Anyone who can find a bicycle is invited to gather around 5:30 p.m. on the last Friday of each month at the foot of Market Street here at Embarcadero. What happens next depends on the month and the era. The officially leaderless group is led each time by those who feel moved to do so, and the ride—which can fill whole city blocks with people of all ages, sometimes in Halloween costumes, sometimes bearing political signs or musical instruments, sometimes in high-tech racing gear—proceeds in a way that halts car traffic, like a parade. The ride is unofficial, without permits. Sometimes police have kept the peace between car drivers and cyclists, and sometimes they have cracked down violently on the unpermitted event, most memorably in 1995 under Mayor Willie Brown.

The practice of Critical Mass spread from here to at least 350 cities around the world, and it has largely defied pressure to formalize. Instead, its character and participants shift over time. Sometimes participants arrive with maps for proposed routes and self-made literature to hand out about the purpose of the event, raising awareness about urban bike safety and climate change (a favorite sign made the point: Bicycling to End Oil Wars). Still, for many the ride has been largely about reclaiming car-centric space for car-free living, or simply finding collective joy. In more recent years, riders have adopted parts of this history and rejected other parts; this shifting focus is part of the Critical Mass ethos. Participating in a ride like Critical Mass can reshape your experience of the city. Riders who normally might walk their bikes up a steep incline can be buoyed by the group effort and find themselves "topping" hills. There is a sense of empowerment and freedom when cars have been chased off a big city street, or when riders fill the Broadway Tunnel with echoing songs. Those moments of inspiration may help people step into their urban lives in new ways, whether through taking up regular cycling or taking other risks and participating in creative acts that challenge the status quo.

San Francisco's bike culture now goes far beyond Critical Mass. The San Francisco Bike Coalition, the Bike Party, and other formations bring attention to cycling in a variety of ways, pushing for the urban infrastructure needed to make cycling easier for more people, with the urgency of the climate crisis driving advocacy. In our car-centric culture, this work has a long way to go, but it has grown over the years, along with the numbers of regular bike riders.

TO LEARN MORE

Carlsson, Chris, LisaRuth Elliott, and Adriana Camarena, eds. *Shift Happens! Critical Mass at 20*. San Francisco: Full Enjoyment Books, 2012.

Henderson, Jason. *Street Fight: The Politics of Mobility in San Francisco*. Amherst: University of Massachusetts Press, 2013.

3.11 Ghadar Memorial

5 Wood Street, San Francisco 94118

New migrants and immigrants have frequently been the driving force of social movements in San Francisco. The radical milieu here also has played a role in furthering revolutionary movements beyond US borders. The Ghadar Memorial (sometimes spelled Gadar) here in the Laurel Heights neighborhood recognizes one case of an effort to build a militant movement to overthrow British rule and establish a free and independent India. Indian nationals had been coming to Northern California since the gold rush, largely to labor in California's agricultural fields. Growers specifically recruited men from the state of Punjab, but federal immigration law restricted Indian migrants from bringing whole families for some time, and they faced fear and racist scapegoating. California newspapers declared that a wave of new migrants constituted a "Hindoo in-

The Ghadar (or Gadar) Memorial on Wood Street.

vasion," although of course many migrants were not Hindu, but Sikh or Muslim.

Yet Indians were among many groups that rejected this ignorance and forged their own paths. In 1913, in response to a series of anti-immigrant actions across the West Coast, members of the Indian diaspora founded the Pacific Coast Hindustan Association in Astoria, Oregon. The group established its headquarters in San Francisco and rose to international importance through the publication of the weekly *Ghadar* newspaper, from which the movement eventually drew its lasting name. Readers were urged not merely to critique Indian colonialism, but to work concretely toward the overthrow of British rule. The membership brought together farmers and students, adherents of many faiths, rejecting religious, ethnic, and caste-based factionalism. To evade surveillance, they memorized the names of their thousands of subscribers.

Ghadar's location in proximity to the Bay Area's overlapping early-twentieth-century radical geographies shaped the party's vision in profound ways. From the office, here at 5 Wood Street (after 1917; they previously used space at 436 Hill Street in Noe Valley and 1324 Valencia), Ghadarites engaged notions of internationalist labor-solidarity of the International Workers of the World (IWW, known as the Wobblies), as well as nationalist armed struggles of the Irish independence movement and the radical feminism and championing of direct action by anarchists, all of whom were quite active in the region.

After the onset of the First World War, Ghadarites put out a call to their readers to head to India to initiate armed rebellion against the British. Some eight thousand responded, in some cases traveling with weapons, ready to fight. Bombings and open uprising terrified the British, who met the rebellion with swift suppression, including conspiracy trials to imprison and kill Ghadarite leaders. Though international papers ran stories on the Indian revolution "launched from California," the Ghadar party failed to ignite the full uprising that had been envisioned. In the long term, though, Ghadar ideas became part of more widely known revolutionary thinking, pushing Gandhi, for example, to refine his nonviolent tactics, which ultimately drove the British out of India. The party was officially dissolved in 1948, but scholars describe cycles of revival of Ghadarite ideas through the Indian Communist Party and through internationalist liberation movements. The monument on Wood Street is open to the public once a week, typically on Wednesdays. Check the website of the Indian consulate for current details.

TO LEARN MORE

Ramnath, Maia. *Haj to Utopia: How the Ghadar Movement Charted Global Radicalism and Attempted to Overthrow the British Empire.* Berkeley: University of California Press, 2011.

3.12 Hotel Whitcomb

1231 Market Street, San Francisco 94103

Key aspects of the devastating expulsion and incarceration of Japanese Americans from the West Coast during WWII were managed directly from this building. The Presidio, site of the US Army's Western Defense Command, was the West Coast center of military authority for the incarceration; General John DeWitt issued the "Civilian Exclusion Orders" from there. The other West Coast administrative hub was the Hotel Whitcomb.

The Whitcomb, a grand center-city hotel built after San Francisco's 1906 earthquake, faces the corner of 8th and Market Streets with seven stories of decoratively finished reinforced concrete. It is likely best known for serving as temporary City Hall, from 1912 to 1915. The Whitcomb's role in 1942 is not evident on any plaque, but that year the Whitcomb housed many of the desks where officials worked out practical details of the mass incarceration, deciding how Japanese Americans would be rounded up and incarcerated in camps like Topaz, Manzanar, and Tule Lake.

On February 19, 1942, President Franklin Roosevelt issued Executive Order 9066, authorizing "exclusion" of "any or all persons" from "military areas." In practice this led to the exile and incarceration of Japanese Americans from the West Coast. The Whitcomb became headquarters for the 1942–43 Wartime Civil Control Administration (WCCA), the military office led by Colonel Karl R. Bendetsen that registered and rounded up Japanese Americans and created the temporary "assembly center" incarceration sites. The WCCA was on the same floor as the first West Coast office of the civilian War Relocation Authority (WRA), which created and primarily ran the large long-term inland camps from 1942 into 1946. Officials working at the Whitcomb originated or relayed many orders whose traumatic effects are still felt in families: imposing special restrictions on previously free people; forcing them to register and receive family numbers in preparation for their own removal; separating them from homes, property, and

The Hotel Whitcomb was once the command and control center where officials designed and carried out the incarceration of people of Japanese descent.

William Kochiyama testified to the Commission on Wartime Relocation and Internment of Civilians regarding his arrival at Tanforan in 1942: "At the entrance . . . stood two lines of troops with rifles and fixed bayonets pointed at the evacuees as they walked between the soldiers to the prison. Overwhelmed with

daily lives; transporting them, mainly by bus, to the so-called assembly centers; sending the inmates, mainly by train, to remote inland concentration camps; keeping them there under guard; setting conditions for their departure after as many as four years of incarceration.

The nearest Bay Area assembly center was the Tanforan racetrack in San Bruno, about fifteen miles south of San Francisco, at the site of the present-day Tanforan shopping mall and San Bruno BART station. Thousands were held in barracks and converted horse stables there until their transfer inland, usually to the Topaz camp in the Sevier Desert near Delta, Utah. Many accounts of the Tanforan camp are available.

Defying the stereotype that Japanese Americans went to the camps quietly, asserting their dignity and US patriotism at the cost of appearing to agree to imprisonment,

bitterness and blind with rage, I screamed every obscenity I knew at the armed guards, daring them to shoot me." Kochiyama later served in the US Army in the legendary Japanese American 442nd Regimental Combat Team, alongside many others who had been incarcerated. He was the husband of activist Yuri Kochiyama. (Martha Bridegam)

TO LEARN MORE

Niiya, Brian. "Wartime Civil Control Administration." In Densho Encyclopedia, http://encyclopedia.densho.org/Wartime_Civil_Control_Administration/.

Personal Justice Denied: Report of the Commission on Wartime Relocation and Internment of Civilians. Washington, DC: USGPO, 1983.

Tanforan Memorial, http://www.tanforanmemorial.org

Moody skies to the southeast reflect the character of the Hunter's Point Naval Shipyard as it awaits redevelopment.

3.13 Hunter's Point Shipyard

Innes Court, San Francisco 94124 (public park at end of court overlooks the industrial shipyard)

Whether you get there by bicycle, bus, or car, the trip to the Hunter's Point Shipyard will take you across socioeconomic realities and through a rapidly changing landscape that has been subject to debate and rebuilding for much of San Francisco's 150-year history. The shipyard itself is at the center of a massive redevelopment project, meant to turn the onetime naval-production site into a residential/commercial dream, complete with sustainable design, massive public art, parks, shopping, and commercial space. Here at the end of Innes Court you can see the beginning of this; the shipyard-themed playground, public art, and housing here represent the first phase of this new develop-

ment. But the project is mired in a major controversy, and has been for decades. Military uses on the site poisoned hundreds of acres, necessitating its designation as a federal superfund site in 1989. By 2018, $1 billion had already been invested to clean up the soils but decades-old concerns were revived by a scandal involving faked soil samples that called into question the safety of the housing developments here that had already been sold to and occupied by new residents. The "fake clean" soil was just one tiny part of the larger challenge of turning the shipyard, which had been the economic engine of the area—as a nineteenth-century private shipbuilding site and then a military-industrial node during WWII—into a livable place.

There are a few key facts you need to know as you walk the area: The WWII

Chinese fishermen harvested and processed shrimp for international and local markets at Hunter's Point, near the shipyard, from the 1860s to the 1940s (1934 photo; photographer unknown).

village akin to the one at China Camp in the North Bay pulled tons of crustaceans from the bay for local and international markets. In the years before San Francisco had fully developed, it was one of the few places where city leaders allowed the Chinese to run businesses outside of Chinatown. After the 1906 earthquake and fire, white city leaders pushed a failed plan to move Chinatown here, but in later years the Chinese presence here was attacked. Locals still tell stories of the public torching of Chinese shacks in the 1930s. The development of the naval shipyard displaced the remains of the shrimp camp, though a few small-scale shrimpers remained through the 1960s.

expansion of the naval yard brought African American migrants here in large numbers. They secured jobs at the shipyard, became rooted in the community, and established a neighborhood that, for a time, nurtured a Black middle class. In moving here, Black families made home and community in a place that had a tangled legacy of isolation. It was the place where the city's old Butcher's Reservation had been sequestered; it was the place where the city dumped its largest sewage plant, and where a polluting power plant hazed the sky for generations; two major freeways pass through, compounding the environmental toxins emitted by the many small-scale industrial sites, like auto body shops. (For more on this community, see Westbrook Court, p. 186.)

Much earlier, Hunter's Point was home to a large Chinese immigrant population that is still represented in the signage for car repairs and other businesses. A shrimping

Today, from the park at the end of Innes, what you see mostly includes the preserved military remnants of the WWII era, surrounded by a perpetually active development site. The layers of history here reveal that San Francisco's race-class geography remains both sociologically and materially under construction. Toxins, as noted above, remain a troubling element. Of the various organizations working to educate the public, the nonprofit Greenaction for Environmental Health may be the most enduring in calling for more robust enforcement of health standards.

TO LEARN MORE

Brahinsky, Rachel. *The Making and Unmaking of Southeast San Francisco*. PhD diss., University of California, Berkeley, 2012.

Dillon, Lindsey. *Waste, Race, and Space: Urban Redevelopment and Environmental Justice in Bayview-Hunters Point*. PhD diss., University of California, Berkeley, 2014.

3.14 International Hotel

848 Kearny Street, San Francisco 94108

The building that stands here at 848 Kearny Street is not the original; a display in the lobby pays homage to the elderly Filipinx and Chinese residents who were forcefully evicted in the middle of the night, some nine years after the first International Hotel eviction notice stirred a mass movement in defense of the place and its residents. The campaign to halt the I Hotel evictions brought people from the city's Manilatown and Chinatown together with some of the most active organizations of the New Left, including student movements at San Francisco State College (later University) and UC Berkeley, as well as groups like the Peoples Temple and Maoist political organizations. The fight for the International Hotel connected urban development struggles across the city, from the Fillmore to SOMA.

In the 1920s Filipinos began living at 848 Kearny, one of the neighborhood's dozens of single-room occupancy hotels. Eventually, some thirty thousand people found housing there during the heyday of San Francisco's Manilatown. Through the 1960s, the hotels provided flexible housing to seasonal workers employed on farms across California and

The new International Hotel, rebuilt as affordable housing after decades of advocacy.

Oregon. The ground-level businesses at the International Hotel—including billiards venues and eventually the well-known Hungry I Club—became home to the community as much as the residential floors above. The density of residents in Manilatown developed into a network of community services, with strong links to the adjacent Chinatown.

In 1968 the firm that owned the building, chaired by real estate mogul Walter Shorenstein, sought to evict all of its tenants to make way for new development. A coalition led initially by the United Filipino Association pushed back, initiating a decade of legal, political, and physical battles over

PERSONAL REFLECTION FROM GORDON
CHIN, FOUNDING EXECUTIVE DIRECTOR,
CHINATOWN COMMUNITY DEVELOPMENT
CORPORATION

Chinatown's history and the history of San
Francisco are very much intertwined, and
leadership in Chinatown has really stood
the test of time since the 1840s. I believe
that we were the first to oppose and con-
front a public effort to move our neighborhood, after the 1906 earthquake. This may
have been the first "we won't move" anti-
displacement campaign in the city's history.
Flash forward to the I Hotel era. This gave
us lessons about coalition building, beyond
individual displacement cases, that have
continued to inform the city for fifty years,
helping to shape things like the first SRO
hotel preservation ordinance in the country.
I learn something every time I'm in Chinatown. I just marvel at the longevity, the
ability of many generations of leadership
to preserve this place. It's a strong community because of the leadership that's
existed for 170 years, and that continues
to be reinforced by newcomers, by visitors.
We didn't start the community development movement; it started way at the very
beginning, in the 1840s.

In the wake of the International Hotel evictions,
community members rallied to support evictees and
to push for replacement affordable housing. This
1978 poster by Rachael Romero depicts activists and
tenants including Tex Llamera, Felix Ayson, My Yip,
Mama Elena, and Etta Moon.

the building. Bolstered by a growing public
distaste for urban renewal projects, and the
fact that Shorenstein's company was already
the largest property owner in SF, the coalition drew a range of supporters from across
the region to use protest and political pressure to delay the evictions. Shorenstein's
firm eventually sold the hotel to a Hong
Kong–based shell company, the Four Seas
Investment Corporation, quietly promising
to cover the costs of eviction. Instead, court

battles and public protest extended the fight
for the I Hotel for another four years. In the
context of a citywide dearth of affordable
housing, supporters sustained the struggle
in part by framing it as the center of a larger
battle for affordable housing and democratic
rights for people of all backgrounds.

The struggle culminated in a highly publicized eviction of 150 remaining tenants on
August 4, 1977. A human barricade of some
3,000 people circled the hotel. Inside, tenants barricaded their doors with whatever
they had, some stuffing wet towels along the
edges of their doors in case of tear gas. Sher-
riff Richard Hongisto first refused to enforce
the eviction but ultimately decided to carry
it out. The human barricade held together

into the early morning, facing beatings by horse-mounted police determined to punish and create chaos. A photograph of Hongisto himself swinging a sledgehammer to split open the doors of elderly residents circulated in the newspapers. The demolition that followed left a hole in the ground for nearly thirty years. Finally, in 2005, the Chinatown Community Development Corporation developed the structure that stands today, offering subsidized housing to seniors and the disabled. In the long decades from SRO to demolition and rebuilding, the I Hotel struggle remains as one of the emblematic challenges through which advocates learned how both to agitate and to build power for an alternative vision in a city where the affordable housing crisis has grown to touch almost every neighborhood.

TO LEARN MORE

Habal, Estella. *San Francisco's International Hotel: Mobilizing the Filipino American Community in the Anti-Eviction Movement*. Asian American History and Culture. Philadelphia: Temple University Press, 2007.

3.15 Japan Center, *Nihonmachi*

Japantown reaches east-west from Laguna to Fillmore and north-south from about Bush to Geary

San Francisco's Japantown was founded as the first and oldest community of *Nikkei* (people of Japanese ancestry) in the continental US. While many visitors will eat a meal and walk the mall, we invite you to dig deeper to learn how Japanese Americans were subjected to repeated attacks on their

rights and presence in the city—and how they fought back.

Japanese immigrants began arriving in San Francisco in the 1860s, and many later settled here in the Western Addition, which escaped the worst effects of the 1906 earthquake and fire. Like the dozens of other Japantowns across the state, San Francisco's grew on a tenuous foundation. Californians passed Alien Land Laws in 1913 and 1920 to prohibit Japanese immigrants from owning property. Despite these and other barriers, by 1940 Japantown housed over five thousand people, more than two hundred businesses, and many community institutions. The WWII incarceration of Japanese Americans abruptly ended this flourishing, as all people of Japanese descent on the West Coast, two-thirds of whom were US citizens, were forcibly removed from their communities and incarcerated under Executive Order 9066.

When Japanese Americans returned to Japantown, they found it largely occupied by wartime defense industry workers, many of whom were African American. Starting over was extremely difficult, and Japanese Americans' tenuous gains were attacked again when the Western Addition became San Francisco's first full-fledged redevelopment project targeting "blight." Despite intense community opposition, eight thousand residents were displaced during the first phase of redevelopment, which established the six-lane Geary Expressway and the Japanese Cultural and Trade Center (now known as the Japan Center). Designed to solicit investment from Japan while creating a tourist

The Peace Plaza is the center of Japantown.

retail destination, the center's initial tenants included Hitachi, Nissan, and Mitsubishi. By the mid-1970s, these corporations no longer needed the center's showrooms to win market share, and a new generation of small-scale retail shops appeared, primarily operated by Japanese nationals who were later joined by Korean immigrants.

The assaults of WWII and redevelopment undermined Japantown's cohesion, but it is still the heart of the Bay Area's Nikkei community, with historic churches, community organizations, and events. During phase two of redevelopment community members argued that Japanese American residents and businesses should be prioritized in development plans north of the Japan Center. In contrast to the massive stripped-down modernism of the Center, the new *Nihonmachi* (Japantown) created an environment that promised an "intimate scale of buildings and spaces." Along the Japantown section of the Buchanan Mall these goals are evident in two-story commercial structures that refer visually to traditional Japanese villages, and a meandering cobblestone river punctuated by artist Ruth Asawa's origami-inspired fountains. Sutter Street retains a mixture of postwar structures and Victorian-era residences that once housed Japanese American residents and businesses. (Donna Graves)

NEARBY SITES OF INTEREST

Japanese YWCA
1830 Sutter Street
Designed by Julia Morgan, the Japanese YWCA was built through fundraising by *Issei* (first-generation Japanese immigrant) women because their daughters weren't welcome at other Y facilities.

Soko Hardware

1698 Post Street and Benkyo Do, 1747 Buchanan Street

Only a few shops in Japantown, including these two, date back to pre-WWII Japantown. Benkyo Do has sold manju and mochi (traditional Japanese sweets) since 1906.

TO LEARN MORE

Lai, Clement. "The Racial Triangulation of Space: The Case of Urban Renewal in San Francisco's Fillmore District." *Annals of the Association of American Geographers* 102, no. 1 (2012): 151–170.

Preserving California's Japantowns, http://www.californiajapantowns.org/index.html

3.16 KPOO Radio, 89.5 FM

1329 Divisadero Street, San Francisco 94115

The sounds of KPOO flow from this unassuming storefront on Divisadero.

In an era when the media landscape is shifting toward digital choose-your-own platforms, KPOO persists as the oldest Black-owned community radio station on the West Coast. The station, which was born through connections forged in the ethnic studies strikes at San Francisco State, maintains a longtime commitment to public-service programming on fundamental urban planning issues and interethnic cultural programs, in addition to shows featuring veterans'- and prisoners'-rights advocates. Pronounced "Kay-Poo" by San Franciscans, KPOO's history is intimately tied to the history of redevelopment in the Western Addition/Fillmore neighborhood. The weekly mix includes some programming that has lasted for more than forty years, such as *Voices of the Native Nation*, alongside newer shows that touch on issues like Middle East and queer-of-color politics and a daily news show that emphasizes working-class stories. DJ shows feature music from the African diaspora in its many forms, from gospel to blues to hip-hop. Terry Collins, a KPOO co-founder, has continued hosting his late-night talk show into his eighties.

The green Edwardian building on Divisadero Street was not KPOO's first home, but its current location on one of the main corridors of the old African American Western Addition is symbolically important. The station was founded in 1971 with the explicit goal of building an institution that would remain community based, giving community members a chance to participate and be heard in ways that mainstream media had not allowed. Originally located at Pier 39 on the waterfront, the station then moved to the South of Market District and then on to multiple Divisadero locations. The 1985 purchase of 1329 Divisadero Street solidified its place in one of its core communities. If you walk south along Divisadero Street (which is uphill) you should still find barbecue restaurants, traditionally African American churches, and barber shops that anchor the Black community, even in an era of Black out-migration and gentrification.

On Sundays you might catch a KPOO broadcast of the sounds of the Saint John Coltrane Church, once located on Divisadero before a move to Fillmore and then Turk, through its show *Uplift*. With a history that brings together key San Francisco legacies, the institution is rooted in jazz-based spirituality and has been influenced by yogic philosophy, Haight-Ashbury rock 'n' roll culture, civil rights politics, and southern Black diasporic traditions. Sunday services are open to the public. If you go, consider taking a walk through the neighborhood toward Alamo Square, noticing that there is much more here than the famous postcard view.

TO LEARN MORE

KPOO, on the radio at 89.5 FM, or online at www.KPOO.com

3.17 Lexington Club

3464 19th Street, San Francisco 94110 (historic site)

San Francisco is storied as a safe haven for LGBTQ communities, and the Castro Dis-

Photographed in 2014, just months before the Lexington closed and this bright marquee disappeared.

trict's gay nightlife is the subject of many guides and historical treatments. The laser focus on tourism in the Castro, however, often obscures the many other queer stories that have made the city tick, from the formation of queer enclaves in the Tenderloin, Polk Gulch, the Mission District, and beyond. In some ways the "big gay story" in this city, and the region more broadly, is about the vastness of queer life—queers in the Bay Area are rich and poor, powerful and everyday, urban and suburban. Still, the concentration of LGBTQ people in San Francisco has been uniquely strong and has produced many subcultures and neighborhoods across the city. The rise and fall of such places has to do with much more than sexuality, as the short life of the Lexington

Club—a lesbian bar that opened here on 19th Street in 1997 and closed in 2015—shows. By the time it shut down, the "Lex" was said to be the last remaining full-time lesbian bar in a city that had birthed waves of queer nightlife as far back as the nineteenth century. The closing was tied to financial troubles in a rapidly gentrifying part of the Valencia corridor.

While the Mission District was never predominantly LGBTQ, post-WWII population shifts in the area made the neighborhood more affordable and thus a magnet for people on the socioeconomic fringe. As largely Irish and German families formed the white middle class and left, lower-income gays and lesbians found their way to the Mission. In doing so, they joined migrants primarily from Mexico and Central America, who expanded the small Latino enclave that had been growing in the Mission for years. Lesbians in particular clustered together as one of several strong minorities in the district, which was close to the male-dominated Castro, but far cheaper, and they began to put down cultural roots in the 1960s and 1970s. Over the years, they reclaimed words like *dyke* and *queer* as positive descriptions, and so we use those terms here in that way as well.

Some of the earliest dyke-oriented businesses included a women's printing-press collective and bookstore in the early 1970s; by the late '70s there were cafés and bars catering to women/lesbians, notably Amelia's (645-647 Valencia Street), which offered space for political events, in addition to music and drinking. The '70s and '80s saw an expansion of the lesbian presence, with fairs and cultural events, craft stores, and the Osento bathhouse, which was based in a Victorian at 953-955 Valencia Street. Good Vibrations, perhaps the nation's first cooperatively owned, feminist sex shop opened up around the corner on 22nd Street (before moving to Valencia Street and expanding around the Bay Area).

By 1997 when the Lexington Club opened, the neighborhood was already feeling the housing and economic pressures of the first dot-com boom. The dominant Latinx population was under siege by rising housing costs, but remained a cultural and demographic majority. The Mission was still a key hearth for the tenants' rights and housing rights movements, with a strong political identity centered around class that bridged race, ethnicity, and sexuality. The working-class and artistic identity of the Mission was evident at the Lexington. For much of its eighteen years it served as a community space, playing host to weddings and domestic partnership ceremonies, meetings, and perhaps thousands of first dates and sexual encounters. In 2015 it fell victim to rising commercial rent, which exacerbated the bar's troubles with changing clientele amid the shrinking lesbian presence in the neighborhood. This demographic shift was in part a product of the gentrification that was pushing lower-rent households to the urban fringe. It was also likely the result of cultural changes, as many dykes that came of age in the 1990s moved on to other things, beyond the bar scene. As the bar closed, a documentary film project was underway, and there were plans to continue event programming under the name of the Lexington at other venues.

TO LEARN MORE

Boyd, Nan Alamilla. *Wide-Open Town: A History of Queer San Francisco to 1965*. Berkeley: University of California Press, 2005.

Graves, Donna J., and Shayne E. Watson. *Citywide Historic Context Statement for LGBTQ History in San Francisco*. City and County of San Francisco, Planning Department, 2016.

Michelle Tea. *Valencia*. Berkeley, CA: Seal Press, 2008.

3.18   Media Moguls Corner

3rd and Market Streets Intersection, San Francisco

In the age of online media, it's sometimes hard to remember that there was a time when newspapers—printed on paper and sold in messy string-tied stacks or later in metal sidewalk boxes—were major players in the physical landscape of cities like San Francisco. Late-nineteenth-century newspaper buildings, like the ones you are surrounded by here on this corner, played a similar function to the headquarter buildings of any other major corporation: They were highly decorated symbols of urban power. Architecture fans will enjoy the dramatic layers of history evident in these grand structures. But the opulence and artistry of this corner is not just a monument to design. It is the material representation of capital, with tentacles that reached from imperial cities like this one to ports of entry all around the world. The media moguls who built this urban corner weren't just allied with powerful interests, they often ran the very businesses that their pages trumpeted. The spoils of mining operations and sugar plantations thus live on in these towers and others like them across downtown.

Michael de Young (whose museum remains a centerpiece of Golden Gate Park) built the first skyscraper in San Francisco at

The stately red de Young building in 2019, with Lotta's Fountain in the foreground.

690 Market as the headquarters for the *San Francisco Chronicle* in 1890. His family controlled the newspaper for more than a century until 2000, when it was sold to Hearst Media. Soon after the *Chronicle*'s building opened, Claus Spreckles commissioned a tower for the *San Francisco Call* across the street at 703 Market. Spreckles is famous as a railroad baron and real estate developer in San Diego, though his fortune originated in the brutally exploitative sugar plantations that his father ran in Hawaii. Competing with the de Youngs, Spreckels demanded a taller building from his development team, and it was later extended even higher. Both buildings were severely damaged in the fires after the 1906 quake but were refurbished in grand style.

To outdo them both, the infamous William Randolph Hearst (whose life story was the basis for Orson Welles's *Citizen Kane*) built his own tower here, even taller than the other two, in 1909. The building still displays a prominent gilded *H* above the door. Hearst transferred family wealth from mining operations across Latin America into the media business, to which he brought a ruthless and often unscrupulously competitive spirit. Long before the era of so-called fake news, Hearst used the pulpit of his own newspaper to win his seat in the US Senate—even as the newspaper itself lost money.

These three papers were the most prominent and longest-lasting broadsheets that emerged from a sea of ubiquitous nineteenth-century news media. Through a variety of name changes, mergers, and acquisitions (the *Call* name disappeared entirely in

the 1960s), the media moguls on this corner channeled their energies into pet causes of national and international import, while also working to ensure that local property values continued to rise. In the 1960s the counterculture revolutions impacted newspapers as well, and a new paradigm of alternative media took root across the country in publications like the *San Francisco Bay Guardian*, which established a critical-journalistic perspective that generally sought to challenge urban power rather than ally with it. As the newspaper industry contracted in the 2000s, many of the weeklies closed, including the *Bay Guardian*. These have been replaced by a landscape of underfunded but persistent online newspapers that get the news out, although without access to the grandeur, or the capital, represented by structures like these.

NEARBY SITE OF INTEREST

Lotta's Fountain

Pedestrian island, Market at 3rd Street

Gifted to the city by gold rush–era performer Lotta Crabtree (one of very few prominent women in San Francisco in the mid-nineteenth century), the fountain is said to have been a meeting site in the postdisaster chaos after the 1906 quake and fire. It has outlived several attempts to move or remove it.

TO LEARN MORE

Brechin, Grey. *Imperial San Francisco: Urban Power, Earthly Ruin.* Berkeley: University of California Press, 1999.

www.48hills.org (online newspaper in the tradition of the *Bay Guardian*)

3.19 Mission Cultural Center for Latino Arts

2868 Mission Street, San Francisco 94110

A vibrant example of the legacy of San Francisco's publicly created network of cultural arts centers, the Mission Cultural Center for Latino Arts (MCCLA) is located on the busy stretch of Mission Street that was once dubbed the Miracle Mile, a popular driving, shopping, and theater corridor. Inside the cultural center there's an atmosphere of creation, where you are likely to be surrounded by sounds of drumming and dancing upstairs or the visuals of brilliantly colored art hanging in the Galería Museo. Today the thirty-three-thousand-square foot MCCLA maintains a theater, the Mission Gráfica printmaking workshop, dance and music classes, space rentals, and a popular annual Day of the Dead exhibit.

The MCCLA opened in 1977 as one node of a wider citywide cultural network called the Neighborhood Arts Program (NAP). The San Francisco Arts Commission (SFAC) had created the program a decade earlier during the eruption of grassroots cultural expression and national attention on the so-called Summer of Love, seeking to bring arts programming to the neighborhood level. The NAP was the first community program of its kind in the country, and it employed organizers and hundreds of local artists to develop neighborhood-specific centers that responded to local needs, offering workshops, performances, and other arts services in a variety of settings.

Beginning in 1973, the arts centers tapped into federal Comprehensive Employment and Training Act funding; the money was intended to support job training and employment opportunities, and San Francisco was the first city to designate these funds for arts-related employment. With this funding, the scale of programs grew with interneighborhood collaboration and interdisciplinary partnerships. In 1974 advocates pushed the city to secure federal funds to acquire buildings—mostly out-of-use, large industrial spaces—in four neighborhoods.

The Mission Cultural Center, a vital community resource.

The Mission Cultural Center, which had been a furniture store, was one of these.

Artists and allies used that same funding to create the Western Addition Cultural Center (now the African American Arts and Culture Complex), which had been a brewery at 762 Fulton Street; the South of Market Union Machine Company factory became the Brannan Street Cultural Center, later named South of Market Art Resource building (now the SOMArts Cultural Center) at 934 Brannan Street; the Bayview Opera House at 4705 3rd Street—a site of cultural programs since its construction in 1888—was converted to a performing-arts workshop space, a dance floor, and a large theater. The range of locations grew to include leased spaces as well, such as the Chinese Cultural Center at 750 Kearny Street, Intersection Arts Center at 756 Union Street, and the Precita Center (now Precita Valley Community Center) at 534 Precita.

While there is not much visible evidence that connects the centers today, in the late 1970s the sites represented a vital part of the landscape of arts programming, helping to make possible a staggering array of activities of the NAP, from visual arts to theater to publications and gardening. The NAP employed hundreds of artists reflecting the cultural identities of the communities in which they lived. Performers like the Pickle Family Circus, the San Francisco Mime Troupe, Intersection for the Arts, and the American Indian Arts Workshop nurtured artists like Bill Irwin, Marga Gomez, Roberto Vargas, Danny Glover, Rene Yañez, and Peter Coyote. Sculptor

Ruth Asawa sat on SFAC's committee on the neighborhood arts in the early 1970s (a public school now bears her name). As NAP funding grew scarce, a number of the services and the individual centers were spun off as independent ventures, but the program still exists under another name as a part of the San Francisco Arts Commission. (LisaRuth Elliott)

NEARBY SITES OF INTEREST

Galería de La Raza

1420 Valencia Street, San Francisco 94103
As a product of the neighborhood arts movement, and a hub for both art and politics, the gallery persists in a rapidly changing Mission District—even after an eviction in 2018 from its longtime home on 24th Street.

The "Google Bus" Protests

Mission and 24th Streets, intersection
The early 2000s were punctuated by artistic, media-grabbing protests at this intersection, which drew attention to the impact that new tech-company shuttles to the South Bay were having on San Francisco neighborhoods. One of the key organizations that became well known through these demonstrations was the Anti-Eviction Mapping Project, which creatively documented the evictions and displacement of the new millennium at https://www.antievictionmap.com.

TO LEARN MORE

See chapters by Alejandro Murguía, Patricia Rodriguez, and Mary Jean Robertson in *Ten Years That Shook the City: San Francisco, 1968–1978*, edited by Chris Carlsson and LisaRuth Elliott. San Francisco: City Lights Books, 2011.

Mosher, Mike. "Artist!," *Bad Subjects*, no. 53, January 2001.

This cemetery is a quiet place in which to question the legacy of the mission system.

3.20 Mission Dolores Cemetery

3321 16th Street, San Francisco 94114

Beyond the often-romanticized Spanish colonial history, which focuses on the original adobe construction and the cultural presence of the church, this two-century-old mission is important for its role in cementing both domination and resistance among Indigenous communities. The Mission San Francisco de Asis is commonly known as the Mission Dolores, a nickname that dates back to the mission's historical location near the Arroyo de Nuestra Señora de los Dolores, a creek that has long since been covered up by urbanization. (At one point it was believed that there had also been a freshwater Dolores Lake here, but researchers have shown that to be a myth.)

Its cemetery, famously featured in Alfred Hitchcock's *Vertigo* (1958), offers a quiet testament to the brutal violence and genocide that was endemic to the Spanish colonial system. Brought to the mission to be "Christianized," the members of Ohlone linguistic groups were forced into hard labor for the Spanish monks and soldiers housed at the Presidio. Although there are important stories of church leaders who rebelled against the violence of the system (see Mission San Jose, p. 103), thousands of Indigenous people were essentially worked to death and exposed to European diseases. By the time the missions were secularized in 1834, the bodies of over five thousand Indigenous Californians were buried here within the mission walls. Only a fraction of the original cemetery remains; it is open to the public, and contemporary exhibits pay respect to the Ohlone, Miwok, and other "first Californians" buried there.

Mission High School

3750 18th Street, San Francisco 94114

In response to California state Proposition 187, which barred undocumented immigrants from services like education and nonemergency health care, students staged a walk-out here in 1993. This was part of a larger tradition of high school student activism in the Bay Area (see reflection below).

PERSONAL REFLECTION BY PRISHNI MURRILLO, COMMUNITY ACTIVIST AND YOUTH ADVOCATE

I had a lot of friends in the Mission who told me that there was this walkout happening, and we went without really knowing what it was to "walk out." It was really mind-blowing to just be there to witness and feel the energy of all the young people gathering at Dolores Park and walking all the way to the school district headquarters in downtown on South Van Ness. I remember the demands were around getting rid of punitive measures that had been targeting all the Raza kids because of the dress code, like wearing flags and certain colors. We were also fighting for ethnic studies, and it was also against Proposition 187. I didn't really know what exactly was going on, but I remember going and catching the energy of it all. The activist stuff was tight to me because I was so mad about the anti-immigrant stuff happening in the '90s. It was just reality for me, being a teen and undocumented and the climate being so different that I couldn't tell nobody, there was like two people that knew I didn't have papers, you know? But then, to go to a protest and then a workshop and be challenged around what does it mean to claim your space or call yourself something. It was almost like a spiritual enlightenment for me.

3.21 Monkey Block

628 Montgomery Street, San Francisco 94111 (historic site)

The transgressions—both political and cultural—at the heart of San Francisco's uniqueness were long rooted on this stretch of Montgomery Street, back when the massive brick Montgomery Block stood here. Originally a nineteenth-century apartment building that housed writers and thinkers like Mark Twain, Emma Goldman, and Jack London, the Montgomery Block served as a residential and cultural center across several eras, including a particularly notable period as home for New Deal–era creatives. The building, known by its low-rent residents as the Monkey Block, was replaced by the Transamerica Pyramid, a building that remains symbolic of the growth of the city as a financial capital.

When the Montgomery Block first opened as a rooming house in 1853, it was the largest building west of the Mississippi, one of a series of boardinghouses and one-room-apartment buildings that matched the needs of the time: bachelor living. The ground level hosted saloons and a public bathhouse originally, and commercial offices in later years. In the midst of the growing financial district, the Monkey Block was close to the Barbary Coast and other "vice" districts over the years, including the edge of North Beach where Beat poets eventually clustered (Lawrence Ferlinghetti's City Lights Bookshop and other famed Beat sites are still just a few blocks away). Other "bohemian" hotels nearby included the Lick House, Russ House, and Occidental Hotel.

(Left) March 1940 view of the Montgomery Block (nicknamed Monkey Block), southwest corner. (A. J. Wittlock photo)

(Below) The Transamerica Pyramid is built on the site of the Monkey Block. Though it is no longer the tallest in San Francisco, you can see its characteristic peak (gray, pointy, on the right side of the 2019 skyline in this image) from points near and far.

The word *bohemian* often signaled that a place was frequented by a great mix of non-conforming San Franciscans and tourists, including LGBTQ people, political radicals, and artists.

The Monkey Block was one of the few downtown buildings to survive the 1906 quake and fire, and it became the cornerstone of a larger arts scene that flowed through North Beach and ultimately the rest of the city. New Deal historian Harvey Smith notes that some seventy-five artists and writers lived or worked in studios there through the

1930s. Artists in the neighborhood included Diego Rivera, Frida Kahlo, Ralph Stackpole, Maynard Dixon, Dorothea Lange, Beniamino Bufano, and Sargent Johnson. In the New Deal era, many made a living working for the federal government when programs like the Works Progress Administration and Federal Art Project funded artistic endeavors across the country. Many focused their artistic lenses on the urgent social problems of the day, often with a strong class analysis.

The Monkey Block was demolished in 1959 for a parking lot. Thirteen years later the Transamerica Corporation completed its landmark pyramid on the site, redefining the San Francisco skyline with a testament not to bohemian life but to international finance, insurance, and corporate power. As with the Bank of America Building, the building was sold off in the 1990s (see p. 133) but remains a downtown focal point.

PERSONAL REFLECTION FROM REBA HUDSON, LONGTIME NORTH BEACH RESIDENT AND SELF-DESCRIBED SAN FRANCISCO BOHEMIAN

Mona [Sargent, who ran Mona's 440 bar, which was central to 1930s–40s lesbian culture] told me that they called themselves the "mad bohemians." Prohibition wasn't lifted until, what, '32, '33? When that was lifted, Mona decided that she'd like to open a bar. She had all these friends she was living with in the Monkey Block—it's famous in North Beach history but was torn down about twenty years ago as part of some high-rise. The Iron Pot was down there, the Black Cat was not too far, and Mona just was going to open a place for her friends. Just a bohemian joint, a little beer and wine place to have a drink and talk and discuss ideas and do what bohemians do, right? Drink and carry on and have intellectual conversations. The bar was already there—it had operated as a bar prior to Prohibition. I think she said she opened it on a hundred dollars or something like that, just enough to buy the beer and wine, because everything was there. And that bar became the Purple Onion. (Excerpted from a 1992 oral history interview in Boyd, *Wide Open Town*.)

NEARBY SITES OF INTEREST

Canessa Gallery
708 Montgomery Street, San Francisco 94111
A forty-plus-year-old gallery featuring artists focused on social critique and public history.

Black Cat Café
710 Montgomery Street (historic site)
Jose Sarria, the country's first openly gay political candidate in 1961, regularly risked arrest in the 1950s by performing in drag here.

Coit Tower
1 Telegraph Hill Boulevard, on top of Telegraph Hill
Monkey Block residents participated in the development of the Coit Tower murals, which were the first artworks to be funded by FDR's New Deal in 1933.

TO LEARN MORE

Boyd, Nan Alamilla. *Wide-Open Town: A History of Queer San Francisco to 1965*. Berkeley: University of California Press, 2005.

Smith, Harvey. "New Deal Artists and Programs during the Depression." FoundSF.org, n.d.

3.22 Other Avenues Food Store Cooperative

3930 Judah Street, San Francisco 94122
This is one of just three remaining food-based cooperatives out of the dozen enterprises that formed the People's Food System in the early 1970s. Back then, communards in hundreds of communal dwellings set up a distribution network across autonomous food-buying clubs they called "food conspiracies." Other Avenues grew out of that network, which aimed to provide locally sourced and mostly organic food.

Free food giveaways in the Golden Gate Park Panhandle by the San Francisco Dig-

The legacies of the 1970s food conspiracies live on in a few parts of the Bay Area, including Other Avenues.

gers in 1966 and 1967 had already set the precedent of a daily run to the Produce Terminal in the Bayview to collect fresh but potentially unsellable vegetable and meat donations from local farmers and distributors. Every day for about a year, the Diggers served free soup to anyone with a bowl and spoon. Commune dwellers began to go directly to farmers markets and nearby orchards and farms, sometimes pooling food stamps or cash. In turn, they provided food for large networks of people at discounted prices, without the markup of distributors and grocery stores. With direct connections to farmers, they were also able to encourage reduced use of chemicals. Seeing an opportunity to further organize wholesale operations, the People's Food System expanded on the food-conspiracy concept, and by 1974 began to collectively organize warehouses, suppliers, and stores, with a distribution hub in the Mission District, while also publishing a

newsletter called *Turnover: Magazine of Politics and Food.*

With the support of People's Food System funding, low rent, and volunteer labor, Other Avenues expanded its food membership operation to a storefront in 1974. Other Avenues incorporated as a worker-owned cooperative in 1999, supported in part by the Inter-Collective Organic Union, which linked the Rainbow Grocery Cooperative, the Inner Sunset Community Store (closed in 1995), the Noe Valley Community Store (closed in 1996), and Veritable Vegetable, a food distribution center in the Bayview District. (LisaRuth Elliott)

NEARBY SITE OF INTEREST

Ocean Beach
Entrance at La Playa Street and Judah Street, San Francisco 94122
Bring your fresh produce—and a warm jacket— to the edge of the continent. The beachfront is managed as a public park, with public restrooms (a rarity in privatized San Francisco).

TO LEARN MORE

Nimbark Sacharoff, Shanta. *Other Avenues Are Possible: Legacy of the People's Food System of the San Francisco Bay Area.* Oakland, CA: PM Press, 2016.

Peirce, Pam. "A Personal History of the San Francisco People's Food System." Drew, Jesse. "Call Any Vegetable: The Politics of Food in the San Francisco Bay Area." Both in *Reclaiming San Francisco: History, Politics, Culture*, edited by Nancy Peters, Chris Carlsson, and James Brook. San Francisco: City Lights, 1998.

3.23 Panhandle of Golden Gate Park

Between Fell and Oak, Stanyan and Baker Streets, San Francisco

It's hard to imagine San Francisco or any contemporary city without the freeways that separate and sequester neighborhoods. But in San Francisco there could have been even more. The story of the preservation of this strip of open space inspired community organizers across the country who were, like residents here, fighting the incursion of the US interstate highway system. The Panhandle is just a few blocks wide, but is large enough for basketball and picnics, and its wending walkways and foliage offer a hint of the shelter from urban life that the entire park itself offers. It is also narrow enough that one is always aware of the four lanes of traffic on each side. The Panhandle itself offers an alternative transit corridor in the midst of the car traffic, with a thick trail of cyclists using its divided bike path to crisscross the city, linking key bike paths in several directions. The bike trail is an important part of what cyclists call "the wiggle," a zigzag trail that enables a crosstown ride with very few hills.

In the 1940s and 1950s, officials sought to create a web of interconnected freeways across San Francisco. Some of that vision was indeed realized, with the development of 101 and 280 on well-worn urban pathways. One of the most contested proposals was for an east-west trajectory that included arterial highways that would have eaten up

Curving paths through the Panhandle connect the Western Addition and Haight-Ashbury to Golden Gate Park as well as bike paths to the Mission and downtown.

some 60 percent of the Panhandle Park to link the Central Freeway (which is the part of 101 that currently dumps onto Market and Octavia Streets) with a proposed "sunset freeway," which would have been an expansion of Highway 1 out at Ocean Beach. In what became known as the Freeway Revolt, a decade of political agitation resulted in the cancellation of the Panhandle freeway project in addition to several others. It was not easy, and the Board of Supervisors voted the project up and then down more than once. The effort spawned important leaders, including Sue Bierman, a Haight-Ashbury resident whose political career was activated by the freeway fight (see sidebar) and who was dedicated to preserving the city's beauty and advocating for the poor and working class.

The preservation of the Panhandle mobilized people in the Haight-Ashbury neighborhood while providing open public space that enabled other mobilizations and activist efforts. In the 1960s the park, just a few blocks north of the commercial district of the Haight, was a magnet for young people and was infamously central to the cultural and political revolutions brewing at the time. Beyond the tie-dye and beads that came to represent the Haight-Ashbury hippies in the media, people here were seeking to create lives in which many different kinds of freedom could be realized, including trying to live outside of the money economy. Groups like the San Francisco Diggers served free food (see Other Avenues, p. 168) at Oak and Ashbury; the daily outpost became a key point of visibility for their efforts to

develop "Free Stores," where they gave away donated goods.

Important institutions emerged out of this political milieu. In 1967, for example, the Haight-Ashbury Free Medical Clinic at 558 Clayton opened up just a few blocks away to help deal with the mass in-migration of young people, which was accompanied by a rise in infectious and sexually transmit-

PERSONAL REFLECTION BY TIM REDMOND, EDITOR/PUBLISHER OF *48HILLS* AND FORMER EDITOR OF THE *SAN FRANCISCO BAY GUARDIAN* WEEKLY NEWSPAPER

Sue Bierman devoted her life to making San Francisco a better place—and to preventing greed and poor planning decisions from ruining it. Sue grew up on a farm in Nebraska, and when she moved to San Francisco with her husband, Art, in the 1950s, she jumped right into the emerging urban environmental movement. She helped organize her neighbors to block a plan to put an elevated freeway over Golden Gate Park and soon became a key part of the efforts to save the beauty of the city. She was also a passionate advocate for poor and working-class people. Sue didn't need to work; she wasn't rich, but the rent on the family farm that she inherited provided more than enough income to live comfortably. But instead of living a society life of leisure, she devoted herself to public service. For sixteen years, Sue was a member of the Planning Commission, and was often the only voice against badly conceived developments that promoted gentrification and overwhelmed the city's infrastructure. She pushed for developers to pay for housing and child care. She spoke up for the neighborhoods when nobody else would.

ted diseases. While much of the Haight has become a commercialized monument to an imagined psychedelic past, institutions like the free clinic contributed to the neighborhood and kept practical visions of the 1960s alive for decades (in 2019 the Haight Street location had closed, but an arm of the clinic persisted at 1563 Mission Street). The Panhandle itself remains a collective open space, dominated by cyclists and dog walkers, and a place to rest for those without homes in a city (and neighborhood) that is increasingly hostile toward houseless people.

NEARBY SITE OF INTEREST

Bound Together Books
1369 Haight Street at Masonic Avenue, San Francisco 94117
An anarchist collective and volunteer-run bookstore.

TO LEARN MORE

Talbot, David. *Season of the Witch: Enchantment, Terror, and Deliverance in the City of Love.* San Francisco: Free Press, 2013.

3.24 "Peoples Temple" Post Office

1859 Geary Street, San Francisco 94115
Most often remembered for the tragic murder-suicides that took place in Guyana, the Peoples Temple and the Reverend Jim Jones played a complicated role in a 1970s San Francisco that was exploding with visions of new politics, cultures, and societies. There is little in the landscape here on Geary to suggest it, but it's worth remembering that this post office rests on the site of the Scottish Rite Temple of the Freemasons, built

in the nineteenth century, which eventually became the Peoples Temple. In the 1970s, Jones began to hold services here next to Bill Graham's Fillmore Auditorium, once an epicenter of American psychedelia. This was also the center of the Western Addition neighborhood, which at that time was about two decades deep into a cycle of urban demolitions and reconstruction that pushed out African American and Japanese American families, and that inspired people to deeply engage in civic life to save their homes.

Jim Jones had preached about an ideal world of interracial cooperation since the 1950s in conservative Indiana. In 1965, plagued by Cold War–fueled visions of a nuclear holocaust, he moved his integrated congregation from Indianapolis to Ukiah, in Mendocino County. He held services in San Francisco for the first time in 1969 in a school gymnasium at 1430 Scott Street. It was a time of uprisings in overpoliced and underinvested urban cores like this one. Meanwhile, civil rights, Black nationalism, and third worldism were actively changing the public conversation on racial inequality.

The professed ideals of Peoples Temple—based on racial harmony and economic egalitarianism—appealed to financially struggling Black San Franciscans from the immediate neighborhood, as well as to Left-leaning people of all backgrounds, who joined Jones here at the Geary Boulevard church. Members formed a multiracial tribe that spanned the city, some living in communal activist households set up by the Temple from Potrero Hill to the Tenderloin to the Western Addition. Jones built this idealism

Jim Jones's appeal to the masses included political activity that revealed important cross-racial alliances. Here Jones is pictured at a multicultural 1977 rally against the planned evictions at the International Hotel on the edge of Chinatown. (Nancy Wong photo)

into political power. Buses full of Temple members would regularly show up at protests around the Bay Area, exemplified most tellingly by the throngs of Peoples Temple members present at the eviction-threatened International Hotel in Manilatown. Jones's political clout reached its zenith in 1977 when the Peoples Temple voting bloc helped elect progressives Mayor George Moscone and Supervisor Harvey Milk.

Soon, however, things took a dramatic and terrible turn. Despite accusations against Jones of abuse and sexual improprieties, his increasingly paranoid behavior, and damaging press, politicians including Willie Brown, Jesse Jackson, and Jerry Brown all professed support for Jones's outward goals. That same year, Jones fled with several hundred members to its agricultural colony in socialist Guyana. It was there, on November 18, 1978, that he ordered the "revolutionary suicide" of everyone at Jonestown. Between self-inflicted poisoning and a series of murders, 918 people died, including Jones himself. A stunning 75 percent of those killed were African Americans from San Francisco and Oakland, four hundred of whom are buried together at Evergreen Cemetery in Oakland. (LisaRuth Elliott)

NEARBY SITES OF INTEREST

Fillmore Street Commercial Corridor
Fillmore Street between Fulton and Geary Streets, San Francisco 94115
This is still an important business corridor for the community, even after redevelopment gutted

the street, bringing on a long-standing economic slump. Watch the sidewalks from Fulton to Geary for names of historically significant neighborhood businesses, musicians, and leaders.

TO LEARN MORE

Scheeres, Julia. *A Thousand Lives: The Untold Story of Hope, Deception, and Survival at Jonestown.* New York: Simon & Schuster, 2011.

Taylor, James Lance. "Bring Out the 'Black Dimensions' of Peoples Temple." Alternative Considerations of Jonestown and Peoples Temple, 2011. https://jonestown.sdsu.edu/?page_id=29462

3.25 Redstone Labor Temple

2940 16th Street, San Francisco 94103

Evidence of the city's historic and contemporary legacy of union labor remains—for now—in the Redstone Building. The massive red brick building here was once called the San Francisco Labor Temple, serving as a node for labor organizing from 1914 to the 1960s. Built by the San Francisco Labor Council (an association representing many unions), the building was a geographic and political center for organizers of several of the city's historic strikes, including the 1917 streetcar strike and the 1934 maritime strike that built power to produce the city's general strike later that year. In the lobby, which is open to the public, a set of murals painted in the mid-1990s memorializes the labor and community struggles that intersected at the Redstone. Several of the labor murals are painted in New Deal realist style; others represent the struggles of the neighborhood in the signature styles of artists affiliated with the nearby Clarion Alley Mural Project.

The Redstone's location just next to the intersection of 16th and Mission Streets has long placed it at the center of heated battles over neighborhood change. The 1960s struggle over the construction of BART was centered there, with ongoing tensions over the control of public space reviving regularly ever since. In the dot-com era, when fights over gentrification challenged the right of poor and working-class people to use the public plaza that surrounds the station, the organizations of the Redstone

The Redstone Building, 2015.

Building rallied to the community side of those struggles. The building itself has changed hands a few times, and there have been several fights with the newest owners over rising rents as the surrounding neighborhood gentrifies. Even so, more than forty community organizations and artists were still there in the 2010s, representing a range of political causes. The Redstone has also housed a local credit union that invested members' dollars back into the Mission District, queer and feminist theater companies, and artist-activists of various tendencies. In 2019 there was a new struggle over ownership underway, with community organizations looking to buy the building to preserve its historic uses.

NEARBY SITE OF INTEREST

Clarion Alley Mural Project (CAMP)

Clarion Alley, between 17th and 18th Streets

CAMP oversees the production and maintenance of the art in this alley, which features a rotation of political and creative works. Among many others, South San Franciscan Barry McGee, an influential figure in the graffiti-art movement, and CAMP founding member Rigo 23 (see "Victory Salute," p. 117), as well as many community-based artists and activists have painted here.

TO LEARN MORE

Jacoby, Annice. *Street Art San Francisco: Mission Muralismo*. New York: Harry N. Abrams, 2009.

Kazin, Michael. *Barons of Labor: The San Francisco Building Trades and Union Power in the Progressive Era*. Champaign: University of Illinois Press, 1987.

3.26 Room 641A

AT&T Building

611 Folsom Street, San Francisco 94107

Long before "netizens" became Big Tech and took over the South of Market District, SOMA was already a key neighborhood for technological development. Some of it took place in rooms like this one, and you were never supposed to find out about it. Stop for a moment on the northern corner of 2nd and Folsom Streets and look at the building diagonally across the street. Most of your personal digital communications probably have been routed here, through room 641A, or rooms like it, where the National Security Agency (NSA) has wiretapped and sifted our information for more than a decade.

The existence of room 641A came to light in 2006, when the San Francisco–based digital rights and privacy organization the Electronic Frontier Foundation (EFF) sued telephone giant AT&T for collaborating with the NSA. AT&T has legitimate technical reasons for routing traffic through its building here. But the EFF was troubled by the unprecedented violation of privacy—and arguably the US Constitution—implied by allowing the NSA to secretly collect and analyze communication between citizens without a warrant. Eventually the lawsuit was dismissed, due to an act of Congress that retroactively immunized AT&T, through an amendment to the Foreign Intelligence Surveillance Act. As of this writing, Congress has renewed the NSA's clearance to monitor all information.

Despite public outcry, political promises, and feigned embarrassment on the part

The mysterious AT&T Building on Folsom Street; they've got your data.

at the rather featureless exterior of 611 Folsom, consider the fact that the largest private companies in the world and almost all Internet businesses everywhere rely on a necessarily open global network running on free, open-source software, big chunks of which were originally developed by people in the Bay Area. UC Berkeley, for example, pioneered an early iteration of this free software beginning in the 1970s with Berkeley Software Distribution (BSD), a free version of the Unix operating system. Not only is open-source software made by volunteer programmers and given away for free, the source code—which is the language you need to replicate it—is open, so anyone can change it to suit their needs. Big Tech has done this for profit, but open-source software (along with the more technically complicated consensus governance structure of the Internet), speaks to the many different paths forward for our increasingly digital world.

Like the secret NSA room that exists in a nondescript office building in San Francisco, so too do the material spaces where a free and open Internet is made. Many of these bright lights in the tech universe are unique to the Bay Area. In addition to the sometimes-controversial digital rights and privacy watchdogs at the EFF, Wikipedia—the ubiquitous, nonprofit, free dictionary fueled by volunteer editors—is located

of corporations making billions off the Internet, the following decade brought a panoply of surveillance and manipulation by tech firms. From the perspective of regular people, it may seem to happen invisibly, but it unfolds in real places like this one. And the companies are not entirely hiding this activity. Google has admitted it reads your e-mail; Facebook admits it subjected users to abuse during the 2016 election season from at least one foreign entity; Twitter admits that bots (which are computer-generated "users") were responsible for driving political activity also during the 2016 political campaigns; and YouTube continues its inflammatory "suggested next video" algorithm, which fans the flames of hatred, racism, and social injustice in the name of optimizing clicks. Even so, very few politicos dare challenge the Big Tech firms that have simultaneously cast themselves as indispensable engines of economic growth, and as willing partners in state-run surveillance from the US to China.

But this is more than a story of top-down power. As you stand on the corner looking

here, along with dozens of small nonprofits dedicated to digital access, such as Girls Who Code, which aims to eliminate gender inequity in tech. And in stark contrast to the NSA's secrecy, the nonprofit Internet Archive preserves the historic Internet, creating open-access backups of the web itself and vast collections of audio, video, and books. They too are collecting information—the stuff people specifically choose to share via the web. You can stop by the Internet Archive for lunch and a glimpse at the massive server bank that archives every page on the Internet in a sea of blinking blue lights (300 Funston Avenue, San Francisco; sign up by Wednesday for Friday lunch). (Bruce Rinehart)

NEARBY SITES OF INTEREST

Prelinger Library

301 8th Street, no. 215, San Francisco, 94103

The private nonprofit library is organized geographically (rather than by the Dewey decimal system) and is open to the public for free. Related, the Prelinger Archive preserves media, especially film, online for free at https://archive.org/details/prelinger.

TO LEARN MORE

Saxenian, AnnaLee. *Regional Advantage: Culture and Competition in Silicon Valley and Route 128.* Cambridge, MA: Harvard University Press, 1996.

3.27 SOMA Pilipinas Streets

Folsom Street and Mabini Street, San Francisco 94107 (continues between 3rd and 4th Streets and between Folsom and Harrison)

Despite having faced displacement and outright racism in local and federal laws, a concentrated community of Filipinos have long called the South of Market District home. The SOMA Pilipinas Streets pay homage to this history and have helped bolster community resilience in a time of dramatic urban change. Filipino men had been coming to California since the early twentieth century when they sought work as agricultural laborers. Their communities grew after the Immigration and Nationality Act of 1965 removed the quota system based on national origins (which had given preference to immigrants from northern and western European countries over Asian and African migrants). San Francisco's already existing Manilatown (north of Market Street) and central SOMA became magnets for new arrivals from the Philippines.

Filipinos were activated around housing and development issues during the redevelopment era (generally 1950s–70s), when this part of the district experienced near-total clearance and reconstruction. A multi-ethnic alliance of largely working-class residents and community organizers challenged the city's plans. A coalition of housing advocates, labor leaders, longshoremen, and seniors organized under the umbrella organization Tenants and Owners in Opposition to Redevelopment (TOOR). TOOR successfully fought for affordable housing for four thousand people, largely immigrants and seniors. TOOR later created a housing development nonprofit, Tenants and Owners Development Corporation (TODCO), which worked with men from one of the local Filipino Masonic lodges to build housing for displaced seniors, including the

Detail from the Ang Lipi Ni Lapu Lapu mural on Lapu Lapu Street (1979, by muralist Joanna Poethig).

Dimasalang House at 50 Rizal Street. They also successfully pressed for the renaming of the surrounding streets to pay homage to Filipino political leaders.

The street names point to early stories that shaped Filipino exile culture. Mabini Street, home to the Mabini Adult Day Health Center, is named after Apolinario Mabini, a revolutionary leader and first prime minister of the Philippines when the First Philippine Republic was established in 1899. Bonifacio Street recognizes Andrés Bonifacio, the "Father of the Philippine Revolution," for his role in creating the Katipunan movement that started the Philippine Revolution. At the corner of Bonifacio and Lapu Lapu, in the Alice Street Community Garden, one can see seniors tending their vegetables and flowers in individual garden boxes. Lapu Lapu, named for the first indigenous Filipino to resist Spanish colonization in 1521, is also the site of the Ang Lipi Ni Lapu Lapu mural, a seven-story visual storyboard of Filipino and Filipino American history painted in 1979 by Philippines-raised Joanna Poethig. Rizal Street, where the former Dimasalang House is now the San Lorenzo Ruiz Center, is named for José Rizal, a Filipino nationalist who was executed by the Spanish colonial government for rebellion inspired by his writings. Tandang Sora Street, which intersects with Rizal, recalls the nickname for the "Grand Woman of the Revolution," Melchora Aquino de Ramos.

In 2006 the continued presence of Filipinx communities here was recognized formally again when the city approved the SOMA Pilipinas–Filipino Cultural Heritage District. One of several similar districts created around that time, the district offers political leverage to fund and preserve spaces of cultural programming to create a bulwark against the rapid development of the tech era, which has been centered in SOMA. The district covers about fifty square blocks, featuring community organizations, businesses, murals, and traditional cultural spaces. (LisaRuth Elliott)

The Gran Oriente Filipino Hotel at the edge of South Park is just one of many historic buildings that line the park, which stands out from the nearby SOMA neighborhood as a calm oasis.

NEARBY SITES OF INTEREST

Bayanihan Community Center
1010 Mission Street, San Francisco 94103
The Bayanihan Community Center, home of the Filipino-American Development Foundation, serves as an anchor for community work in SOMA, including cultural events and projects like the Filipino Mental Health Initiative.

The Martin Luther King Jr. Memorial
750 Howard Street. San Francisco 94103
(in Yerba Buena Gardens Complex)

TO LEARN MORE

Hartman, Chester. *City For Sale: The Transformation of San Francisco*. Berkeley: University of California Press, 2002.

Macabasco, Lisa Wong. "Filipino Americans Make a New Name for Their San Francisco Neighborhood." Center for Asian American Media, May 2016.

San Francisco Planning Department. "Recognizing, Protecting and Memorializing South of Market Filipino Social Heritage Neighborhood Resources," July 13, 2011.

3.28 South Park

1 South Park Street, San Francisco 94107
(between 2nd and 3rd Streets and between Brannan and Bryant)

The historic trajectory of South Park offers a useful barometer for broader urban change in the city—from its elite nineteenth-century residential origins to decades serving local industry and its most recent iteration as a home to the tech sector. Conceived in 1852 by English entrepreneur George Gordon as a four-section fireproof cluster of town houses with a view of the bay encircling an oval park, South Park's original residents represented the city's white elite. Several early San Francisco mayors were based here; in the 1860s the "South Park accent" was heard widely at City Hall. But only a fourth of the planned area, or a half block, was complete before an economic downturn caused the project to fail in 1855. As the broader neighborhood became more of an industrial center in the late 1800s, the char-

The SF Recreation and Parks Department completed a major renovation of South Park, San Francisco's oldest official city park, in 2017.

acter of the park changed, with workers of all ethnicities, including many Japanese men, moving in to be close to their jobs.

The entire built area of the original development was destroyed in the 1906 earthquake and fire. The once-exclusive park became a site of earthquake refugee cottages; these were the only two-story emergency cottages to be built following that disaster. Working populations began to solidly settle this area as it was rebuilt in the early twentieth century, with a Filipino presence as early as the 1920s, joined by African Americans during WWII. The Gran Oriente Filipino Hotel (106 South Park Street) represents a collaboration that evaded racist real estate markets. The hotel was established in the 1920s, at a time when Filipinos were restricted by law from purchasing real estate. Forty Filipino seamen pooled their money and created several fraternal orders under the aegis of the Masons—who were not prohibited from the market—to purchase this hotel and a nearby property across the park. The hotel contin-

ued to provide stable housing for elderly Filipinos and was restored by an affordable housing developer in 2018 so that it will continue to provide affordable housing.

The character of the neighborhood changed again in the 1990s. *Wired* magazine made its home on the park, using this space as its perch from which to tell the new metanarrative of the tech world. The area became a magnet for the nascent Internet start-up culture and was known through the 1990s as the heart of "Multimedia Gulch." After a lull during the recession of the late 2000s, South Park was once again ringed with tech firms, which spread throughout SOMA much more broadly beginning around 2004. South Park's oval public green was relandscaped in the 2010s and is a lovely place to visit. Although quite a few parkside buildings have been renovated, the historical character of the buildings around the park stands out dramatically from the warehouses and high-rises of the neighborhood. (LisaRuth Elliott)

TO LEARN MORE

Northern California Coalition on Immigrant Rights. No date. "South Park Filipinos," Foundsf.org. http://www.foundsf.org/index.php?title=SOUTH_PARK_FILIPINOS

Shumate, Albert. *Rincon Hill and South Park: San Francisco's Fashionable Neighborhood*. San Francisco: Windgate Press, 1988.

The warehouse on the left is one of the few structures on the historic site of The Farm; the Potrero del Sol community garden is in the foreground.

3.29 The Farm

1499 Potrero Avenue, San Francisco 94110 (historic site)

Remembered as a performance venue, a youth-centered agricultural project, and an experiment in urban utopia, the Farm was an institution that bridged several worlds. Founded as a combination art space and agricultural project in 1974 by artists Jack Wickert and Bonnie Sherk on the ruins of a dairy farm, in the shadow of the 101 freeway overpass, the Farm linked the vibe of 1960s counterculture and the youth rebellions of the 1970s to the early 1980s punk rock scene and the DIY Mission District. People stopped by to visit cows, goats, ducks, chickens, and other livestock and to work or play in the gardens. Kids created performances with staff, watched SF Mime Troupe or Make-a-

La Familia mural, in Potrero del Sol park, former site of the Farm.

Circus rehearsals, while adults built model urban-agricultural spaces, curated art shows, and put on their own musical and theatrical performances.

Many accounts remember the Farm with nostalgia as a utopian project, with few rules and a sense that anything was possible, but the space was not immune from the woes that plague many such communities. Organizers dealt with everything from aggressive livestock to internal political disagreements and the ongoing struggle to keep the project funded. It was this last issue that led Andy Pollack, the director in 1983, to begin booking punk rock shows at the Farm. In what was effectively a barn that legally held 299 people, four times that number regularly crammed in for long shows that showcased dozens of bands. Profits went to keeping the space open for youth and agricultural programming.

Between 1983 and 1987, the Farm hosted hundreds of shows with some of the most influential punk bands of the era as well as hundreds of less famous groups that emerged from the liberatory DIY orientation of punk. Echoes of the radical politics of Bay Area '60s activism came through in performances of pioneering feminist punk groups like Frightwig and far-Left groups like the Dead Kennedys and MDC. The overlapping politics of the Farm are exemplified in a 1987 double fundraiser to support a nascent food policy organization and to help cover medical bills for Brian Willson. Willson, a Veterans for Peace activist, had been hit by a train near the Concord Naval Station in the North Bay; he and other

The all-women, feminist punk band Frightwig headlines this 1987 "Day at the Farm" show, with twelve bands for $8.

activists sought to block the train from carrying weapons bound for right-wing Central America paramilitaries. Ultimately, after legal disputes over rent payments, the property owners evicted the Farm, and the space cleared out. Today the site is home to an alternative school and for-profit creative spaces. The freeway still looms above.

NEARBY SITE OF INTEREST

Potrero del Sol Park
Potrero Avenue and Cesar Chavez,
San Francisco 94110
A section of this well-used park, skate park (the city's largest), and community garden once served as garden space for the Farm.

TO LEARN MORE

Boulware, Jack, and Silke Tudor. *Gimme Something Better: The Profound, Progressive, and Occasionally*

Pointless History of Bay Area Punk from Dead Kennedys to Green Day. New York: Penguin Books, 2009.

Katz, Kathy, and Mike Kavanaugh, directors. *The Farm.* San Francisco: GitSpin Productions, 1990. (Documentary film)

3.30 Trans March

March begins around Dolores Street at 19th Street, San Francisco 94114

LGBTQ people in the Bay Area continue to push the national conversation on rights and on the meaning of gender, sexuality, and naming. The Trans March—which begins here at Dolores Park annually on the last Friday in June—is one of the ways people have built power and acceptance, through naming, seeing, and being seen. San Francisco's annual LGBTQ Pride weekend began as a rebel event in 1970, marking the anniversary of the Stonewall uprising in New York City, in which trans people resisted the police raid of a gay bar in an act of defiance that escalated into what has been characterized as a series of riots. It was a time in which nonconformity with mainstream gender and sexual norms was still criminalized. Stonewall and the new scale of resistance it represented are credited with inspiring the expansion of the gay rights movement nationally. Engaging in a physical fight with armed police may have been rare, but it was not new to queer San Franciscans at that time; three years prior to Stonewall, trans people here had also rebelled against an all-too-typical police raid at Gene Compton's Cafeteria, then at 101 Turk in the Tenderloin.

Fast forward a few years and San Francisco Pride began formally as the Gay Freedom Parade, with a strong call for basic rights, and an end to antigay violence. Commemorating the fighting impulse of Stonewall, each year the event highlighted the

The annual Trans March (Friday of Pride weekend), 2018.

issues of the day, including the fight against the Briggs Initiative (Proposition 6) in 1978, which sought to criminalize gay school teachers. The parade evolved over the years to be both more inclusive and, to some observers, less rebellious. One part of the challenge was its success: Pride became massive, attracting thousands and then hundreds of thousands, becoming the event at which local politicians could not afford not to be seen, riding on floats with feather boas. Over time, in the activist tradition of the original call to march, queer women created their own event in 1993. The Dyke March struck an independent political note, typically led by the motorcycle-riding Dykes on Bikes.

In 2004 something shifted again. While the larger Pride event itself was titled inclusively (the full name, as of 1995, was the San Francisco Lesbian Gay Bisexual Transgender Pride Celebration), transgender people began to look for their own space. They had been working for recognition and rights for years, and were increasingly politically active. Already they recognized victims of violence through the Transgender Day of Remembrance; by 2004 they wanted to find a way to also celebrate trans life without solely focusing on violence. Even so, as organizers tell it, the first Trans March almost didn't happen. It started with an anonymously authored announcement circulated by e-mail that called for a transgender-oriented march. Concerned that a leaderless march might leave attendees vulnerable to antitrans violence, Cecilia Chung and others decided to organize their own march at the same time and place, to try to create a safe

> PERSONAL REFLECTION BY CECILIA CHUNG, SENIOR DIRECTOR OF STRATEGIC INITIATIVES AND EVALUATIONS, TRANSGENDER LAW CENTER, AND COFOUNDER OF THE TRANS MARCH
>
> Up until that point we really didn't have a space that we could claim. We said, "Why do we have to wait until somebody dies before we show up?" We were thinking about celebrating, creating a new space. It was both inspirational and overwhelming to be physically there in that first year, and seeing the enormity of the crowd. What we realized was the importance that we see one another, connect to one another, and love one another. Now Trans March has become its own animal. Even if we didn't step up to organize, it would still happen. People know that on Friday of Pride weekend, they will find our community there. When we come together, it's because we see the value of connecting trans people who would otherwise be isolated, and demonstrating our power as one community.

event. Chung raised money for permits and portable toilets, which ultimately served a crowd of about five thousand. The next year New Yorkers replicated the march, and the twin events drew international media attention. By the time of its fifteenth anniversary in 2018, the event brought marchers on a route that extended from the park, through the Civic Center, to the site of Compton's Cafeteria.

The impact of one event is hard to quantify. Trans people still face discrimination and violence. At the same time, acceptance has grown, from political participation to Hollywood representation. In San Francisco,

Compton's Cafeteria has been proposed for historical landmark status, and the neighborhood around it has been transformed into the formally recognized and city-funded Compton's Transgender Cultural District, the first of its kind. These days the Trans March is filled with young hopeful faces: It is a political event, a social gathering, and an urban happening.

TO LEARN MORE

Screaming Queens: The Riot at Compton's Cafeteria. Directed by Victor Silverman and Susan Stryker, 2005. (Documentary film)

Stryker, Susan. *Transgender History.* Berkeley, CA: Seal Press, 2008.

3.31 "Twitter Tax Break" Zone

Twitter Headquarters, 1355 Market Street, San Francisco 94103

This part of Market Street is a case study in the pitfalls of "growth machine" urban boosterism, particularly since city leaders embraced a tax incentive in 2011 to lure tech firms. Targeting this slice of mid-Market and an even larger part of the nearby Tenderloin (on the northwest side of Market), former Mayor Ed Lee joined venture capitalist Ron Conway in promoting the sweetheart deal as a partnership that would yield long-term benefits for the city at large. In the years that followed, Twitter's gleaming headquarters became a beacon to the industry—even as Twitter continued to hemorrhage money in the boom-and-bust tech economy (founded in 2006, the company did not record a profit until 2018). Soon the so-called Twitter Tax Zone lured other flagship tech companies—

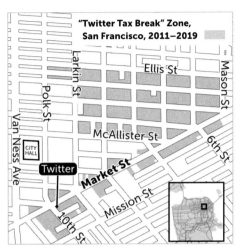

"Twitter Tax Break" Zone, 2011–2019. This rendering of the government-defined zone, which may bring to mind gerrymandered voting districts, reveals the effort to which the city went to lure tech firms to specific blocks in the Tenderloin and Civic Center.

Uber, Square, Zendesk, and many others—as well as new bars and restaurants catering to their highly paid workers.

But the development here was uneven. The new economic activity certainly transformed an area that had once been cruelly described by the *San Francisco Chronicle* as the "mess on Market," turning a corridor with long-standing vacancies into a jam-packed zone of opportunity for those with the wealth to take advantage of it. In fact, just about every corner of the tax-break zone covered city blocks where working-class and houseless people lived. But the people that the city hoped tech would sweep away remained, and the area morphed into a disturbing concentration of the city's growing extreme inequality, with high-end eateries amid growing homelessness and hunger. At first the tax deal was not a huge loss to the city treasury, when balanced against other economic trends. But seven years later, the city's own analysis showed that companies in the zone withheld $34 million from city coffers in just one year of the tax exemption.

Meanwhile, as his employees built his tweeting empire, Twitter CEO Jack Dorsey asserted himself as a political player in San Francisco. In 2018 he loudly fought a proposal to tax the richest corporations in the city to pay for housing and support services for homeless people (some of those same people sleeping on his company's doorsteps). He lost that fight when the measure passed, in part because activists convinced Salesforce CEO Marc Benioff that the new tax was fair, and Benioff threw millions into the campaign. Benioff's support for the tax was notable; he is one of a surprisingly small group of tech magnates who have channeled wealth into philanthropic causes. You can find a cluster of futuristic towers, including the city's Transbay public bus terminal, with the Salesforce name in SOMA. But even these generous gestures have not undone the tidal wave of wealth (generated in part by the tax break) that has hardened the city's now famous wealth inequality.

NEARBY SITES OF INTEREST

Before it was known as a tax-break zone, the **Tenderloin** was home to a diverse community of immigrants, seniors, and families. There are many great organizations throughout the area that you may want to support. While you're there, consider a visit to the **Tenderloin National Forest** (Cohen Place, San Francisco 94109), a former public alley turned into a neighborhood park with redwood trees and eco-

nomically accessible programming. Nearby, the **Windows into the Tenderloin** mural (86 Golden Gate Avenue, San Francisco 94012) offers a great example of community-oriented public art, with a utopic future that includes the faces of people who actually live here. (Nearby site research by LisaRuth Elliott.)

3.32 Westbrook Court and Hunter's Point Hill Street Names

Westbrook Court at Hudson Avenue,
San Francisco 94124

Here on Hunter's Point Hill, on streets that many San Franciscans have never traversed, the names of women who transformed the neighborhood glint in the sun. The street names represent neighborhood self-determination—or at least the potential for it. Urban memory is marked and kept alive by naming. When names aren't focused on what geographer Paul Groth calls "useful trees" (like Oak, Pine, Lombard, Ash), evocative place names (Yosemite, Sonoma, Nevada), or numbers, street names record the values of a community at the time of naming. They are our everyday monuments to power and history. As in most US cities, many San Francisco streets inscribe a good deal of local history into residents' everyday language, commemorating early Spanish explorers, nineteenth-century mayors, city surveyors, and gold rush heroes. The vast majority are male, typically representing top-down power through race or class position.

These Hunter's Point streets were named in the early 1970s as this hill was transformed through a massive redevelopment effort that installed hundreds of affordable

Westbrook Court is one of several streets nearby named after community activists. From here, you can see the downtown skyline from the southeast.

housing units on curvilinear cul-de-sacs. The housing resulted from a multiyear campaign to redirect city redevelopment after a similar effort produced widespread demolition and displacement in the Fillmore District (see Buchanan Mall, p. 135). Hunter's Point activists, led by a group of women known as The Big Five, advocated for community-driven change, lobbying a Nixon-era Congress to fully fund neighborhood development plans. But the development funds focused almost entirely on housing, leaving out the other institutions needed for jobs and community development. Hunter's Point thus followed a path of economic decline, even with the new hilltop housing. This became particularly poignant as the nearby naval shipyard shuttered (see Hunter's Point Shipyard, p. 152).

The streets that recall the era of The Big Five include Westbrook Court, named for Elouise Westbrook, who was the lead matriarch of the movement and who is also recognized in other parts of the city for her

work on affordable health care (including a South of Market health clinic). Ethel Garlington, Julia Commer, Marcelee Cashmere, Oceola Washington, Bertha Freeman, and others are represented in these streets; they worked on the redevelopment effort and also fostered a culture of activism in the community, which continues today, often with African American women providing the leadership. Espanola Jackson, who spoke of herself as a daughter of The Big Five, described being a young mother who, under Westbrook's tutelage, sharpened her analysis of government assistance and the complexities of the welfare state. She later also worked on housing and environmental justice struggles; her street is around the corner from Westbrook Court. Other streets on the hill recognize national figures involved in civil rights, like Whitney Young, who ran the national Urban League, and the writer and social critic James Baldwin.

TO LEARN MORE

Brahinsky, Rachel. "The Making and Unmaking of Southeast San Francisco." PhD diss., University of California, Berkeley, 2012.

Brahinsky, Rachel. "'Tell Him I'm Gone:' On the Margins in High Tech City." In *A Political Companion to James Baldwin*, edited by Susan Jane McWilliams. Lexington: University Press of Kentucky, 2018.

3.33 Women's Building

3543 18th Street, San Francisco 94110

The Women's Building (TWB) occupies an intersection of multiple political and social movements; it is a place where struggles for women's rights are linked to other struggles, including those of marginalized racial/ethnic communities, LGBTQ people, and immigrants. It's difficult to miss: Originally constructed in 1910 as a hall for San Francisco's German American community, the building's main facades are enveloped by a mural titled *Maestrapeace*—a play on the word "masterpiece" (*maestra* is the Spanish term for a woman teacher or master). Created by a collective of seven artists (Juana Alicia, Miranda Bergman, Edythe Boone, Susan Kelk Cervantes, Meera Desai, Yvonne Littleton, and Irene Perez), the mural reflects a feminist vision that is transnational and trans-historical, depicting real and mythical women around the world and across time.

Opened in 1979, the Women's Building describes itself as "the first women-owned and women-operated community center in the U.S." Having scrambled to find a location for a conference on violence against women, the San Francisco Women's Centers realized they needed to control their own space, but purchasing the large building presented a significant challenge. Prior to the 1974 passage of the Equal Credit Opportunity Act, women needed a man to cosign any credit applications, regardless of their own income, and discrimination against women in bank lending was standard practice until 1988. Yet TWB founders forged ahead with broad community fund-raising support and purchased the building, which was then the mostly dormant home to the Sons and Daughters of Norway.

The Women's Building is a powerful example of the places created by second-wave feminists of the 1960s and '70s to establish women's rights and to envision a more equitable society. Women's centers, which appeared in various forms and occupied a variety of building types across the US at that time, were especially important manifestations of this grassroots movement for gender equality and social transformation. San Francisco's is one of a very few that have lasted into the twenty-first century, in large part because TWB bought the building.

The building is also significant for its reflection of the evolution of feminism toward a linked understanding of identities and oppression. Popular narratives of the women's movement put white, privileged women at the center of the story. Yet TWB was birthed at a time and place in which many women were imperfectly but seriously grappling with what a feminism centered outside of heterosexual, white, middle-class experiences would look like. You can read

As part of the early wave of women-centered feminist institutions, the Women's Building has become an anchoring neighborhood place, serving people of all genders and backgrounds.

this in the building's exterior, from the bilingual sign over the entry to the enormous portrait of Guatemalan activist Rigoberta Menchú on the Lapidge Street side of the mural. Today the Women's Building still offers community support such as a food pantry, legal and immigrant rights clinics, and a computer lab; it houses nonprofit groups at below-market rents, and makes spaces available for a multitude of community events. (Donna Graves)

TO LEARN MORE

Alicia, Juana, Miranda Bergman, Edythe Boone, Susan Kelk Cervantes, Meera Desai, Yvonne Littleton, and Irene Pérez. *Maestrapeace: San Francisco's Monumental Feminist Mural*. Berkeley, CA: Heyday Books, 2019.

4

The North Bay and Islands

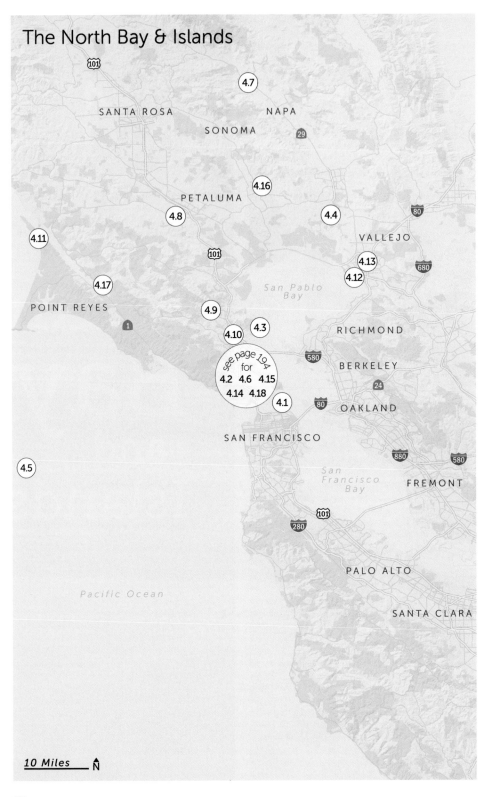

The North Bay & Islands

4.7

SANTA ROSA

NAPA

SONOMA

29

4.16

PETALUMA

4.8

4.11

101

VALLEJO

4.13

4.12

San Pablo
Bay

4.17

80

680

POINT REYES

1

4.9

4.10 4.3

RICHMOND

580

BERKELEY

24

see page 194
for
4.2 4.6 4.15
4.14 4.18

4.1

80

OAKLAND

SAN FRANCISCO

880

580

4.5

San
Francisco
Bay

FREMONT

101

280

PALO ALTO

Pacific Ocean

SANTA CLARA

10 Miles   N

Introduction

Winery-filled valleys. Towering coastal redwoods. Steep cliffs plunging to a wild ocean. The Golden Gate Bridge emerging from the fog. These North Bay geographies define much of the popular imagination of Northern California. These iconic images, however, reveal only part of the North Bay story, and in their beauty they often obscure the contradictions that abound in this dreamy landscape. The famed wineries of Napa and Sonoma, for example, are hardly idyllic, old-world family affairs, but are often designed by wealthy landholders and corporations to evoke a pastiche of Tuscany, Southern France, and colonial California. The faux chateaus keep visitors' eyes away from the working landscapes where thousands of mostly migrant workers spend lifetimes skillfully pruning, tending, and harvesting the vineyards, all for wages far below what the price of a nice California chardonnay would suggest.

Similarly, the towering redwoods of places like Muir Woods are a stunning treasure and well worth the visit. But the fact that this redwood preserve is so small is a tragic legacy of the wholesale destruction of a coastal ecosystem that once had tens of thousands of such trees, felled for use in urban development and mountain mining operations. Similarly, the iconic Golden Gate Bridge gleams a sense of connection across the water, yet the bridge also represents an important invisible barrier. As you'll read in this chapter, the agency that operates the bridge fought to stop the Bay Area Rapid Transit system from linking San Francisco to Marin. This decision has kept thousands of people from affordable, clean public transit, which would give them access to jobs and opportunities, and which would also reduce the carbon footprint of residents and tourists alike.

In this chapter we travel through the North Bay and largely through narratives like this, where we take you to the difficult histories of people and places, and we ask you not to look away. The region is afflicted

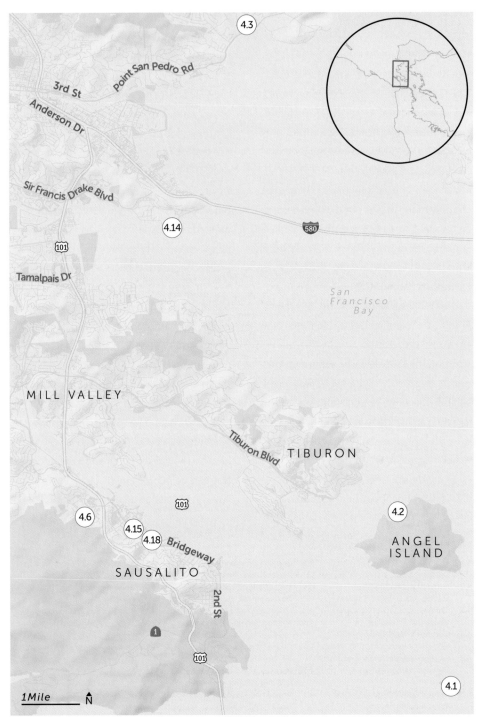

DETAIL FROM PAGE 192

with the toxicity of widespread pesticide use in the wineries and orchards, waste from decommissioned military and industrial spaces, and a marine ecosystem still impacted by legacies of upstream mining. The North Bay struggles against a legacy of labor exploitation that persists today, and that is bound tightly to the affordable-housing dearth that forces workers to commute long hours for low-wage jobs. California's racism and its impacts linger here, alongside the long legacies of conquest and colonial domination. Much of this is intentionally hidden from the casual observer.

In some ways, the North Bay occupies an especially muddled place in the geography of the San Francisco Bay Area. These towns and cities and the agrarian and rural spaces can feel disconnected both from each other and the rest of the Bay Area. Often they are separated, sometimes strategically, by topography. But as the sites in this chapter reveal, the pastoral landscapes and sweeping vistas obscure long-connected histories of struggle over land, labor, and the environment that intricately tie together the places of the North Bay, and the islands we've included here as well, to each other and the whole Bay Area.

Lately the future of the North Bay has felt even less certain, as the wildfires that have long plagued Californians began making unprecedented incursions into urban areas in 2017. In a matter of days, the Tubbs, Nuns, Atlas, and Cherokee fires consumed whole communities, gutting wineries, multi-million-dollar homes, working-class suburbs, and businesses alike. Santa Rosa lost entire

PERSONAL REFLECTION FROM ELLEN GREEN, FAMILY PHYSICIAN AT SANTA ROSA COMMUNITY HEALTH

I could hear something that sounded like bombs. It was people's propane tanks exploding. Part of the issue at the time was there wasn't a good system for alerting the public to the status of the Tubbs Fire. We evacuated with our two small children because we didn't know where the fire was going. I could see that my clinic was in the fire zone on the map; the roof had caught fire and the sprinklers went off, which is what really caused all the damage. We lost the flagship building, which was our space for primary care and specialists. After the fire, we were effectively doing walk-in appointments wherever we could, like priority visits for pregnant mothers and urgent care for people with respiratory issues from the smoke. Our community has not recovered. The clinic will reopen, but we are struggling since so many patients moved away. People lost their homes. Businesses closed, and people lost jobs. We already had a housing crisis before the fire, and now it is prohibitively expensive to live in Santa Rosa. I have many patients that have become homeless, or are on the verge of it, not because their house burned down, but because the fire made it impossible to afford life here.

neighborhoods; forty-four people perished. People as far away as Oakland suffered asthma attacks as air quality plummeted while the scorched foundations of suburban houses smoldered. One year later, more tragedies would unfold as California fire season peaked again with the destruction of the entire northern California town of Paradise, which is northwest, at the foot of the Sierra Nevada mountains (beyond the scope of the North Bay, but within air-quality distance). By 2019, the cycle of terrifying fires, evacuations, and destruction plaguing the North Bay appeared increasingly as the new normal.

Each year, the fires reveal a great deal about overlapping connections between the rural/suburban North Bay and the rest of the Bay Area and even the state itself. Centrally, even with their reputation as some of the most consciously "green" places in the nation, North Bay counties are in no way immune to the intense effects of anthropogenic climate change—that is, climate change caused by humans. The sprawling built environment that North Bay residents have created, and their collective "management" of nature, have created an immensely dangerous landscape. This context seems to make the work of documenting what is here and what has been here before even more important.

■ ■ ■

4.1 Alcatraz Island

Alcatraz Island, San Francisco, CA 94133

Beyond the kitschy "I Escaped Alcatraz" T-shirts for sale at every tourist shop in San Francisco lies the story of the immensely brutal beginnings of federal maximum-security prisons, and, not unrelated, of the center of a powerful moment in the American Indian struggle for self-determination. If you visit, you'll be regaled with stories of how the federal government locked men in cages, with notoriously poor living conditions and strict control by violent guards.

You'll be asked to find a thrill in imagining yourself locked up with "America's worst criminals." You'll join the company of about 1.4 million people that annually visit the island, now under the control of the National Park Service. Indeed, alongside trolley cars and the Golden Gate Bridge, the prison-island is among the best-known icons of the San Francisco Bay.

Throughout its modern history, Alcatraz has been a site of interwoven moments of tragedy and revolutionary resistance by Indigenous people. The first two American Indian prisoners known to be incarcerated there were part of a group of Modoc leaders captured by the US Army near the modern California-Oregon border. In the 1890s, Alcatraz caged a group of Hopi men who had refused to send their children to federal schools (where their language and culture would be ripped from them) and refused to abandon their own collective agricultural practices for US-style private property. The traces of these histories took on a different valence in the 1940s when the federal government implemented an official set of policies of terminating recognition of Native communities and demanding complete subsumption into US society.

In 1964, when the future of the island as federal property was uncertain, Sioux activists occupied Alcatraz for four hours to demand that it be turned into a Native university and cultural center. Five years later, a group using the moniker Indians of All Tribes, organized by Richard Oakes (Mohawk), returned to the island for one day to declare a similar set of demands.

Alcatraz Island, Alcatraz National Park, photographed from the Larkspur ferry, 2019.

Reinforced by nearly a hundred other activists, including many college students from UCLA's American Indian Studies Center, they returned again later that month to launch an occupation that would last nearly eighteen months, from November 20, 1969, to June 10, 1971. For over a year, the occupiers ran a consensus-based community on the island with widespread local and national support. When federal agents swarmed the island to forcibly remove the last fifteen people, the symbolic work of the occupation had already been immense. It made the continued existence of Indigenous communities as an autonomous group demanding self-determination visible to mainstream US society, while galvanizing the "Red Power" movement in connection with the emergent Black and Brown Power and Third World Left movements.

The National Park Service, to its credit, has preserved and promotes the history of the occupation as part of the island's history in both interpretive material at the park and on its accompanying website—though in uneven and frequently problematic ways. Native activists and supporters continue to gather at Alcatraz on Thanksgiving and Indigenous Peoples' Day (still "Columbus Day" in many places) for sunrise ceremonies. They insist that stories of Native American resistance are not just historical traces to note in a museum. These are significant moments in five centuries of defiance against settler-colonial genocide, and they continue. The island is accessible via ferry from San Francisco, located at Piers 31–33, Embarcadero and Bay Street, San Francisco.

TO LEARN MORE

Johnson, Troy R. *The American Indian Occupation of Alcatraz Island: Red Power and Self-Determination.* Lincoln: University of Nebraska Press, 2008.

Smith, Paul Chaat, and Robert Allen Warrior. *Like a Hurricane: The Indian Movement from Alcatraz to Wounded Knee.* New York: The New Press, 1996.

The National Park Service website for Alcatraz contains several essays on the Hopi men imprisoned at Alcatraz, written by Wendy Holliday, historian at the Hopi Cultural Preservation Office, https://www.nps.gov/alca/learn/historyculture/hopi-prisoners-on-the-rock.htm

4.2 Angel Island Immigration Station

Angel Island, Tiburon

The anti-immigration tactics of the early twenty-first century are rooted in the exclusionary enforcement that took place here at Angel Island from 1910 to 1940. Chinese immigrants may have borne the worst of it, though they were not alone in experiencing harsh tactics at the island station, where migrants faced extended detention and deportation. Despite this, the immigration station here also represents a primary port of entry for Chinese Americans, who have played a major role in shaping the Bay Area since the beginning of the gold rush. Today Angel Island is protected as a state park. Most of the island is open space, with hiking, overnight camping, and stunning views in all directions. But there's a tension in the beauty here. Like many secluded places of beauty in California, this place has a history of violence that goes back to the Spanish expulsion of the Hookooeko, a tribe of the coastal Miwok peoples who used this island seasonally for at least a thousand years. Following its restoration as a museum in the 1970s, the immigration station still stands on the northeast corner, a testament to this long legacy of ethnoracial tension. If you visit, you can see poems etched on the walls by detained immigrants, aching to escape.

Built to enforce the rules stemming from the federal 1882 Chinese Exclusion Act, which sharply restricted Chinese immigration, the Angel Island station was completed in 1910. Prior to the completion of the station, would-be immigrants were held in squalid, inhumane conditions on San Francisco's Pier 40 while awaiting permission to enter the country. The new island station isolated would-be immigrants from local support (for example, relatives already living in Chinatown), and new arrivals faced intense scrutiny. Some made it through in a few days; others were held for months before deportation. Officials based their decisions on a set of evolving criteria that assessed whether newcomers had family in the US, whether they were healthy, and whether they appeared to be fit for labor (which was presumed to be their sole potential contribution). Chinese and others, particularly South Asians, were subject to invasive physical examinations and detailed interrogations, all based in racist ideas about their humanity, including the backward notion that they were particularly likely to bring and breed disease.

The island is often described as the Ellis Island of the West, and over time it was indeed a portal to the country for about half a million immigrants and refugees from eighty countries. But scholars note that while Ellis Island served mostly to process and naturalize, Angel Island served more often to exclude, including through deportation hearings against immigrants already living in California. The island station closed in 1940 after a fire and was turned over to the

(Above) The Immigration Station was built on Angel Island to isolate newcomers from the city, which also meant isolation from friends, family, employers, and legal counsel.

(Left) A crowd of people on a dock at Angel Island, 1920. (Photographer unknown)

US military, which used it to detain Japanese and other foreign nationals during WWII, further embedding the use of this place as a site of fear and xenophobia. In the 1960s, the state began converting much of the island into a park, and in the 1970s a park ranger alerted researchers to the poetry-etched walls that remained in the deteriorating abandoned buildings. That discovery eventually led to the establishment of the existing museum and ongoing research on the lives of the people who passed through Angel Island. Ferries run from San Francisco and Tiburon.

TO LEARN MORE

Lai, H. Mark, Genny Lim, and Judy Yung. *Island: Poetry and History of Chinese Immigrants on Angel Island, 1910–1940*. Second edition. Seattle: University of Washington Press, 2014.

Lee, Erika, and Judy Yung. *Angel Island: Immigrant Gateway to America*. Oxford: Oxford University Press, 2010.

China Camp State Park, 2018.

4.3 China Camp

100 China Camp Village Road, San Rafael
94901

Once a place of work and refuge for Chinese immigrants and their descendants, China Camp offers rare physical evidence of the maritime history of Chinese Americans. It also reflects an all-too-common history in which California's Chinese-descendant communities were forced to fight for survival. Amid the old wooden buildings, shrimp boiling equipment, and pier at the heart of the China Camp State Park, a plaque commemorates Frank Quan, whose ancestors started the village. Until Quan died in August 2016, just a few days before his ninety-first birthday, he was the last direct link to the nineteenth-century shrimping businesses that once anchored here. It's fitting that his name is remembered here, but the plaque is a telling monument to the ways that China Camp's history has been oversimplified in public memory, and how the racial and economic violence of Marin County is written out of that story.

At the end of the nineteenth century, many of the Chinese-born immigrants who had been recruited to the United States to work in mining and railroad construction began moving into Western cities to find new work. The backlash from white workers and political leaders was brutal; many neighborhoods were burned (see Heinleinville, p. 92), and people were terrorized into leaving. In the Bay Area, one site of refuge was this self-built village on the coast of the San Pablo Bay. The village expanded to include infrastructure for harvesting and processing the two

View of the bay through the shed, China Camp, 2018.

This boat named for Frank Quan's mother, Grace, is a reconstruction of the boats historically used here by shrimpers. China Camp, 2018.

species of shrimp still living in the San Pablo and San Francisco Bays at that time. At its height in the 1920s, China Camp was home to approximately five hundred people.

By the early twentieth century, there were at least twenty-six such camps, including one at Hunter's Point in San Francisco. These were home to complex systems of shrimping that produced hundreds of tons of shrimp—both fresh and dried—for local and global networks. Without modern tools to keep seafood fresh, shrimpers boiled most of their catches in huge vats as soon as they were brought in. Large fresh shrimp were sold to San Francisco restaurants. The majority were dried, bagged, and shipped in a labor-intensive process that drew on commercial-family networks headquartered mostly in San Francisco. The shrimpers sold the leftovers locally for fertilizer and chicken feed. But the success of the business drew white shrimpers' jealous ire. The Chinese shrimpers employed particularly effective nets, and white officials used this fact as a pretense to attack the industry. From initiating seasonal harvesting limits to shutting down exports and eventually banning the nets themselves, the California state legislature actively drove the Chinese shrimpers out of the industry. It was true that the shrimpers were harvesting an estimated five million pounds of shrimp and bycatch from the bay ecosystem annually, with untold consequences. But the disingenuous and racist concerns of the legislature were revealed

PERSONAL REFLECTION FROM RENE YUNG, ARTISTIC AND FOUNDING DIRECTOR, CHINESE WHISPERS

You hear about the railroad, you hear about the mines, you hear about laundry and restaurants, but somehow Chinese maritime history has been a hidden story, and there is a strong relationship between the loss of this history and the loss of the landscapes where these events happened. There were other Chinese camps in the Point San Pedro area, and they were all burned down by arson. Hunter's Point had a very large fishing village; it was eliminated through what I call official arson, when the San Francisco Health Department burned it down in 1939. I love China Camp, and I'm so glad it survived. But it can be tempting to romanticize its weathered buildings and picturesque beach. Meanwhile, I think the complete absence of any relics, artifacts, or even recognition of all of these other sites is even more powerful. How does one memorialize elimination or disappearance? . . . There's also the ecological piece, when you think back to the abundance of wildlife on the bay back then, compared to the daunting information about species disappearing today. The timeworn planks and the fragile pier that Frank Quan so loved and took care of are in a way a visual reminder of the entire ecosystem change.

after 1915—when new nets were approved for use and better records kept—and the actual number of shrimp harvested continued to increase well into the 1940s.

In the 1950s massive state projects to redirect fresh water from the Sacramento River Delta into agriculture and drinking water for the Bay Area altered the salinity of the bay, and the shrimp population shrank too much to support commercial operations. Quan, for example, mostly gathered a small amount of shrimp to sell as bait to fishermen at his China Camp shop. Suburban developers consumed a good portion of the surrounding hillsides, but their expansion stalled when the city of San Rafael raised objections about plans to add thirty thousand new units without any waste treatment facilities. In the 1970s, new plans for development of China Camp, and the last undeveloped stretch of land that ran from the water to mountains, sparked one of several environmentalist campaigns to preserve open space across the bay.

RELATED SITE OF INTEREST

McNear Brick and Block
1 McNear Brickyard Road, San Rafael 94901
McNears Beach Pier
201 Cantera Way, San Rafael 94901
The McNear family bought twenty-five hundred acres of Point San Pedro in 1868 to operate this brick factory and run a large dairy operation. They employed the Chinese migrants who built the China Camp shrimping village on the McNears' land. The factory delivered millions of bricks via shallow boats throughout the Bay Area. The brick plant still operates, but most of the land was sold off for development;

both McNears Beach and China Camp are now public parks.

TO LEARN MORE

Chinese Whispers Project, http://chinese-whispers.org

4.4 Cuttings Wharf Housing

100 Block of Cuttings Wharf Road (at Moore's Landing), Napa 94559 (historic site)

In many ways, the beauty of the North Bay landscape is the product of the historical dispossession of poor and working-class people. The housing that once stood here is a case in point. Today Moore's Landing is a bucolic spot from which to launch a kayak into the bay's "Water Trail," a growing series of stops along the Bay Area's water systems meant to expand the region's open-space trails into the water for nonmotorized recreation. It is also an important location from which to see how the "natural" landscapes of the bay are produced for leisure through the erasure of many different kinds of work and people.

At the end of the WWII economic boom, twenty-four surplus military buildings were floated up the Napa River and placed along Cuttings Wharf Road, just past Moore's landing. Over the next sixty years, as Napa filled with wine-fueled wealth, the Cuttings Wharf cottages represented some of the only affordable housing for low-income families in Napa County. The owner neglected the place, as often happens with

The historic housing (now demolished) near Cuttings Wharf in 2014. (Photographer unknown)

With the housing gone, a visit to Cuttings Wharf is purely recreational.

institutionalized low-income housing, and by the early 2000s county officials declared the buildings in serious violation of health and safety codes. The landlord, faced with a choice of bringing the buildings up to code or evicting families and demolishing the homes, went for the latter. The county tried to put the homes into third-party receivership—which would have created a fund for repairing the homes—but a judge ruled that the landlord had the legal right to simply demolish the noncompliant structures. The landlord declined to cover relocation fees for tenants, who found themselves adrift in the unaffordable 2012 housing market, which forced many to choose between extra-high rents or extra-long commutes to their Napa County jobs. In the wake of the demolition, visitors to Moore's Landing embarking on a water-trail excursion will not have their views of natural landscape interrupted by dilapidated housing.

TO LEARN MORE

See the *Napa Valley Register* newspaper's extensive coverage of the fight and demolitions from 2010 to 2012.

4.5 Farallon Islands

Farallon Islands National Wildlife Refuge, San Francisco

The dual life of the Farallon Islands offers a stark reminder of the Bay Area's hydra-headed role in both militarism and environmentalism. Home to at least 44,750 barrels of radioactive waste below the surface, the islands also offer a rare, protected home for seabirds above. Some thirty miles west of

the Golden Gate Bridge, the Farallons are visible from both San Francisco and Point Reyes on a clear day, and some whale watching tours will take you near the uninhabited islands. In the nineteenth century, Russian trappers and US colonists exploited the island's wildlife as a major source of fur and eggs. Today the island wildlife refuge is protected by the US Fish and Wildlife Service. Visitors are not allowed on, or even very close to, the steep Farallon cliffs.

The radioactive waste at the Farallons came from several sources. Immediately following World War II, as US politicians ramped up the Cold War, the configuration of military, manufacturing, and medical research that we refer to as the military-industrial complex began producing unprecedented amounts of radioactive waste. Unsafe for regular disposal, everything from paper towels and clothes to used lab equipment and lab samples were packed into fifty-five-gallon drums, capped with concrete, and shipped to the naval shipyard at Hunters Point. Atomic Energy Commission workers then sunk the barrels in the waters at the edge of the Farallons. In 1951 the navy added to the dump, filling the already contaminated hull of the USS *Independence* with waste and sinking it out near the islands; the ship had been used in nuclear-weapons testing in the Bikini Atolls (in the Marshall Islands near Micronesia). Dumping continued unabated until 1960 and was officially banned in 1972, when monitoring of the two dump sites was transferred to the National Oceanic and Atmospheric Administration (NOAA) and the federal Environmental Protection Agency (EPA).

The *San Francisco Call-Bulletin* described this 1945 photograph as "the secret wartime radar station on the largest of the Farallon Islands, Southeast Farallon." (Photographer unknown)

Rich and abundant sea life up close with the Oceanic Society boat tour of the Farallons.

The EPA and environmental monitoring groups have continued to debate the possible effects of the waste. Barrels are definitely leaking, but the EPA has argued for years that attempting to move the waste would potentially cause more problems. Much of the waste had low levels of radioactivity that should have decayed to safe levels. But the military also dumped undisclosed amounts of waste containing plutonium, which will outlive us all and could take several hundred thousand more years to reach currently designated "safe" levels. In the meantime, scientists continue to study whether fish and other wildlife harvested from the area are safe to eat, and what long-term effects will emerge in the marine ecosystem from the slow release of radiation into the sea.

But although the military waste remains a mysterious undersea concern, the reason you can't visit the islands is specifically to protect the wildlife. The place is home to a stunning array of birds—including puffins, cormorants, and several nocturnal species—who, alongside colonies of seals and sea lions, whales, great white sharks, and more, thrive in this place that is so carefully protected from human contact.

TO LEARN MORE

Colombo, P., and M. W. Kending. "Analysis and Evaluation of Radioactive Waste Package Retrieved from the Farallon Islands 900-Meter Disposal Site." Upton, NY: United States Environmental Protection Agency, 1990.

4.6 Golden Gate Village

429 Drake Avenue, Sausalito 94965
(in unincorporated Marin City)

Marin County is not known for its affordable housing, but unincorporated Marin City remains home to a public housing project that is protected as a historic site. The place is a rare bulwark against the cost of living in Marin. If you cross the Golden Gate Bridge to the north and drive the iconic 101 highway, a row of incongruously tall buildings with stylized modernist facades and bright red roofs appears to the west. These are the main apartment complexes of what used to be called Marin City Public Housing, known as Golden Gate Village since the 1990s. The site hosts 292 units of federally subsidized housing for seven hundred people, abutting the Golden Gate National Recreation Area on one side, with bay views on the other. Residents continue to pay low federally determined rates based on their incomes, while all around them real estate is on the rise. In 2017 the site was placed on the National List of Historic Places; advocates for this designation relied in part on photos from the 1960s that showed the value of the place for African American families. That same year, the median home price in Marin County was $1.14 million.

The predominantly African American residents of Marin City enlisted the help of local architects to apply for the National Historic Place listing, which effectively prevents the county or state from demolishing the buildings for mixed-income or market-rate housing. The historic designation was won primarily because the complex was designed by Frank Lloyd Wright's West Coast representative, Aaron Green, and by star landscape architect Lawrence Halprin; the intent of its construction matters even more. First, the county levied federal money via the FHA (an agency that is more famous for its use in building white-only suburbs) to explicitly hire top architects to design a community that brought together the open natural spaces and beautiful buildings for working-class people of color. Second, the housing was intentionally constructed to help some of the thousands of African American families who had been

(Left) Golden Gate Village in 2019.

(Below) A 1961 photograph of children in the Golden Gate Village playground, with housing and the Marin hills to the northeast. This photo was one of several that were used to successfully argue for the inclusion of the village on the National List of Historic Places. (Photographer unknown)

recruited to work in the Marin shipyards during World War II stay in the area, even after their wartime jobs disappeared.

Marin City had housed shipyard workers since 1942, and when Marin City Public Housing opened in 1959—as a replacement for some of the deteriorated wartime buildings—officials and residents imagined a diverse and democratic Marin County. But as the county grew whiter (as of the 2010 census the county was 71 percent white) and wealthier, Marin City became more isolated, cut off by the highway and river to

the north. Federal funding for public housing shrank from the early 1970s onward, and by the 1990s, young rappers from Marin were calling Marin City "The Jungle." Most famously, Tupac Shakur launched his career from these projects, where he'd relocated from the East Coast with his mom for the last two years of high school.

Because of the National Historic Registry designation, tenants of Golden Gate Village (many of whom have been in the community for decades) have some protection at a time when federal commitments to public housing continue to shrink. However, the buildings need tens of millions of dollars in repairs and upgrades, and, although the Marin County Housing Authority is starved for funds, the broader community has not yet stepped in to save the public housing that is the one pocket of racial and ethnic diversity at the southern end of Marin.

NEARBY SITES OF INTEREST

Marinship Park
Testa Street at Marinship Way, Sausalito 94965
The park and street that bear the name of the Marin Shipbuilding Division of W. A. Bechtel Company, known as Marinship, only hint at the massive shipbuilding operation that ran here from 1942 to 1945. In 1944 a young Thurgood Marshall won a California Supreme Court case on behalf of Black workers at Marinship, arguing they could not legally be excluded from joining unions based on race and thus denied higher paying jobs.

Marin County Civic Center
3501 Civic Center Drive, San Rafael 94903
Now one of ten UNESCO World Heritage Sites designed by Frank Lloyd Wright (though it was constructed a year after his death in 1959), the center is home to the Marin County Superior Court, where an attempt to free the Soledad brothers in 1970 led to a shootout that killed four people. Subsequently, the FBI pursued radical activist and scholar Angela Davis when she fled California, having been accused of providing the weapons used in the shootout; Davis was eventually arrested, inspiring the famed "Free Angela" campaign of the early 1970s.

TO LEARN MORE

Wollenberg, Charles. *Marinship at War: Shipbuilding and Social Change in Wartime Sausalito.* Berkeley, CA: Western Heritage Press, 1990.

4.7 Greystone Cellars
2555 Main Street, Saint Helena 94574

From the perspective of the workers in the field, Greystone Cellars is far more than just a grand winery with historic architecture. This 1889 towering castle on a hill, built by the son of a wealthy mine owner, is the site where the United Farm Workers (UFW) established the first union-contracted vineyard in Napa-Sonoma. The landscape here has the visual effect of many of the other grand towers scattered across the Napa Valley: It draws the visitor's eye to the winery and away from the vineyard itself, lending a sense of grandeur to the mythology of artisanally crafted wines and avoiding the stories of the men and women who toil at growing and harvesting. This particular building, and the grounds, are admittedly better crafted than many of the newer faux-Tuscan tasting rooms and may be of interest to those looking for a glimpse of Napa before its aesthetic was driven by global capital.

Tending vines and harvesting grapes is backbreaking and highly skilled work. The hot, dry conditions that produce the best wine grapes also produce long, exhausting days for the predominantly migrant workers that Napa and Sonoma wineries depend on. Strong and sharp clippers used to carefully prune branches vine by vine over hundreds of acres can easily take off fingers with an accidental slip. Exposure to pesticides and fungicides designed to kill every living thing around the grapevines can cause rashes, burns, and other problems for workers. But because the United States structures agricultural labor as supposedly low-skill

The palatial Greystone Cellars.

work, compensation for field workers—even in highly profitable niche commodities like California wine—has historically been abysmally low. Regular health insurance, pensions, stable homes, and educational spaces for children were long essentially nonexistent.

It was under these conditions that the UFW first began organizing workers in Napa in the mid-1960s, encouraging workers to sign union cards, while picketing and lobbying growers to recognize the union. One of their first targets was Greystone Cellars, owned and operated since the 1940s by the La Sallian Catholic order, the Christian Brothers, which had moved production to Napa during Prohibition to make sacramental wines, and which had become a driving force in the growth of the Napa wine region by the 1960s. For a nascent wine industry

looking to be taken seriously on world markets (it's hard to imagine now, but most California wines still came in jugs and were not seen as on par with French and Italian imports), the threat of the kind of boycotts the UFW had successfully organized in the Central Valley was meaningful. On March 13, 1967, the Christian Brothers signed the first union contract for workers in their fields. They were followed shortly by several other wineries.

Other growers, wary of the UFW, formed a "Winegrowers Foundation" to coordinate among themselves. They offered higher wages than the UFW contracts called for and established a winery-controlled pension plan for workers. This provided a short-term boon to some workers but left them with little control over their work or future agreements. The growers' strategy, paired with their increased use of subcontracted labor, prevented the UFW from gaining a significant toehold in Napa and Sonoma. Even though the winery itself was sold in 1989 to a corporate owner, and passed through many stages of mergers and acquisitions over the next decade, the UFW maintained a contract for the workers in the Greystone fields. But due to a combination of changes in the labor structure of the industry, antiunion campaigns by growers, and changes within the UFW, thirty-nine out of sixty workers voted to reject UFW representation in 2008. Today only two UFW contracts remain in Napa.

The Greystone Cellars is currently occupied by the West Coast branch of the Culinary Institute of America (CIA), a nonprofit academy that trains chefs, cooks, and entrepreneurs in the art and business of haute cuisine, as it has come to be defined, in no small part through the tastes and culinary fashions of the San Francisco Bay Area. Visitors are welcome on the grounds to see the remodeled building, demo kitchens, extensive gift shop selling all things high-end foodie, and a display of several hundred bottle openers collected by the former head winemaker of the Christian Brothers. Just don't forget to stop and look out into the fields.

TO LEARN MORE

Bardacke, Frank. *Trampling out the Vintage: Cesar Chavez and the Two Souls of the United Farm Workers.* New York: Verso, 2012.

NEARBY SITE OF INTEREST

The French Laundry
6640 Washington Street, Yountville 94599
If you stop by here, note that the famed restaurant occupies a former "French laundry," thus named in the early twentieth century to reassure prospective customers that the workers at the laundry were white, and not Chinese. Today the most affordable meal without wine pairing starts at $300 a head; the name remains unchanged.

4.8 Jewish Community Center
740 Western Avenue, Petaluma

California has a long-hidden history of vigilante mob violence. Whole towns of Chinese Americans were driven out by racist mobs in the nineteenth century, for example. And there was a time, during the fraught 1930s when economic pain was widespread, that being Jewish and Communist—and supporting union labor—incurred terrifying violence. On the night of August 21, 1935, chicken farmer Sol Nitzberg awoke to find several hundred vigilantes surrounding his home in Petaluma, shouting, "Lynch him, lynch him!" Despite the best efforts of Sol and his wife, Millie, to fend off the mob, Sol was captured, beaten, tarred and feathered, and left at the town border and told to leave Sonoma.

The Nitzbergs were just one of several hundred Jewish families who made their way from Tsarist Russia to Petaluma in the early twentieth century to take up "chicken ranching," mostly producing eggs for nearby cities. Many of the first wave were fleeing poverty and the brutal violence of escalating pogroms (organized massacres) in the last

The former JCC, now B'Nai Israel.

years of Tsarist control. They took circuitous routes, settling and resettling across the globe in any region that allowed Jews to farm and form communities. Eventually, some learned that there was land that they could buy in California, where they could engage in agriculture and work for themselves. Established ranchers regularly signed for new immigrants to get loans for land and credit with feed stores, and trained them in the new and hard work of raising chickens. In 1925, with the support of a loan from the Haas family (of the Levi Strauss company), the community built the small Jewish Community Center that still stands at 740 Western Avenue, marked only with a small Star of David above the front door.

Petaluma Jews intentionally built a community center, not a synagogue. The refugees and immigrants who set up their operations in Petaluma were not particularly religious, but they shared a sense of *yiddishkeit*—a Jewish cultural identity. The center became the de facto meeting place for the International Workers Order (who organized support for the dockworkers in San Francisco, Left educational programs, and Yiddish drama clubs), for the Yiddish Choir (frequently accused of singing Soviet songs), and Nitzberg's Communist Party. In the '30s, at the height of the Great Depression, Communists supported and worked to organize apple pickers in a strike against orchard owners. It was this political work that drew the ire of the vigilante mob in 1935 and subsequently led to Nitzberg losing the credit and insurance needed to run the chicken farm. It was not just vigilantes and reactionary businessmen that radical Jews had to look out for; historian Kenneth Kann notes that just two blocks west of the Community Center on Western Avenue, Hermann Sons Hall was a regular and public meeting place for Petaluma's Nazis.

The Depression took its toll on the egg-producers. The Holocaust brought a second wave of Jewish refugees to Petaluma. The political dynamics of Petaluma began to shift. Sol, Millie, and the large group of left-wing Jews found themselves at odds with not only conservative elements of the North Bay, but also with a growing number of conservative-leaning Jews. There had long been rifts in the community along political lines, especially around left-wing resistance to Zionism. But now, in the anti-Communist McCarthy Era, the conservative elements of the community had support for pushing out the radical Left. After many tense meetings at the Community Center, with hundreds in attendance, the now conservative-controlled board voted to expel any "subversive" group from meeting at the center—from the IWO to the Yiddish Choir. The expulsion caused a lingering rift in the community.

The legacy of Jewish ranchers was further undone by the industrialization and consolidation of egg production. The ranchers' well-educated children left or went into other lines of work, and the JCC was effectively converted, against the wishes of many of the older generation, into a religious center with a rabbi. Today the center has a renewed mission that is more in line with its original purpose, to be home to a wide variety of Jewish-identifying people.

NEARBY SITE OF INTEREST

Scott Ranch
700 Hardin Lane, Petaluma 94954
Scott Geber, a grandchild of one of the one-time ranchers, sings Yiddish labor songs at Scott Ranch, where he continues the agrarian tradition and manages a herd of organically fed cattle.

TO LEARN MORE

Kann, Kenneth. *Comrades and Chicken Ranchers: The Story of a California Jewish Community.* Ithaca, NY: Cornell University Press, 1993.
Withington, Jack. "Days of Tar and Feathering." *Sonoma Historian* no. 3, 2006.

4.9 Lucas Valley Eichler Development

Lucas Valley Road and Mount Shasta Drive, San Rafael 94903

The California suburbs have a long history of race-class exclusion. In Lucas Valley, the suburban story took a slightly different turn; it wasn't perfect, but the Eichler development represents a shift in the exclusionary practices used throughout the state that laid the groundwork for today's persistent racial segregation. In 1963 the blacklisted socialist writer-turned-photographer Albert E. Kahn took a photo of an African American boy and a white boy walking to school with their arms around each other's shoulders, headed to school in the newly opened Lucas Valley suburb of San Rafael. At the time, the neighborhood was still under development by the famed father-son development team Joseph and Ned Eichler. The Eichlers would go on to use Kahn's photo on billboards to promote future developments in San Francisco, on holiday cards to congressmen, and as a prominently featured image in their Palo Alto offices. The image perfectly captures the liberal dream that racial harmony could be achieved simply through shared middle-

(Above) Lucas Valley (named as such before George Lucas bought a property just up the road from the Eichler development, which is shown here in the foreground).

(Left) One of the classic Eichler designs that brought "high-style" modernist architecture to the masses. (Ernest Braun photo)

class achievements like homeownership (rather than through remaking power dynamics). Still, in the geographic context of the postwar Bay Area, the photo of interracial friendship in a middle-class development also symbolizes a radical departure from the status quo of California suburbanization.

Often simplified as white flight—in reference to the departure of middle-class and wealthy white families and business from cities—midcentury suburbanization also meant excluding people of color from the new housing that was sprouting up all over

the state. Developers, real estate agents, and white home owners, often with the explicit backing of local, state, and federal officials, used legal and financial strategies, along with direct intimidation at times, to prevent people of color from buying homes. In this context, the Eichlers—who are more famous for their commitment to bringing high-design modernist architecture to the middle-class masses than for their progressive views on race—provided an important, but limited, exception. As architectural historian Ocean Howell has shown, the Eichlers were not civil rights activists, but they worked to shape government policies toward open housing, pushed back against racist realtor associations, and in developments like Lucas Valley they maintained a de facto nondiscrimination policy.

The Eichlers began selling to Asian American buyers starting 1949, without significant pushback from white home owners; they delayed openly selling to African American buyers until 1954, having frequently met hostile responses from white neighbors. In one telling incident that Howell describes, a Black air force officer bought a house in Terra Linda, the development just to the north of Lucas Valley, prompting complaints by eight white neighbors. Incensed at the complaints, Joe Eichler offered to buy their houses back if they didn't want Black neighbors, telling them they'd already underpaid for their houses; no one took him up on the offer. The Eichlers maintained friendships with prominent African Americans in the region. They built a home for lead NAACP counsel Frank Williams in Palo Alto and designed (though never built) a house for baseball legend Willie Mays when he came to San Francisco with the Giants. Around the same time, Mays was refused the right to purchase a home in Sherwood Forest, a white development on San Francisco's west side. After media attention and political pressure, the Mays family bought the home, but they left in less than two years, citing a racially hostile neighborhood. In a white-supremacist real estate market, the Eichlers thus crossed a meaningful line.

The development remains one of the best places to see a collection of midcentury-modern homes, but over time, the Eichlers' interracial vision for Lucas Valley has evaporated. The 2010 US census reported residents there as 95 percent to 99 percent white. Eichler-built homes regularly sell for well over a million dollars each, and they come with strict restrictions from the Lucas Valley Homeowners Association on how property is to be maintained and buildings historically preserved.

TO LEARN MORE

Howell, Ocean. "The Merchant Crusaders: Eichler Homes and Fair Housing, 1949–1974." *Pacific Historical Review* 85, no. 3 (Aug. 2016): 379–407.
Eichler Design, http://www.eichlermidcentury.com

4.10 Mission San Rafael Archangel

1104 Fifth Avenue, San Rafael 94901

The myths that bolster the idea of California as a place rooted in a romantic Spanish past are alive in San Rafael. Like much of the state's mission-style architecture, the Chapel of Mission San Rafael is a replica. It was built under the direction of an Irish Catholic priest, with support from the Hearst Family Foundation, to visibly situate mythic mission history in San Rafael. The towers of the parish church of San Rafael (built 1919) and the surrounding modern buildings of downtown San Rafael are built atop acres of territory once controlled by California's second-to-last Spanish mission. The former cemetery, now a parking lot, was the burial site of Chief Marin, born around 1781, the

Mission San Rafael, 2019.

Miwok rebel for whom Marin County was named; Marin's people had lived here long before Europeans arrived.

The mission at San Rafael was originally built as a dedicated space to send sick and dying Indigenous people from San Francisco's Mission Dolores starting in 1819. Romanticized Anglo myths now celebrate it as California's first sanatorium, a hospital of sorts. The problem with that idea is that it ignores the fact that the mission system itself was creating the very sicknesses that needed curing—from exposing Native people to European disease and the physical abuses of forced hard labor, poor food, and violent disciplining, to the public-health damage done by destroying tribal social systems. Without these atrocities, there may have been no need for San Rafael's mission. Later, San Rafael was granted full mission status in 1821, as a productive agricultural center. During the Miwok revolts of 1829 (see Mission San Jose, p. 103), San Rafael was the object of several raids and was a site from which rebels drove soldiers back to the San Francisco Presidio multiple times.

At the end of Mexico's war for independence, San Rafael was the first mission to be secularized, with its rich and valuable agricultural lands turned over to private owners. Mexican ranchers used the chapel for religious purposes for a few years, and John Frémont (who massacred hundreds of California Indians before becoming California's first US Senator) used it as a headquarters briefly in 1846, when the United States seized California. By the 1870s the original mission buildings were so thoroughly abandoned that they were demolished to make way for the city of San Rafael.

Tule elk roaming freely at Pierce Point Ranch.

4.11 Pierce Point Ranch

Pierce Point Road, Inverness 94937

Point Reyes National Seashore

For many visitors to Point Reyes National Seashore, one of the park's most striking features is the cows, whose presence signals the unique status of the park as a space of both recreation and production. In fact, cows have grazed the national seashore pastures since the 1800s, when the Mexican ranchos on the peninsula supported huge herds of cattle. This is mentioned in the Bear Valley Visitor Center exhibits, which also describe the Miwok presence on the peninsula, the early Spanish explorers along the coast, and the history of ranching on the peninsula. But the park is short on information about the contemporary ranching experience. This is unfortunate because the working landscape is foundational to the park and the surrounding towns of West Marin.

You can learn more about the historic ranches at Pierce Point Ranch, about sixteen miles from the Visitor Center, at the end of Pierce Point Road, near the trailhead for a 9.7-mile round-trip hike to Tomales Point (also one of the best places in the park to view tule elk). A visit to the well-kept ranch, which is on the National Register of Historic Places, offers a glimpse into the dairying history of Point Reyes. On your way there, you will pass some of the six dairies and nine beef ranches that operate in the park. The stench of cow manure may be evident, your tires will rumble over the cattle guards on the road, and you may see young calves getting their footing. The ranch homes are modest, with trucks, tractors, and often trailers that shelter workers—all signs of a working ranch. Picturesque or not, they are fundamental to the landscape, and they are cornerstones of the agricultural economy of West Marin.

The working ranches recall a long history of human interaction with the landscape. The perennially green, treeless moors of the peninsula were once cultivated by Coast Miwok practices of burning, pruning, and harvesting. Herds of tule elk and, later, cattle grazed the hillsides, keeping coyote bush, poison oak, and other shrubs at bay. In the 1980s, the park service designated much of the previous ranchland acreage as wilderness, with trails built from old ranch roads, and camps on the sites of old ranches, as the occasional eucalyptus tree and flowers planted by ranchers indicate. During the gold rush, Portuguese, Swedish, Italian-Swiss, and Irish immigrants settled in West Marin and began dairy ranching. By the late 1900s, Point Reyes ranches were producing more butter than anywhere else in the state. Many immigrant families who started out as tenant farmers eventually bought their ranches and continued operations.

The continued existence of working ranches in a national park is controversial. In the 1960s when the federal government bought the land to incorporate into Point Reyes National Seashore, ranching families were granted leases for twenty to forty years, after which most leases were extended, but for a shorter time and with less autonomy. A 2016 lawsuit charged that the cows caused environmental damage to the park's scenic resources and raised questions about the role of national parks, who they serve, and who decides. The ranches are also in tension with the elk, who compete for forage with the cows, frustrating ranchers. (Jessica Lage)

TO LEARN MORE

Watt, Laura A. *The Paradox of Preservation: Wilderness and Working Landscapes at Point Reyes National Seashore.* Berkeley: University of California Press, 2017.

RELATED SITE OF INTEREST

Headlands Center for the Arts
944 Simmonds Road, Sausalito 94965

This arts center provides unique studio and exhibition space, along with precious funding, to emerging Bay Area artists. The Marin Headlands, where the center is located, is covered in former military installations, including Nike missile silos and artillery batteries once capable of sinking any ship entering the bay. The National Park Service transformed barracks into this artists' space, providing a hopeful example of military landscape repurposing. Excellent hikes, Rodeo Beach, and unique views of the Golden Gate Bridge are all easily accessible from here. Visiting hours are posted here: http://www.headlands.org.

4.12 Port Chicago Sailors' Strike

Vallejo Sanitation and Flood Control District, 450 Ryder Street, Vallejo 94590 (note: this is the nearest address)

This industrial corner of the Vallejo waterfront was the site of a little-known antisegregation struggle, when Black military personnel used their collective power to draw attention to the Jim Crow structure of the US military—which officially relegated Black personnel to menial tasks, with white officers always in charge—and its long history of racial violence. It was August 9, 1944, and more than 250 African American navy personnel massed outside their barracks on Ryder Street here in Vallejo. Ordered to march aboard a vessel to make the short Napa River crossing to the Mare Island ammunition depot, they refused to move. It was a wildcat (unauthorized) labor strike, staged by survivors of a catastrophic munitions explosion that had, just three weeks before, killed 320 people at the racially segregated Port Chicago naval ammunitions storage site. The military barracks where the strike was planned was near here, approximately at the intersection of Ryder Street and Sonoma Boulevard. Ryder Street ends at an off-limits yard that now belongs to the city's sanitation district. The barracks were a short march from the shoreline, and it's likely that construction of this 1950s-era wastewater treatment plant covers the site of the strike.

The Port Chicago explosion, about fifteen miles to the east, had rocked the navy, but the Black personnel who were wounded or killed were treated as mere collateral damage. Official records show that 202 African American stevedores died, and 233 were wounded. Percy Robinson survived the blast, describing it this way to the *Los Angeles Times*: "My face was mutilated. When you passed the mirrors, the skin was hanging off your face and you couldn't recognize yourself. After you were wounded, you were supposed to go home for leave." But, said Robinson, "after we were wounded, they made us go back to work. That's why I struck." The pain of the explosion compounded a long history of racial violence, including a 1942 incident in which white shore patrol shot two unarmed Black sailors in Vallejo's "Gold Coast" wartime nightlife district.

The Twelfth Naval District detained the strikers for three days aboard a barge, where the highest-ranking admiral addressed the strikers and threatened them with death by firing squad. Ultimately the navy punished over two hundred with dishonorable discharges—a status that was later reduced but not reversed. The navy charged fifty other men ("the Port Chicago Fifty") with organizing mutiny in a trial before an all-white panel of retired naval officers at Treasure Island. The NAACP sent head attorney Thurgood Marshall to observe the proceedings. According to sociologist Robert Allen, Marshall remarked: "This is not 50 men on trial for mutiny. This is the Navy on trial for its whole vicious policy toward Negroes. Negroes in the Navy don't mind loading ammunition. They just want to know why they are the only ones doing the loading!" On October 24, 1944, the tribunal handed down a guilty verdict. The courts-martial drew letters and protests that contributed to the integration of the armed forces, a shift that became official with President Truman's 1948 Executive Order 9981, which ended legal discrimination in the military. Even so, the "victory" over Jim Crow remained elusive, and the navy has left the convictions standing up to the present, despite numerous appeals over the decades.

In 1994 the National Park Service installed a memorial for those killed at the site of the Port Chicago explosion that triggered the strike. The memorial describes the explosion but is devoid of visual references to the strike itself, and the park doesn't have easy access, given its location in an active military base. The Pentagon continues to use the base for shipping deadly weapons; access is denied whenever ships dock, and US identification is required at other times. (Javier Arbona)

TO LEARN MORE

Allen, Robert L. *The Port Chicago Mutiny: The Story of the Largest Mass Mutiny Trial in U.S. Naval History*. Berkeley, CA: Heyday Books, 2006.

Arbona, Javier. "Anti-Memorials and World War II Heritage in the San Francisco Bay Area: Spaces of the 1942 Black Sailors Uprising." *Landscape Journal* 34, no. 2 (February 1, 2015): 177–192.

Doss, Erika. "Commemorating the Port Chicago Naval Magazine Disaster of 1944: Remembering the Racial Injustices of the 'Good War' in Contemporary America." *American Studies Journal* 59 (June 3, 2015).

4.13 Prince Hall Masons Firma Lodge No. 27

1209 Georgia Street, Vallejo 94590

Founded by African American Masons, Vallejo's elegant two-story Prince Hall Masons Firma Lodge No. 27 is modest and practical in comparison to the more ornate Scottish Rite temples at the center of many cities. The hall stands as an important reminder of both the exclusion of nonwhites from institutions and the long history of independent Black institutional development. The Prince Hall Freemasons, founded in Massachusetts in the 1780s by Black abolitionist and revolutionary war veteran Prince Hall, were denied recognition by the main branch of American Freemasons,

an organization that held significant power and influence in early American history. The Prince Hall Masons nevertheless went on to found lodges and halls throughout the United States as one strategy for building and maintaining Black communities.

Many of the early Black residents of Vallejo had been brought to California as enslaved persons, and despite the popular perception of California as a "free state," many had to wait years—while working, unpaid, in the gold fields and on white-controlled homesteads—before liberation and independence. No more than a generation or two removed, their children and grandchildren, as well as those of other Black immigrants to the state, understood quickly that Anglo power structures in the region would not be welcoming to them. Chapters of fraternal organizations like the Prince Hall Freemasons, as well as Oddfellows, in addition to churches in the AME and Baptist traditions, offered ways for people to pool resources, financial or otherwise, to build and share networks and integrate new migrants into their communities.

Prince Hall Mason's Lodge, 2019.

Black veterans, many of whom had served in the segregated Buffalo Soldier companies deployed by the US government against Natives in its imperial incursions into Puerto Rico, Mexico, and the Philippines, served as the primary organizers of the hall between 1914 and 1917. This became an important gathering point for them, as well as for veterans of color from subsequent wars. Within months of its completion, the hall became an important meeting place for other community organizations and functions—dinners and dances—including the founding of the Firma Lodge. The Prince Hall Freemasons officially bought the building from the veterans association in 1946.

Throughout the years the presence of the lodge has attested to the importance of Black-owned city spaces. As historian Sharon McGriff-Payne writes, over time the building housed a temporary USO office during WWII (providing a safe space for Black soldiers to gather) as well as the Prince Hall Masons' credit union (helping Black families establish credit and equity outside of predatory/exclusionary conventional banking), and the Black-owned and -focused Golden State Mutual Life Insurance Company. The significance of the Freemasons has declined over the years, but the lodge is still used for regular meetings and has looked much the same for over a century on Georgia Street.

TO LEARN MORE

McGriff-Payne, Sharon. *John Grider's Century: African Americans in Solano, Napa, and Sonoma Counties from 1845 to 1925.* New York: iUniverse, 2009.

NEARBY SITE OF INTEREST

Vallejo Rising mural (historic)
401 Georgia Street, Vallejo 94590
From 2012 to 2017, the Marin Street side of this building displayed a mural, painted by local youth and a high school teacher, celebrating Vallejo's multicultural history and its return from municipal bankruptcy in the early 2000s, and commemorating the lives of young people who have died here. Paramount Pictures painted over the mural while shooting a *Transformers* movie in 2017, but has promised to help fund a new mural. See if it is up yet, and check out Vallejo's growing public-art scene, at http://vallejoartandarchitecture.com/map/.

4.14 San Quentin Prison

1 Main Street, San Quentin, CA
"San Quentin, you've been a livin' hell to me." So sang country music legend Johnny Cash to a room full of cheering San Quentin prisoners not once but twice during his 1969 set at "the Q." Cash went on: "San Quentin, I hate every inch of you. You've cut me and you scarred me through and through. And I'll walk out a wiser, weaker man; Mister Congressman you can't understand." The live album and accompanying documentary cemented the aging prison's reputation as a place of hard living, and like its neighbor in the bay, Alcatraz, this prison maintains an unsettling mystique in popular culture. But unlike Alcatraz, San Quentin State Prison remains open after 166 years. And inmates continue to describe it as a living hell. On the waterfront and set against the rolling hills of the North Bay, with its Spanish Revival facade and peeling paint, San Quentin looks more like the prewar film set it was

San Quentin Prison, 2019.

once used for in the Humphry Bogart film *San Quentin* than a facility where California keeps over 4,000 men locked in cages. The prison is meant to hold 3,082, and like almost all of the state's prisons, regularly crowds over 50 percent more people into cells.

In 2013 prisoners here joined thirty thousand others across the state in a hunger strike and refusal to go to work. The strike was initially called by prisoners at Pelican Bay, near the Oregon border, where indefinite solitary confinement (widely recognized as a form of torture) had become the norm. The call resonated at San Quentin not just because of inhumane conditions in deteriorating buildings, but also because the prison held, at that moment, over seven hundred men on death row. All men sentenced to be killed by the state of California live in purgatory at San Quentin, where the lethal-injection room has gone unused since 2006 because of legal disputes over how the state

should develop a protocol that is somehow not cruel and unusual—yet still kills. Instead, the state of California burns through tens of millions of dollars a year keeping people locked alone in solitary confinement, causing incalculable psychosocial damage and effectively doing nothing to heal prisoners or their communities. Prisoners and their families and allies continue to organize against the use of solitary confinement and life without parole, often as part of holistic efforts to abolish prisons entirely, led by the Oakland-based organization Critical Resistance.

Lest San Quentin be understood only as a place of tragedy and oppression, it is also a remarkable site of resistance and refusal to accept what scholars call "the carceral state" as the status quo. It is home to the Prison University Project, a volunteer-based program bringing college education into prison, an education that is often denied to prisoners even upon release because of their inability to access federal grants. The PUP succeeds in part because of San Quentin's proximity to progressive activists and university-affiliated people in the Bay Area, and has become a model for programs around the country. Prisoners at San Quentin, along with formerly incarcerated people from across the state, publish newspapers and magazines to showcase the creativity and lives of the people kept out of public view inside its walls. But the ultimate goal is to do away with prison altogether. Back to Johnny Cash: "San Quentin, may you rot and burn in hell. May your walls fall and may I live to tell. May all the world forget you ever stood. And may all the world regret you did no good."

RELATED SITE OF INTEREST

Critical Resistance
4400 Telegraph Avenue, Oakland 94609
Across the bay in Oakland, Critical Resistance runs campaigns and produces events, publications, trainings, and more—all aimed at the total abolition of not just prisons but the linked institutions known as the prison-industrial complex. Founded in 1998 in the East Bay, CR's founders included Ruth Wilson Gilmore, Rose Braz, and Angela Davis. This organizational address reflects an important stabilizing move in 2019, when a donor helped CR buy its own building.

NEARBY SITE OF INTEREST

Red Rock Island
Visible from San Rafael Bridge (I-580) or Vallejo-bound ferries
Unlike most of the islands in the bay, which are publicly owned, this still-undeveloped island is privately held. Rumored to have once held pirate treasure, imagined as both a mining outpost

and resort-hotel destination, the six-acre island remains both empty and for sale, split between Contra Costa, Marin, and San Francisco counties.

TO LEARN MORE

CR10 Publishing Collective. *Abolition Now! Ten Years of Strategy and Struggle against the Prison Industrial Complex.* Oakland, CA: AK Press, 2008. http://criticalresistance.org/wp-content/uploads/2012/06/Critical-Resistance-Abolition-Now-Ten-Years-of-Strategy-and-Struggle-against-the-Prison-Industrial-Complex.pdf

Gilmore, Ruth Wilson. *Golden Gulag: Prisons, Surplus, Crisis, and Opposition in Globalizing California.* Berkeley: University of California Press, 2007.

4.15 Sausalito BART Stop

Nevada and Bridgeway Streets, Sausalito 94965 (never built)

While this corner never became the Sausalito BART station, as proposed, this high-style bus stop serves at least eight bus lines.

In the original designs for Bay Area Rapid Transit (BART), this corner was to be the first stop in the North Bay on the Marin train line that would have run from downtown San Francisco to San Rafael or perhaps even much farther north. The bus stop that currently occupies the corner of Nevada and Bridgeway could certainly be lauded for

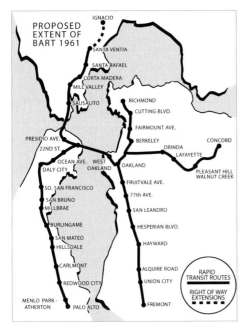

PROPOSED
EXTENT
OF BART 1961

IGNACIO
SANTA VENTIA
SANTA RAFAEL
CORTA MADERA
MILL VALLEY
SAUSALITO
RICHMOND
CUTTING BLVD.
FAIRMOUNT AVE.
PRESIDIO AVE.
22ND ST.
BERKELEY
ORINDA
LAFAYETTE
CONCORD
OCEAN AVE. WEST
DALY CITY OAKLAND
OAKLAND
PLEASANT HILL
WALNUT CREEK
SO. SAN FRANCISCO
FRUITVALE AVE.
SAN BRUNO
MILLBRAE
77th AVE.
SAN LEANDRO
BURLINGAME
HESPERIAN BLVD.
SAN MATEO
HILLSDALE
HAYWARD
CARLMONT
ALQUIRE ROAD
RAPID
TRANSIT ROUTES
REDWOOD CITY
UNION CITY
RIGHT OF WAY
EXTENSIONS
MENLO PARK -
ATHERTON
PALO ALTO
FREMONT

A February 1961 plan for the BART system reached into the North Bay beyond San Rafael. Alas, the proposal also included many more stops in San Francisco and Oakland, but they were never built. Not all planned stops are noted here. (Map reproduced from BART public records.)

its high-style design, with interior lighting and protection for waiting bus riders. But the design is not much comfort for bus-reliant people in car-centric Marin, who will note that the buses here stop just once an hour during weekdays and less frequently on nights and weekends.

The promise of BART predates contemporary articulations of "transit justice," which is the overarching idea that social and racial justice should include accessible mobility for all people, regardless of age, ability, or income, while also not exposing communities to air pollution. This is very much what regional planners initially promised the people of Marin in the 1950s, and

multiple studies had shown that the Golden Gate Bridge would be capable of supporting the trains. But in a move to maintain their own agency's power, and worried that public transit would cut into their district's lucrative tolls from the bridge, officials from the Golden Gate Bridge and state highway division killed the plan to run BART north. A quiet campaign over several years convinced planners that the proposal was unfeasible. Public outrage was not enough to stop their schemes to wall off Marin county from the city, and by 1962, BART's plans officially dropped the North Bay from development.

NEARBY SITE OF INTEREST

No Name Bar

757 Bridgeway, Sausalito 94965

This bar opened in 1959 without a name and still does not have one. Having spent decades as a gathering spot for Beat generation writers and psychedelic rock and jazz musicians, and after a stint as the mailing address of sex-worker advocate Margot St. James, this bar has survived the gentrification of Sausalito. There are still regular jazz shows.

TO LEARN MORE

Dyble, Louise N. *Paying the Toll: Local Power, Regional Politics, and the Golden Gate Bridge.* Philadelphia: University of Pennsylvania Press, 2011.

4.16 Sonoma Plaza

453 1st Street E., Sonoma 95476

This plaza is the site of the Bear Flag Revolt of June 14, 1846, which catalyzed Anglo-American control over California. While the symbol of the bear flag stands as a ubiquitous brand for the state today, its origin

A monument reflecting California's white supremacist roots at the center of Sonoma Plaza, installed by the "Native Sons of the Golden West."

the rape and lynching of Indigenous peoples and Mexicans, and a massive land grab. The "republic" lasted less than a month, but the event is credited with igniting the Mexican-American War, also known as the American War of Invasion, which resulted in US rule over this territory.

The public narrative of the Bear Flag Revolt went through some revision in the early 1990s when the commemoration of five hundred years of European contact elicited a critical response. Echoing the cries of Indigenous movements south of the US border, activists and educators "decolonized" mainstream historical narratives. That is, they wrote history in a way that no longer sanitized the violence of conquest and that no longer silenced Indigenous experiences. On June 14, 1996, Republican Governor Pete Wilson participated in a 150-year tribute and reenactment of Frémont's moment here at Sonoma Plaza, which recalled the revolt as part of a perceived glorious beginning of the US state of California. When they learned about plans for the event, Indigenous peoples of the Napa and Sonoma Valleys united with Chicanx activists to create a Bear Flag Resistance Committee, which organized a "March for Peace and a Bear Flag Alternative" to counter the governor's official celebration, raising their own flag over the plaza. The largely young activists organized a "whistle drive" prior to the action to ensure that everyone in attendance had a whistle that could help drown out the speeches on the main stage. They had an impact: Governor Wilson's speech was cut off by the overwhelming noise from the protest-

and the site of the revolt are often glossed over in California history lessons, leaving out their role in rooting white supremacy in the state. An armed US militia led the revolt, having moved westward following the territorial and social ideology of Manifest Destiny. Calling themselves Osos after the region's fierce grizzly bears, and led by Captain John Frémont, Ezequiel Merritt, and "frontier legend" Kit Carson, they claimed Sonoma, which was still under Mexican rule, as the California Republic. The raising of the bear flag over the plaza—a moment that is typically described as the beginning of US rule in California—was followed with the Bear Flag Manifesto, calling on white Americans to join the Osos in their new republic in exchange for land. Written accounts of the period document how these militias carried out premeditated thefts of cattle and horses,

ing crowd. Years later, though, the bear flag remains a widely used symbol of California and a hidden-in-plain-sight symbol of white supremacy. (Diana Negrín da Silva)

TO LEARN MORE

Heidenreich, Linda. *This Land Was Mexican Once: Histories of Resistance from Northern California*. Austin: University of Texas Press, 2007.

Walker, Dale L. *Bear Flag Rising: The Conquest of California, 1846*. New York: Forge Books, 1999.

4.17 Tomales Bay Trailhead

Golden Gate National Recreation Area

Highway 1, 1.7 miles north of Point Reyes Station

Foodie tours take visitors across West Marin to sample the area's specialties, like cheeses made from local organic milk, baked goods, grass-fed beef, honey wine, and Tomales Bay oysters. It may be delicious, but life here contains many of the standard contradictions of the US foodscape, where the laborers who make the landscape are ignored by

those who consume its bounty, or worse. This may come as a surprise in the midst of rhetoric that paints the unique beauty of this area as both progressive and productive. Here at the Tomales Bay Trailhead, you won't find these delicacies, but the trail offers sweeping views of a landscape largely built by immigrants linked to the same people that make this productive agricultural landscape possible. The trail takes you through the wetlands at the southern tip of the bay, originally converted to dairy pasture in the 1940s and purchased in 2000 by the National Park Service for restoration.

The area's agricultural history is indeed remarkable—from the gold rush, when West Marin butter was hailed as the best in the state, to the 1950s and 1960s struggles to preserve agriculture against suburban encroachment and competition from large-scale Central Valley operations. Creative land-use practices in the 1970s and 1980s, including the formation of the Marin Agricultural Land Trust (MALT), a partnership

A pastoral scene on the Tomales Bay trail; note both the bay and farm buildings in the distance.

225

The cows at Tomales Point signal that this beautiful place of recreation is also a working landscape.

between ranchers and environmentalists, saved numerous family farms and ranches. Many ranches converted to organic production and began making new products that spurred the growing Bay Area alternative food movement. This is typically hailed as a tremendous success story, but the difficult working conditions that maintain the dairy ranches and oyster farms near this trail remain largely invisible.

One of the core issues for workers is housing, which is intimately tied to labor here. Workers on the dairy ranches usually live on site, but on-ranch housing is inadequate for those with families, and it is often informal, converted from barns or recreational vehicles, in substandard condition. Plus, workers that depend on employers for housing are especially vulnerable, and the majority here are Mexican immigrants. Many have multigenerational connections to the area going back to the 1960s; even so, many longtime and recent arrivals alike are undocumented, and thus more vulnerable. Those who work as cheesemakers, oyster farmers, and other food service providers don't have the option of on-site housing,

and after the 2008 financial crisis many were pushed farther afield, as short-term rentals sapped the area of affordable rental housing and as rural gentrification spread through West Marin. By 2018 many were commuting up to two hours a day. What's more, though they make the foods that tourists love, West Marin workers struggle to feed themselves. Local markets don't match the needs or incomes of working-class West Marin families and often don't accept food assistance programs. (Jessica Lage)

TO LEARN MORE

Fairfax, Sally, et al. *California Cuisine and Food Justice*. Cambridge, MA: MIT Press, 2012.

Hart, John. *Farming on the Edge: Saving Family Farms in Marin County, California*. Berkeley: University of California Press, 1991.

Kelly, Nancy, and Kenji Yamamoto, directors. *Rebels with a Cause: How a Battle over Land Changed the Landscape Forever*. Cotati, CA: KRCB North Bay Public Media, 2012. (Documentary film)

Lage, Jessica. "Gentrification on the Urban Fringe: Prosperity and Displacement in West Marin, California." PhD diss., Department of Geography, University of California, Berkeley, 2019.

4.18 US Army Corps of Engineers Bay Model

2100 Bridgeway, Sausalito 94965

The massive, working-scale model of the San Francisco Bay-Delta's waterways and flows, which you can visit in Sausalito, embodies the military-metropolitan complex in the Bay Area. The Army Corps of Engineers built the model between 1956 and 1957 to test the feasibility of defense and

The warehouse-sized Bay Model includes a tiny Golden Gate Bridge.

development plans, including the infamous but never implemented Reber Plan, which sought to dam and pave over much of the bay. In 2000, official research using the model ended, and it became an educational showcase for the Army Corps. Its continued presence is a monument to the influence of the military in shaping the urban fabric of the region.

Composed of hundreds of twelve-foot-by-twelve-foot concrete slabs, the physical model is spread out over a full acre in a former shipbuilding warehouse. A labyrinth of miniature channels, levees, dikes, bridges, and technical elements, the model offers a landscape to traverse as much as a view to behold. Over the course of its four-decade working life, research there generated important new ways for understanding the bay and delta as an interconnected system. As a planning tool, the model was used to highlight how the fate of different Bay Area communities are entwined by their ecological connections, and it creates a sense that the entire region is an appropriate scale of

environmental governance (rather than the individual slices of land that we call cities and counties). A variety of contending political actors—land developers, municipal agencies, and environmentalist organizations like Save San Francisco Bay Association (later renamed Save the Bay)—used data from the model, and the way of comprehending the region that it provided, in debates over development and regulation. Ultimately, analysis based on the model supported the formation of regulatory institutions, including the San Francisco Bay Conservation and Development Commission, which plays a major role in regional development decisions that impact the bay. The model's visitor center is free and open to the public, but hours vary by season; you can call ahead to request a demonstration. (John Elrick)

TO LEARN MORE

Wollenberg, Charles. "The Man Who Helped Save the Bay by Trying to Destroy It." *Boom: A Journal of California,* April 14, 2015.

5

Thematic
Tours

Practical Notes

WHAT'S IN THESE TOURS AND HOW LONG WILL THEY TAKE?

This chapter offers five tours that link sites from the previous chapters across regions. We are not offering point-by-point directions because our assumption is that most readers have access to phone or computer map-navigation tools, or that you'll enjoy using a paper map to develop your own route. That said, we have organized each one in a geographically logical way to facilitate a coherent excursion, or perhaps several on each topic. See our accompanying maps to give you a sense of the possible journey.

These are all regional tours that could take you through all four quadrants of the Bay Area; shorter tours can be pulled from each by focusing just on the sites that represent a single chapter. You can of course also make your own more concentrated tours that touch on multiple themes by working with the maps in each chapter.

Each tour uses a theme to curate a collection of sites, all of which correspond to more detailed information you can find in earlier chapters; we include the entry number here for easy reference. There are infinite ways to draw connections between sites. We have chosen a few, and only a fraction of the sites in the book, but we hope as you read and explore you will make your own connections and collections.

WHAT'S FOR LUNCH?

As you wander the Bay Area, you'll find many wonderful options and opportunities for side journeys, including the quest for delicious food. We encourage you to branch out, knowing that the region offers an extraordinarily wide range of regional and international foods. Whenever you can, consider patronizing local businesses rather than national chains in order to have a positive impact on the local economy and get a better feel for what the locals are making. Most of the bay has low-budget options, but in some places you have to search harder for those. In San Francisco you'll notice an additional fee on your bill that funds health care for staff; until we have a functional national health care system, this is part of the cost of living and visiting there.

PRACTICALITIES: BATHROOMS, TRANSPORTATION, AND CONTRIBUTING

PUBLIC BATHROOMS are not as widespread as we'd like, but they are indeed all around the region. Beyond the cafés or restaurants that you may visit along the way, look for public library branches and public parks, both of which tend to have good public bathrooms throughout the Bay Area. Any given city hall, government building, or public university should be open to you as well. In the urban centers, big hotel lobbies can be an easy place for a quick break; in the suburban fringes gas stations can serve the same purpose.

You'll notice that the inequalities of our society extend to bathroom access. In San Francisco, Oakland, and Berkeley, you're more likely to find gender-neutral bathrooms (in some public buildings, universities, and LGBTQ-centered institutions). This is one of the unfinished projects of domestic human rights work: Every town needs public toilets, available without discrimination by gender expression, economic status, race, or any other human difference.

TRANSPORTATION decisions involve so many factors, including ability and time. These tours cover a lot of regional ground. Still, many of these geographies can be reached by bicycle, walking, and public transit, from trains to buses to ferries. And if you have the time and capacity, car-free modes of travel tend to make the landscape come alive in special ways.

Some Bay Area cities are better equipped for cyclists. Thanks to a strong history of advocacy, the East Bay and SF are currently the best in this way, with more bike lanes, bike racks, and programs where you can rent bikes by the hour or day. The South Bay is also packed with bike lanes along its newer, flat roads, and the completed parts of the Bay Trail, but you may be traveling long suburban-sprawl distances. North Bay biking involves stunning beauty, often on narrow roads without designated bike lanes.

Like cycling, riding public transit can help you develop a nice feel for places and cultures and helps keep open the possibility of noticing the quirks in the landscape and having spontaneous conversations with people. Many transit systems in the bay are fairly well equipped to handle wheelchair or stroller needs—for example, with electric lifts on many buses—but transit on heavily used bus lines, for example, can be harder to navigate when buses are full.

If you are relying on taxis (or ride-hailing companies), please tip as generously as you can, using cash so that drivers receive the full weight of your generosity. Many, if not most, drivers in the gig economy are struggling, and the compensation system of the ride-hailing companies remains inadequate (Bay Area cities are working on regulations to change this; see groups like Gig Workers Rising for the latest, https://www.gigworkersrising.org).

If you drive, you'll certainly cover the most ground in the shortest time. These cities are indeed still car-centric, although the rapidly rising impact of climate change may well change this more quickly than previously expected. Note that parking in the denser cities can be challenging and expensive, but there are ample paid parking lots; street parking is easiest outside of San Francisco.

Finally, we encourage you to **CONTRIBUTE** to the places you visit. Whether through volunteering, monetary donations, or other means, find a way to support and engage with the Bay Area. Throughout this book we mention organizations, and there are hundreds more that we haven't mentioned. Find the ones that speak to you; ask questions and learn; give in the ways that you can.

The Intertribal Bay Tour

Native Americans, representing dozens of tribes, live and work across the Bay Area, and their stories are California's. The sites in this tour largely represent difficult histories and should not be construed as a complete representation of Native American life. We hope, however, that these sites offer an important view into the legacies and traces of the long arc of Native resistance to colonization itself and to the ways that contemporary urbanism still relies on settler-colonialism (that is, colonization that involves the occupation of other people's territory, not just the extraction of their resources). It's a history we must reckon with and acknowledge as we push the society toward recognition, reparations, and more.

SOUTH BAY

You might begin at the **NEW ALMADEN MINE AREA** (2.17 • 21350 Almaden Rd., San Jose), looking north across the Santa Clara Valley, where a network of interconnected groups made their lives for thousands of years before colonization. The rocks here were an important source of cinnabar, a mercury-based red pigment, used in various art forms. Cross the valley to the **MISSION SAN JOSE** (2.15 • 43300 Mission Blvd., Fremont), where a Yokut leader led an open revolt against the mission system.

EAST BAY

Head north to Oakland along the flatlands alongside a bay once filled with abundant sea life and hills with flora and fauna that contributed to Indigenous diets. Some pre-colonial plants are cultivated at the **PERALTA HACIENDA HISTORICAL PARK** (1.22 • 2465 34th Ave., Oakland) in a calming garden where you can read an Ohlone poem inscribed here. **JINGLETOWN** (1.12 • 2611 E. 11th St., Oakland) can be visited through a stop in Union Point Park, with its monument to Indigenous and immigrant women in Oakland and to spiritual burial shellmounds that were here. The **INTERTRIBAL FRIENDSHIP HOUSE** (1.11 • 523 International Blvd., Oakland) is the "urban reservation" that has, since 1955, offered intergenerational and intertribal resources. Check the online calendar for events, connections to other active organizations, or to donate. The **EMERYVILLE SHELLMOUND MEMORIAL** (1.8 • 4597 Shellmound St., Emeryville) is a testament to the troubling societal disdain for Native American places, as well as to the refusal on the part of Indigenous communities to be erased.

NORTH BAY

If you head to the North Bay, Interstate 580 will bring you to **MISSION SAN RAFAEL** (4.10 • 1104 5th Ave., San Rafael), a tragic memorial to the violence of Spanish conquest.

SAN FRANCISCO

You can follow the route that Spanish troops took back to San Francisco after being defeated—several times during what colonizers called the Miwok Wars of 1829—to the heart of Bay Area colonialism. Some five thousand American Indians were buried in the **MISSION DOLORES CEMETERY** (3.20 •

The Intertribal Bay

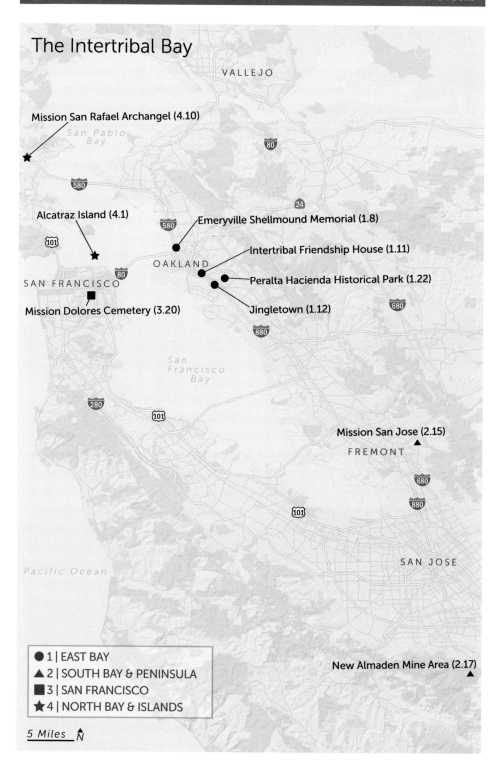

VALLEJO

Mission San Rafael Archangel (4.10)

San Pablo Bay

80

580

Alcatraz Island (4.1)

580

Emeryville Shellmound Memorial (1.8)

101

Intertribal Friendship House (1.11)

OAKLAND

SAN FRANCISCO

80

Peralta Hacienda Historical Park (1.22)

Mission Dolores Cemetery (3.20)

Jingletown (1.12)

680

880

San Francisco Bay

280

101

Mission San Jose (2.15)

FREMONT

680

880

101

SAN JOSE

Pacific Ocean

● 1 | EAST BAY
▲ 2 | SOUTH BAY & PENINSULA
■ 3 | SAN FRANCISCO
★ 4 | NORTH BAY & ISLANDS

New Almaden Mine Area (2.17)

5 Miles N

3321 16th St., San Francisco). Take the ferry to **ALCATRAZ** (4.1 • Alcatraz Island), where you can find traces of the American Indian Movement's 1973 occupation of the island, which inspired people to forge alliances for self-determination. As you reflect on these sites, consider contributing to the Bay Area's only Ohlone community land trust, Sogorea Te', at sogoreate-landtrust.com.

Capital & Its Discontents Tour

Capital—as a class of people, a process of accumulation, and the circulation of wealth— relies on the exploitation of laboring people and nature. Workers, meanwhile, have a long history of creatively challenging such exploitation and forging better lives through collective action. This tour traces a few of these struggles, many of which were foundational for the contemporary expansion of the labor movement that was underway as we wrote this book, including the hotel workers, teachers, and many others who have been in the streets in the 2010s demanding respectful workplace conditions and genuinely livable wages.

SAN FRANCISCO

In San Francisco's financial district at the **BANK OF AMERICA BUILDING** (3.4 • 555 California St., San Francisco), you can stand at the cold, black sculpture colloquially known as "Banker's Heart" and ponder the wealth accumulation necessary to build such a tower. Head out to the Embarcadero, where the nineteenth-century working port was established, and then to **"AN INJURY TO ONE . . ."**

(3.3 • Steuart and Mission Sts., San Francisco), a memorial to the 1934 general strike. While you're downtown, you'll pass hotel sites where workers sustained a successful two-month strike for better wages in 2018. Then head to the **REDSTONE LABOR TEMPLE** (3.25 • 2940 16th St., San Francisco), a historic home of unions and social justice organizations. It's a good place to think about the connections between various community-organizing projects—on housing, homelessness, gender justice, and so on—and the labor movement. One organization working to specifically make these kinds of links is Jobs with Justice, jwjsf.org.

SOUTH BAY

A long trek south will take you to **SAINT JAMES PARK** (2.22 • 2nd St. at E. Saint John St., San Jose) and the adjacent **SAN JOSE LABOR COUNCIL** (2.19 • Between 70 and 82 N. 2nd St., San Jose), with echoes of the radical unionism of the 1930s. Cesar Chavez expanded that legacy on the other side of town at **MCDONNELL HALL** (2.14 • 2020 E. San Antonio St., San Jose), where he developed the organizing skills to take on industrial agriculture across the state. Heading north brings you to Tesla, formerly the **NUMMI AUTO PLANT** (2.18 • 45500 Fremont Blvd., Fremont), which was the last union auto factory on the West Coast.

EAST BAY

In downtown Oakland, enjoy the public seating in **LATHAM SQUARE** (1.15 • Broadway and Telegraph Ave., Oakland) site of Oakland's 1946 general strike, led by a

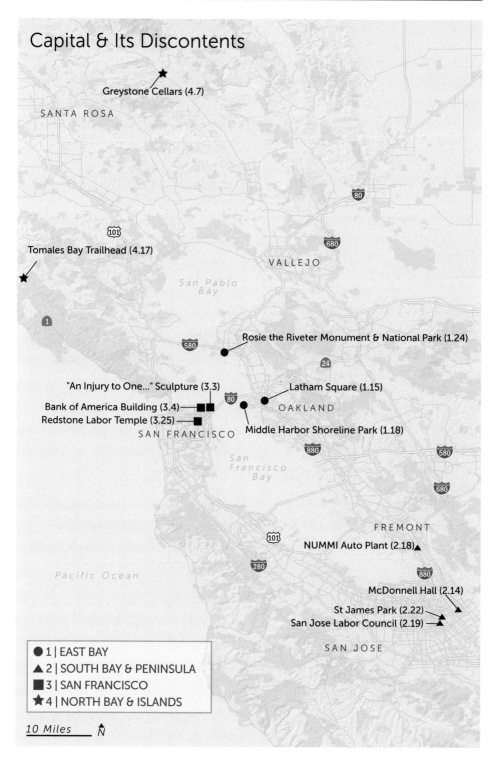

Capital & Its Discontents

Greystone Cellars (4.7)

SANTA ROSA

Tomales Bay Trailhead (4.17)

VALLEJO

San Pablo Bay

Rosie the Riveter Monument & National Park (1.24)

"An Injury to One..." Sculpture (3.3)

Latham Square (1.15)

Bank of America Building (3.4)

OAKLAND

Redstone Labor Temple (3.25)

SAN FRANCISCO

Middle Harbor Shoreline Park (1.18)

San Francisco Bay

FREMONT

NUMMI Auto Plant (2.18)

Pacific Ocean

McDonnell Hall (2.14)

St James Park (2.22)

San Jose Labor Council (2.19)

SAN JOSE

● 1 | EAST BAY
▲ 2 | SOUTH BAY & PENINSULA
■ 3 | SAN FRANCISCO
★ 4 | NORTH BAY & ISLANDS

10 Miles   N

largely female workforce of retail clerks. Then reach Oakland's westernmost point at **MIDDLE HARBOR SHORELINE PARK** (1.18 • 2777 Middle Harbor Rd., Oakland) with relaxing views and proximity to Oakland's port. This node in the global commodity chain has motivated important contemporary efforts like the Clean Ports Campaign. Visit the **ROSIE THE RIVETER MONUMENT AND NATIONAL PARK** (1.24 • 1414 Harbour Way, Richmond), where the capital flows of militarism were harnessed toward racial and gendered justice at work, with a ripple effect throughout society.

NORTH BAY

Crossing the bridge into the North Bay takes you to the **GREYSTONE CELLARS** (4.7 • 2555 Main St., Saint Helena), where the United Farm Workers organized the first winery contract, and to the **TOMALES BAY TRAILHEAD** (4.17 • Highway 1, 1.7 miles north of Point Reyes Station), which sits in a landscape made by low-wage workers. If you partake of the locally produced chardonnay, locally harvested oysters, or cheese from the well-tended cows you can see in the distance, consider the workers that produce the wealth of this place and indeed the entire Bay Area. What work remains to be done to make this experience equitable?

Ecological Imagination Tour

While hiking, environmentalism, and organic food are often cast as elite, this tour will help you think about everyday connections between open-space preservation, environmental activism, and food politics. These places may show you another view of foodies and food co-ops and offer opportunities to think about alternative ways to live, while noting challenges that have come with those alternatives. Finally, though corporate power has produced toxic landscapes, we find communities that are working to bring environmental justice to the region.

EAST BAY

Start at the worker-owned **MANDELA GROCERY COOPERATIVE** (1.16 • 1430 7th St., Oakland), where you might stock up on snacks for the tour ahead. The short trip from here to North Oakland will give you a good sense of why food justice, in the form of places like Mandela and the urban garden at **"BLACK PANTHER PARK"** (1.6 • Dover St., between 57th and 58th Sts., Oakland), has been central to Bay Area politics. Further north, the **"FOSSIL FUEL CORRIDOR"** (1.9 • 413 San Pablo Ave., Rodeo) offers a view of the region's sprawling petrochemical complex. Environmental justice advocates here continue to fight for cleaner energy solutions that don't poison workers, community members, or the land.

NORTH BAY AND ISLANDS

You can't take a train to the **SAUSALITO BART STOP** (4.15 • Nevada and Bridgeway Sts., Sau-

Ecological Imagination

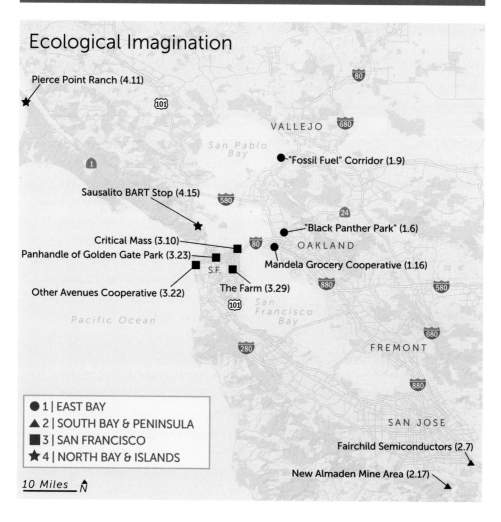

Pierce Point Ranch (4.11)

VALLEJO

San Pablo Bay

"Fossil Fuel" Corridor (1.9)

Sausalito BART Stop (4.15)

"Black Panther Park" (1.6)

Critical Mass (3.10)

OAKLAND

Panhandle of Golden Gate Park (3.23)

Mandela Grocery Cooperative (1.16)

S.F.

Other Avenues Cooperative (3.22)

The Farm (3.29)

San Francisco Bay

Pacific Ocean

FREMONT

● 1 | EAST BAY
▲ 2 | SOUTH BAY & PENINSULA
■ 3 | SAN FRANCISCO
★ 4 | NORTH BAY & ISLANDS

SAN JOSE

Fairchild Semiconductors (2.7)

10 Miles N

New Almaden Mine Area (2.17)

salito), which was never built, but if you go there, you can catch a bus to San Francisco. Further north, **PIERCE POINT RANCH** (4.11 • Pierce Point Rd., Inverness) offers hiking potential and lessons about the connections between open-space preservation and regional development.

SAN FRANCISCO

OTHER AVENUES FOOD STORE COOPERATIVE (3.22 • 3930 Judah St., San Francisco) keeps the legacy of the 1970s People's Food System

alive. The **PANHANDLE OF GOLDEN GATE PARK** (3.23 • Between Fell and Oak, Stanyan and Baker Sts., San Francisco) persists because of the "freeway revolts" that halted development here. These winding Panhandle paths are frequented often by the cyclists of **CRITICAL MASS** (3.10 • Market St. and Embarcadero, San Francisco) and by everyday bicycle riders. The former urban agriculture, art, and performance venue **THE FARM** (3.29 • 1499 Potrero Ave., San Francisco) is gone, but the Potrero del Sol park and community garden it helped spark at this site remains an excellent place to visit.

SOUTH BAY

The **FAIRCHILD SEMICONDUCTOR** (2.7 • 101 Bernal Rd., San Jose) superfund site provides a stark reminder of the "externalities" of Silicon Valley, which has one of the largest concentrations of federally designated toxic sites in the country. For a historical perspective on the same issue, visit the **NEW ALMADEN MINE AREA** (2.17 • 21350 Almaden Rd., San Jose), where you can also hike to find views of Santa Clara Valley.

Youth in Revolt Tour

Young people are often dismissed as apolitical or too immature to know what's good for themselves or the society at large. With a sharply contrasting view, this tour highlights the many different ways young people have been at the forefront of political change in the Bay Area. Educated by their elders at times and rebelling against them at others, people in their teens and twenties continue to take risks to transform the conditions of educational institutions and reshape the very trajectory of the places in which they live.

SOUTH BAY

Start in San Jose, where the **"VICTORY SALUTE" STATUE** (2.23 • San Jose State University campus, San Jose) commemorates the moment that two student-athletes woke the world with a Black power salute as they won gold and silver medals at the 1968 Olympics. Pick-

ing up that torch, the young people who run **SILICON VALLEY DE-BUG** (2.21 • 701 Lenzen Ave., San Jose) challenge dominant narratives about San Jose and its power structures. Head up the peninsula past the proliferation of tech campuses to the community that birthed the **NAIROBI SCHOOL SYSTEM** (2.16 • 85 Runnymede St., East Palo Alto), where an Afrocentric curriculum supported young people's educational development. Though it's now a movie theater, you can pass by the site of the **DALY CITY TEEN CENTER** (2.3 • 1901 Junipero Serra Blvd., Daly City), which was a product of Bay Area–wide student walkouts in the 1990s that included Mission High (3718 18th St., San Francisco).

SAN FRANCISCO

The **CESAR CHAVEZ STUDENT CENTER** (3.8 • 1600 Holloway Ave., San Francisco) marks the 1968 strikes that helped launch ethnic studies programs across the US and that drove home the power of intersectional organizing. This history inspired activism in later years at Bay Area high schools.

EAST BAY

Across the bay, **SPROUL PLAZA** (1.26 • Telegraph and Bancroft Aves., Berkeley) and its legacy persists, from free speech and antiwar to the Occupy and Defend Public Education movements of the 2000s. **BERKELEY HIGH SCHOOL** (1.4 • 1980 Allston Way, Berkeley) birthed alternative curricula, which inspired waves of new activism in later generations, around racial justice and immigration. Check the performance schedule and consider a stop by **924 GILMAN STREET** (1.2 • Berkeley),

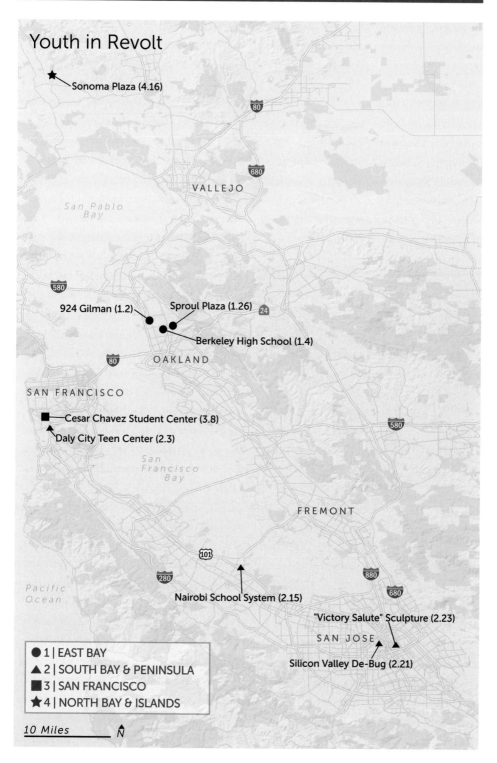

Youth in Revolt

★ Sonoma Plaza (4.16)

VALLEJO

San Pablo Bay

● 924 Gilman (1.2) — ● Sproul Plaza (1.26)

● Berkeley High School (1.4)

OAKLAND

SAN FRANCISCO

■ Cesar Chavez Student Center (3.8)

■ Daly City Teen Center (2.3)

San Francisco Bay

FREMONT

Pacific Ocean

Nairobi School System (2.15)

"Victory Salute" Sculpture (2.23)

SAN JOSE

Silicon Valley De-Bug (2.21)

● 1 | EAST BAY
▲ 2 | SOUTH BAY & PENINSULA
■ 3 | SAN FRANCISCO
★ 4 | NORTH BAY & ISLANDS

10 Miles N

the all-ages, volunteer-run cooperative venue for punk rock, misfits, outcasts, and young people in revolt against the limits of society.

NORTH BAY AND ISLANDS

The mythos of California's founding is represented at **SONOMA PLAZA** (4.16 • 453 1st St. E., Sonoma), a site of US military incursion into lands occupied largely by Mexicans and Native Americans. Here a youth-led political action raised public awareness about the legacies of colonialism.

Militarized States Tour

Militarism has shaped the Bay Area at least since the Spanish arrived, and its impacts linger in the urban fabric, in the cultural landscape, in its ecosystems, and in its world-famous technology. If you are using an Internet-based mapping tool to navigate this tour, then you're already deeply entwined in the military-industrial complex (just like us).

SOUTH BAY

The company that first developed spy satellites with CIA funding also funded **KEYHOLE** (2.11 • 1100A La Avenida, Mountain View) to build the software that underlies Google Maps and similar platforms. A visit to the Keyhole building itself may be interesting only to a limited audience, but it's a great jumping-off point to see Silicon Valley, and it's just minutes from the Computer History Museum (1401 N. Shoreline Blvd., Mountain View).

SAN FRANCISCO

The **HUNTER'S POINT SHIPYARD** (3.13 • Innes Court, San Francisco) is easily recognized by the ship-size crane that dominates the horizon. Community members are still fighting to ensure the cleanup of this site; meanwhile, new development has already begun. Workers here packed up radioactive materials to float out to a dump near the **FARALLON ISLANDS** (4.5 • San Francisco). On Bernal Heights, a memorial that should never have been needed may be formalized by the time you get there. Now called **ALEX NIETO PARK** (3.2 • 3450 Folsom St., San Francisco), this is one of the everyday places in the urban landscape where police have treated San Franciscans like enemy combatants. Downtown, the **HOTEL WHITCOMB** (3.12 • 1231 Market St., San Francisco) served as one of the command centers for planning and carrying out the incarceration of hundreds of thousands of Japanese and Japanese Americans during WWII. Meanwhile, you can stare up the AT&T building to try to find **ROOM 641A** (3.26 • 611 Folsom St., San Francisco); your private information just might be routing through there right now.

NORTH BAY AND ISLANDS

Catch a ride from the Ferry Building to **ANGEL ISLAND** (4.2 • Tiburon), where the old immigrant detention and processing center, which was designed largely to prevent immigration rather than to welcome newcomers, has been transformed into an educational museum. To the west you can see **ALCATRAZ ISLAND** (4.1 • San Francisco), which has a brutal history as a military prison, once used

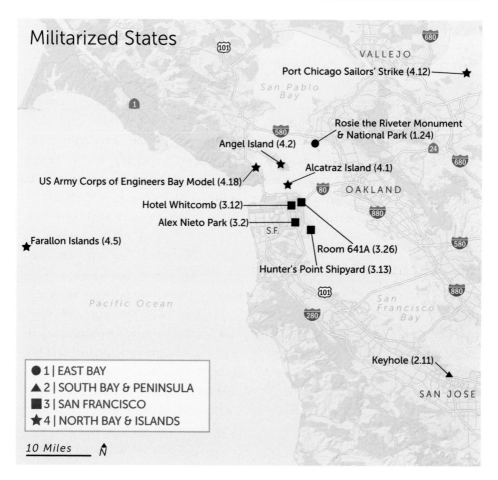

Militarized States

Port Chicago Sailors' Strike (4.12) ★

VALLEJO

San Pablo Bay

Rosie the Riveter Monument & National Park (1.24)

Angel Island (4.2) ●

Alcatraz Island (4.1)

US Army Corps of Engineers Bay Model (4.18)

OAKLAND

Hotel Whitcomb (3.12)

Alex Nieto Park (3.2)

S.F.

Farallon Islands (4.5) ★

Room 641A (3.26)

Hunter's Point Shipyard (3.13)

Pacific Ocean

San Francisco Bay

Keyhole (2.11) ▲

SAN JOSE

● 1 | EAST BAY
▲ 2 | SOUTH BAY & PENINSULA
■ 3 | SAN FRANCISCO
★ 4 | NORTH BAY & ISLANDS

10 Miles   Ν̂

to hold Indigenous leaders who dared to resist American colonization. Alcatraz also holds the history of an inspirational occupation that is commemorated annually on the island. Sometimes military technologies get repurposed in ways that serve other means; one example is the **US ARMY CORPS OF ENGINEERS BAY MODEL** (4.18 • 2100 Bridgeway, Sausalito). Once used to imagine how nuclear waste would move through the region in case of an attack or accident, now the model can be used as a tool for understanding the ways that we are connected across the region. Meanwhile, the **PORT CHICAGO**

SAILORS' STRIKE (4.12 • 450 Ryder St., Vallejo) represents a moment in which resistance to military operations shaped the civil rights movement.

EAST BAY

Finally, the **ROSIE THE RIVETER MONUMENT AND NATIONAL PARK** (1.24 • 1414 Harbour Way, Richmond) offers a window into the role of industrial wartime production in shaping our region and a look at the intersection between militarism and opportunity for marginalized people.

Acknowledgments

This book is the product of a dedicated collective effort. About a quarter of the site entries were written by contributors: Simon Abramowitsch, Javier Arbona, Ofelia Bello, Martha Bridegam, LisaRuth Elliott, John Elrick, Jennifer Fieber, Donna Graves, Jessica Lage, Diana Negrín Da Silva, Will Payne, Bruce Rinehart, and Katja Schwaller. Three of them gave us multiple entries and helped shape the book as a whole. Diana Negrín Da Silva authored ten site essays; LisaRuth Elliott authored seven; Donna Graves authored four. Diana also played a central role in the book's conceptual development, shaping ideas and themes with us over many conversations. We are so thankful to all of them for their insight, care, and generosity in sharing their expertise. Their names appear at the end of the entries they wrote (all have been edited for consistency with our style).

Most of our contemporary photographs were taken by Bruce Rinehart, who traveled hundreds of miles by bike, foot, bus, boat, rail, and car to document every site, often several times. We also benefited from the generosity of photographers around the Bay Area who shared their images with us. Their names are listed in the photo credits. Others helped connect us to photos and in some cases helped research their origins, including Barnali Ghosh, Donna Graves, Nolizwe Nondabula, Jan Novie, Tim Rowe, Daniel Ruark, and Sean Scully.

In service of creating a text that is both regional in scope and broad in topical reach, this book samples the historical and political geographies of the Bay Area. A generous group of people who have lived in and through these histories were kind enough to share their stories with us, which are included as reflection sidebars throughout the book. These include Sergio Arroyo, Cecilia Chung, Amy Dean, Jason Ferreira, Jennifer Freidenbach, Liz Gonzalez, Ellen Green, NTanya Lee, Ivy McClelland (interviewed by John Stehlin), Susan Moffatt, Prishni Murillo, Viet Ngyuen, Tim Redmond, and Rene Yung. There are infinitely more people and organizations in the Bay Area doing the work of organizing and building spaces of justice that we would have loved to include.

The University of San Francisco's Faculty Development Fund and the Mary Brown Summer Research Fellowship supported the work of wonderful student researchers: Ofelia Bello, Amy Dundon, Jennifer Fieber, Michael Heffernan-Zelaya, Alicia Lehmer, Sean McCarthy, Dan Raile, Katja Schwaller, and David Woo. The University of San Francisco Faculty Development Fund also provided essential support for cartography.

The remarkable staff and collections at many libraries and archives were essential to our efforts. These include the Bancroft and Earth Sciences and Map Libraries at UC Berkeley, San Francisco Public Library, San Jose Public Library, History San Jose, Solano County Library, San Francisco State University's Labor Archives and Research Center, Stanford University Library, California Historical Society, the Prelinger Archive and Prelinger Library, and the digital collections of the Online Archive of California. We have greatly benefited from the research-friendly portal at Archive.org and its "Wayback Machine," which makes so much of the Bay Area's ephemeral digital history available. Many archivists and holders of historical information went above and beyond to find information under tight deadlines, including Amy French, Michael Marie Lange, Christina Moretta, and Catherine Powell.

We are grateful to *People's Guide* series founders and editors Laura Pulido, Laura Barraclough, and Wendy Cheng for bringing us into this project, believing in our interpretation of the *People's Guide* effort, and supporting us all the way through. They have played many different roles, from helping conceptualize what a guide to such a large, complex region would look like, to aiding with the difficult task of finalizing the list of sites, all while developing the broader framework for the *People's Guide* series, which includes many more books and ideas than just this one.

Our wonderful editor at UC Press, Kim Robinson, and her staff—including Summer Farah, Benjy Malings, Archna Patel, Francisco Reinking, and many others whose names we may not have known along the way—have been unflagging shepherds of this book. That the *People's Guide* series is indeed coming to fruition is in no small part due to Kim's belief in it. We sincerely thank copyeditor Holly Bridges, who brought beautiful precision to the book, and our terrific indexer Susan Storch.

Mentors and teachers of ours over the years will recognize their imprint in this text. We particularly thank Paul Groth and Richard Walker, whom we both have worked with and learned from for many years. They helped us look at the landscape of the Bay Area in critical ways through long walks and lectures, and continually offered examples of ways to find, in the most ordinary places, extraordinary stories of the struggle over power. We also want to thank our own students at UC Berkeley and the University of San Francisco who have taken our field courses and who often asked questions that lead us to research deeper and better. They pushed our curiosity in ways they couldn't have known.

Charles Wollenberg and Peter Richardson generously read the manuscript carefully and gave us incredibly helpful and detailed peer reviews. Jason Henderson and an anonymous reviewer offered generous and incisive comments on the book at an early stage. We are thankful to have benefited from the combined breadth and depth of their regional knowledge and historical sensibility. Colleagues at the California Studies Association have been central to our intellectual growth as scholars of California, and their interest in bringing academic richness to public conversations is reflected in this text.

RACHEL BRAHINSKY'S THANKS: My commitment to this project is academic but also personal, having developed my interest in San Francisco history and geography alongside a cohort of people who are dedicated to learning about places through experiences like walking and biking, and who are committed to sharing knowledge beyond the academy. Mary Brown inspired me with long walks across the city and her fascination with the deep study of everyday landscapes. The public history approach promoted by Shaping San Francisco has long supported the idea that knowledge and history are actively made by all of us; that philosophy lives in this book as well. Much of my early knowledge of the Bay Area came through my years as a newspaper reporter

for the *San Francisco Bay Guardian,* an experience that continues to shape my approach to public history and geography. Since becoming a professor, just about every class I've taught has provided a space to develop and refine the ideas in this book, and I thank all of my students and thesis advisees for sharing in the work of unpacking the theory and practice of the Bay Area. Too many dear colleagues to name in the world of critical geography, too, have inspired and shaped my thinking and helped me better learn how to find and articulate connections and meaning.

At the University of San Francisco, supportive colleagues and friends have had a direct impact on this book, including Kresten Froistad-Martin, Candice Harrison, Stephanie Sears, Annick Wibben, Sonja Poole, Kathleen Coll, Corey Cook, and Tim Redmond, who have supported this project in specific ways. Kathy's ongoing generosity, from articles referenced to analysis shared, has been essential in the evolution of my thinking about the meaning of the Bay Area and social justice more broadly. I thank Pamela Balls-Organista and Marcelo Camperi, the Faculty Development Fund, and USF's invaluable faculty writing retreats, where I worked on aspects of this book. So many other wonderful colleagues at USF— too many to name, and I apologize for all omissions—have made it a truly special professional home base that is supportive of public scholarship, and a place where I personally feel welcomed and at home.

I am lucky to have friends across the Bay Area who work each day to make this place and other places more just. Many of them shared their ideas over the years in ways that seeped into this text, and I'm grateful for that and even more for the work that they continue to do toward a better world. Some of that work is reflected in this book, and I hope they'll forgive the inevitable omissions that they will surely notice. Over the years dear friends who are also activists have created a sense of possibility for a project like this; activists who have become friends have shared ways to extend care and love into political and academic work and to refuse to give up on making those connections.

My family, especially Naomi, David, Josh, and Michelle, inspire me with their own commitments to work and life that matters; those dreams are threaded through this text. In addition to the material contribution of his photographs, Bruce Rinehart has been a daily interlocutor on this text, and on all things, offering a steady reminder of why a "people's guide" might matter.

Alex Tarr has become a dear friend and dedicated teammate on a project that truly seemed to grow over time. This book wouldn't be complete without the optimism, humor, and creative strategizing that he brought to it (in addition to research, writing, cartography, geographic depth, and more). His continued willingness to seek out and understand new corners of the bay made this a richer and far better book.

ALEX TARR'S THANKS: I have often told friends that I undertook this book precisely because I felt no great love for the Bay Area as outsiders imagined it (myself included),

but have grown a deep admiration for the people who make the real, lived place. In Berkeley, the first glimmer of ideas and a great deal of ongoing encouragement came from Gina Acebo, Tripti Bhattacharya, Alicia Cowart, John Elrick, Sarah Knuth, Will Payne, John Stehlin, Alberto Velazquez, and many more inspiring colleagues at UC Berkeley. Both Paul Duguid and Scott Saul offered sincere curiosity and guidance to a wayward geographer. Tali and the Weinberg family made it possible to start the project at all. Danny, Eric, Jackie, Jesús, Jessica, Kristen, Lauren, Lys, Nate, Mai, Matt, Patrick, Rosten, Sabrina, Sharon, and Yelena have provided an unbroken thread connecting me to California for over a decade, providing analysis, occasional levity, and daily reminders of why this kind of work is necessary.

In Houston, a year as a Mellon postdoc fellow in the Spatial Humanities at Rice University gave me the time and space to focus on *People's Guide* work almost exclusively. I thank Farès El-Dahdah and Melissa Bailar for the opportunity, and Ted and Rachel Geier, Rex Troumbly, Carolyn Adams, and everyone at the Humanities Research Center for making a community from which to continue the work.

Colleagues and students at Worcester State University have supported my enduring fixation with the "other coast" with sincere curiosity and encouragement, especially fellow human geographer Pat Benjamin and Dean Linda Larrivee. My new comrades in organizing for democratic unions, and the radical scholars of the Women's, Gender and Sexuality Studies Board have kept a flame alive in these dark times and been a constant reminder that this project reverberates far beyond the times and places it covers. Alan Wiig, Renee Tapp, and Vicki Gruzynski have, at various times, made sure there was a roof over my head and food in my fridge, and been tireless sounding boards. Along with Jessa Loomis, they have lovingly seen to it that this near infinite project arrived at a finite and meaningful place.

Throughout the project, my family has graciously endured many visits unexpectedly consumed by both the joyous and heartbreaking work of this book and provided untold support of all kinds. I am very fortunate that my parents, Nina and Stuart, and sister, Michaela, both understand and believe in the politics, purpose, and need to do this kind of book.

More than anything, I thank Rachel for inviting me to coauthor this book. She has been an extraordinary collaborator across my many changes in geography, the thousands of collective decisions we've had to make about the book, writing and rewriting each other's words (especially my run-on sentences), dedicating each spare minute between semesters to our deadlines, and always keeping us dedicated to the goal of sharing people's stories of struggle and victories with clarity, respect, and a sense that they can give us all hope.

Timeline

A Brief and Incomplete Outline of Bay Area History

The fast pace of change in California can be a hard thing to grasp. Imagine a person born into an Ohlone household in 1776, the year Spanish troops first set foot on what would they would eventually call San Francisco. If that person lived seventy-five years, in their lifetime they would have seen the Spanish conquest of Alta California, Mexican independence, US conquest, the gold rush, and California's induction as the thirty-first US state in 1850. A person born in 1850 might then see the region go from a few small industrial and agricultural towns to a massive, multi-centered, diverse metropolis connected by rail and bridges across the bay.

The uneven movement of time vis-à-vis space is hardly unique to California—and perhaps a topic better left to metaphysics than a guidebook dedicated to historical-geographic landscapes—but as this guide moves you from place to place, it may be easy to lose track of the historical moment in which an event took place. We try to include context throughout, but to help situate the site narratives we include here a broad outline of California's territorial history, with a few important dates included, for easy reference as you use the guide.

Approximately by **13,000 BCE**, but possibly earlier: First People arrive in the Americas (the exact period remains a topic of research)

~ 9000–5000 BCE   End of last Ice Age, glacial melt and sea-level rise (300 feet) form the San Francisco Bay, more or less, as we know it now

~4000 BCE   Villages of first Ohlone-speaking people established in bay (based on history of shellmounds)

1776   Spanish begin conquest of Bay Area region, first missions established

1821   Mexico gains independence, Alta California designated a territory (not a state)

1833   Mission system secularizes and lands are turned over to large, private ranches

1846–1848   US uses military to annex California territory

1849   Gold discovered upriver from the San Francisco Bay, and—as historians would later say—"the world rushed in," with waves of new migrants flooding into the state in the decades that followed

1850 California becomes thirty-first state

1869 First transcontinental railroad connects Bay Area to rest of US by rail

1882 Anti-Chinese agitation centered in the Bay Area culminates in federal laws strictly limiting Chinese immigration, followed by others to limit other nationalities

1906 Earthquake and major fire destroy much of San Francisco's built environment, spurring development of East Bay and South Bay cities

1936–1937 Bay Bridge and Golden Gate Bridge open amid Great Depression

1940 Second Great Migration of African Americans begins to reshape racial geography in the region

1942 Executive Order 9066—people of Japanese descent dislocated from their communities by US government and held in remote concentration camps

1942–1945 World War II—war industries, especially shipbuilding, boom in the Bay Area, luring thousands of new workers and residents

1950s–1970s "Urban renewal" schemes, especially freeway development and "slum clearance," dramatically reshape Bay Area cities

1965 Immigration and Naturalization Act opens the door for new groups from across Asia and Latin America to emigrate

1960s–1980s US-backed wars in Southeast Asia and Central America displace millions of people, large numbers of whom rebuild communities in Bay Area

1995–2000 First dot-com boom signals major changes in regional economic geography

2007 Great Recession begins, waves of foreclosures displace many communities

2010s–PRESENT Second tech boom accelerates the reach of Silicon Valley and its impact on everyday landscapes and people of the entire Bay Area

2020 In a Bay Area home to more than seven million people, communities continue to demand justice

Resources

These resources extend beyond the "to learn more" citations throughout the book. Given space constraints, we include here only a selection of books, websites, and tours that we have found useful in understanding the Bay Area.

PUBLIC HISTORY WEBSITES AND BAY AREA WALKING TOURS WITH STRONG "PEOPLE'S HISTORY" TENDENCIES

Berkeley South Asian Radical History Walking Tour, http://www.berkeleysouthasian.org

East Bay Yesterday, https://eastbayyesterday.com

Internet Archive, https://archive.org

Prelinger Archive, https://archive.org/details/prelinger

Shaping San Francisco, http://www.shapingsf.org

Think Walks, http://www.thinkwalks.org/

Also, check Bay Area college and university course listings for many interesting, affordable options, including field courses that tour the region.

FURTHER RECOMMENDED READING ON SAN FRANCISCO BAY AREA "PEOPLE'S HISTORY" AND "PEOPLE'S GEOGRAPHY"

Just a sampling of what's out there

Allen, Robert L. *The Port Chicago Mutiny: The Story of the Largest Mass Mutiny Trial in U.S. Naval History*. Berkeley, CA: Heyday Books, 2006.

Almaguer, Tomás. *Racial Fault Lines: The Historical Origins of White Supremacy in California*. Berkeley: University of California Press, 2008.

Bagwell, Beth. *Oakland, the Story of a City*. Novato, CA: Presidio Press, 1982.

Bloom, Josh, and Waldo Martin. *Black Against Empire*. Berkeley: University of California Press, 2016.

Boyd, Nan Alamilla. *Wide-Open Town: A History of Queer San Francisco to 1965*. Berkeley: University of California Press, 2005.

Brahinsky, Rachel. "The Making and Unmaking of Southeast San Francisco." PhD diss., University of California, Berkeley, 2012.

Brechin, Grey. *Imperial San Francisco: Urban Power, Earthly Ruin*. Berkeley: University of California Press, 1999.

Brook, James, Chris Carlsson, and Nancy J. Peters, eds. *Reclaiming San Francisco: History, Politics, Culture*. San Francisco: City Lights, 1998.

Chin, Gordon. *Building Community, Chinatown Style: A Half Century of Leadership in San Francisco Chinatown*. San Francisco: Friends of Chinatown Community Development Center, 2015.

Cordova, Cary. *The Heart of the Mission: Latino Art and Politics in San Francisco*. Philadelphia: University of Pennsylvania Press, 2017.

Early, Steve. *Refinery Town: Big Oil, Big Money, and the Remaking of an American City*. Boston: Beacon Press, 2017.

Elinson, Elaine, and Stan Yogi. *Wherever There's a Fight: How Runaway Slaves, Suffragists, Immigrants, Strikers, and Poets Shaped Civil Liberties in California*. Berkeley, CA: Heyday Books, 2009.

Fairfax, Sally, et al. *California Cuisine and Food Justice*. Cambridge, MA: MIT Press, 2012.

Gilmore, Ruth Wilson. *Golden Gulag: Prisons, Surplus, Crisis, and Opposition in Globalizing California*. Berkeley: University of California Press, 2007.

Gowan, Teresa. *Hobos, Hustlers, and Backsliders: Homeless in San Francisco*. Minneapolis: University of Minnesota Press, 2010.

Groth, Paul. *Living Downtown: The History of Residential Hotels in the United States*. Berkeley: University of California Press, 1999.

Habal, Estella. *San Francisco's International Hotel: Mobilizing the Filipino American Community in the Anti-Eviction Movement*. Asian American History and Culture. Philadelphia: Temple University Press, 2007.

Hartman, Chester. *City for Sale: The Transformation of San Francisco*. Berkeley: University of California Press, 2002.

Henderson, Jason. *Street Fight: The Politics of Mobility in San Francisco*. Amherst: University of Massachusetts Press, 2013.

Hobson, Emily K. *Lavender and Red: Liberation and Solidarity in the Gay and Lesbian Left*. Oakland: University of California Press, 2016.

Howell, Ocean. *Making the Mission: Planning and Ethnicity in San Francisco*. Chicago: University of Chicago Press, 2015.

Johnson, Marilynn S. *The Second Gold Rush: Oakland and the East Bay in World War II*. Berkeley: University of California Press, 1993.

Kamiya, Gary. *Cool Gray City of Love: Forty-Nine Views of San Francisco*. New York: Bloomsbury, 2013.

Lai, H. Mark, Genny Lim, and Judy Yung. *Island: Poetry and History of Chinese Immigrants on Angel Island, 1910–1940*. Second edition. Seattle: University of Washington Press, 2014.

Lobo, Susan, ed. *Urban Voices: The Bay Area American Indian Community, Community History Project, Intertribal Friendship House, Oakland, California*. Tucson: University of Arizona Press, 2002.

Ma, L. Eve Armentrout. *Hometown Chinatown: The History of Oakland's Chinese Community, 1852–1995*. Studies in Asian Americans. New York: Garland Publishing, 2000.

Matthews, Glenna. *Silicon Valley, Women, and the California Dream: Gender, Class, and Opportunity in the Twentieth Century*. Palo Alto, CA: Stanford University Press, 2003.

Miranda, Deborah A. *Bad Indians: A Tribal Memoir*. Berkeley, CA: Heyday Books, 2012.

Moore, Shirley Ann Wilson. *To Place Our Deeds: The African American Community in Richmond, California, 1910–1963*. Berkeley: University of California Press, 2000.

Mozingo, Louise A. *Pastoral Capitalism: A History of Suburban Corporate Landscapes*. Cambridge, MA: MIT Press, 2016.

Murch, Donna Jean. *Living for the City: Migration, Education, and the Rise of the Black Panther Party in Oakland, California*. Chapel Hill: University of North Carolina Press, 2010.

Pellow, David N., and Lisa Sun-Hee Park. *The Silicon Valley of Dreams: Environmental Injustice, Immigrant Workers, and the High-Tech Global Economy*. New York: NYU Press, 2002.

Pitti, Stephen J. *The Devil in Silicon Valley: Northern California, Race, and Mexican Americans*. Princeton, NJ: Princeton University Press, 2004.

Rhomberg, Chris. *No There There: Race, Class, and Political Community in Oakland*. Berkeley: University of California Press, 2004.

Richardson, Peter. *A Bomb in Every Issue: How the Short, Unruly Life of "Ramparts" Magazine Changed America*. New York: The New Press, 2009.

Rothstein, Richard. *The Color of Law: A Forgotten History of How Our Government Segregated America*. New York: Liveright Publishing, W. W. Norton & Co., 2017.

Saxenian, AnnaLee. *Regional Advantage: Culture and Competition in Silicon Valley and Route 128*. Cambridge, MA: Harvard University Press, 1996.

Schrag, Peter. *California: America's High-Stakes Experiment*. Berkeley: University of California Press, 2006.

Scott, Mel. *The San Francisco Bay Area: A Metropolis in Perspective*. Second edition. Berkeley: University of California Press, 1985.

Self, Robert O. *American Babylon: Race and the Struggle for Postwar Oakland*. Princeton, NJ: Princeton University Press, 2003.

Solnit, Rebecca, ed. *Infinite City: A San Francisco Atlas*. Berkeley: University of California Press, 2010.

Stryker, Susan. *Transgender History*. First edition. Berkeley, CA: Seal Press, 2008.

Summers Sandoval, Tomás F. *Latinos at the Golden Gate: Creating Community and Identity in San Francisco*. Chapel Hill: University of North Carolina Press, 2013.

Tea, Michelle. *Valencia*. Berkeley, CA: Seal Press, 2008.

Tracy, James. *Dispatches against Displacement: Field Notes from San Francisco's Housing Wars*. Oakland, CA: AK Press, 2014.

Turner, Fred. *From Counterculture to Cyberculture: Stewart Brand, the Whole Earth Network, and the Rise of Digital Utopianism*. Chicago: University of Chicago Press, 2006.

Walker, Richard A. *The Country in the City: The Greening of the San Francisco Bay Area*. Seattle: University of Washington Press, 2007.

Walker, Richard A. *Pictures of a Gone City: Tech and the Dark Side of Prosperity in the San Francisco Bay Area*. Oakland, CA: PM Press, 2018.

Watt, Laura A. *The Paradox of Preservation: Wilderness and Working Landscapes at Point Reyes National Seashore*. Oakland: University of California Press, 2017.

Wilson, Chris, and Paul Groth, eds. *Everyday America: Cultural Landscape Studies after J. B. Jackson*. Berkeley: University of California Press, 2003.

Wollenberg, Charles. *Marinship at War: Shipbuilding and Social Change in Wartime Sausalito*. First edition. Berkeley, CA: Western Heritage, 1990.

Wollenberg, Charles. *Golden Gate Metropolis: Perspectives on Bay Area History*. First edition. Berkeley: Institute of Governmental Studies, University of California, 1985.

Credits

PHOTOS BY BRUCE RINEHART UNLESS
CREDITED OTHERWISE.

Page iv, 34: 1.7, Black.Seed demonstration, Brooke Anderson Photography

Page 37: 1.8, West Berkeley Shellmound site, Scott Braley

Page 39: 1.9, Historical Chevron photo, Bancroft Library, University of California, Berkeley, photographer unknown

Page 41: 1.10, Frances Albrier and Sacramento Market, Bancroft Library, University of California, Berkeley, Photos by Presley Winfield, and historical ephemera

Page 43: 1.11 Mural photographed by Bruce Rinehart with permission from the Intertribal Friendship House

Page 51 & Cover: 1.15 Demonstration in Latham Square, Labor Archives and Research Center, J. Paul Leonard Library, San Francisco State University, photographer unknown

Page 58: 1.19, Occupy Oakland camp, Myles Boisen

Page 59: 1.20, Pacific Center front steps, Sharat G. Lin

Page 65: 1.23, Map by Alexander Tarr

Page iv, 70: 1.26, Free Speech Movement, Bancroft Library, University of California, Berkeley, Steven Marcus

Page 91: 2.8 Alviso "toll booth," Al Magazu for the *San Jose Mercury News*

Page 93: 2.9, Chinatown fire, History San Jose, *San Jose Mercury News*, photographer unknown

Page 99: 2.12, Lawrence Tract map, City of Palo Alto, Planning Department

Page 100: 2.13, 2006 May Day march, Sharat G. Lin

Page 108: 2.17, New Almaden miners, Laurence E. Bulmore Collection, History San Jose, photographer unknown

Page 113: 2.20, Imagine 7 marquee, Francisco Padorla

Page 115: 2.20, *De-Bug Magazine* cover, Silicon Valley De-Bug

Page 128: 3.1, 829 Fell newsletter, Calvin Welch, personal files

Page iv & 130: 3.2, Alex Nieto memorial, Labor Video Project, Steve Zeltzer

Page 147: 3.10, Critical Mass ride, Dave Snyder

Page 153: 3.13, Fishermen at Hunter's Point, San Francisco History Room, San Francisco Public Library, photographer unknown

Page 155: 3.14, I-Hotel poster, linoleum cut made for the IHTA by Rachael Romero, SF Poster Brigade

Page 167: 3.21 Montgomery Block building, Historic American Buildings Survey, Library of Congress, A. J. Wittlock

Page 173: 3.24, Jim Jones and crowd, San Francisco History Room, San Francisco Public Library, Nancy Wong

Page 182: 3.27, Farm event poster, Cornell University Archive, artist unknown

Page 185: 3.31, "Twitter Tax Break" Zone map by Alexander Tarr

Page 199: 4.2, Crowd on Angel Island dock, San Francisco History Room, San Francisco Public Library, photographer unknown

Page 203: 4.4, Cuttings Wharf housing, staff photographer, *Napa Valley Register*

Page 205: 4.5 Farallon Islands, *SF Call-Bulletin,* San Francisco History Room, San Francisco Public Library

Page 207: 4.6, Golden Gate Village, Aaron Green Archive, photographer unknown

Page 213: 4.9, An Eichler home in Lucas Valley, Ernest Braun Photography

Page 233: 4.15, BART map by Alexander Tarr

Index

oppression: history of, in geography, 5; in identities, 188–89; and resistance, 7–8, 12, 221–22
Orange, Tommy, 12–13
Osento bathhouse, San Francisco, 160
Other Avenues Food Store Cooperative, 168–70, *169*, 237
Otis, Johnny, 42
Our Lady of Guadalupe Mission Chapel, San Jose, 101

P

Pacific Center, Front Steps, Berkeley, 59–60, *59*
Pacific Gas and Electric Company, 146
Pacific Islanders/Pacific Islander communities, *142*
Palo Alto, 78–79, 85–86, 98–100, *99*, 104–6, 238
Palo Alto Fair Play Council, 98
Panhandle of Golden Gate Park, 170–72, 237, *170*
Paradise, fires in, 195–96
Parchester Village, Richmond, 60–62, *61*
PARK(ING) Day, 139–40
Parr, Fred and Chester, 61
"participatory defense" model against police violence, 115
Pat, Luis Góngora, 130
Payne, Will, 64–65
peace movement, 70–71
Peace Plaza, San Francisco, *157*
Pelican Bay Prison, 221
People's Food System, 168–69
People's Guide to Los Angeles, A (Pulido, Barraclough, and Cheng), 5
People's Park, Berkeley, 71
"Peoples Temple" Post Office, San Francisco, 172–74
Peralta, Luis, 62–63
Peralta Hacienda Historical Park, Oakland, 62–64, *63*, 232
Pergola at Lake Merritt, 48–49, *49*
Phat Beets food justice collective, 32–33
Piedmont-Oakland Border, 64–65
Pierce Point Ranch, Inverness, 216–17, *216*, 236–37
Pilipinas-Filipino Cultural Heritage District, 178

Pilipinas Streets, SOMA, San Francisco, 177–79
pipelines, oil, 38–39
plutonium waste, 205–6
Poethig, Joanna: Ang Lipi Ni Lapu Lapu mural, 178, *178*
Point Pinole Regional Shoreline, 62
Point Reyes National Seashore, 216–17, *216*, 225–26, *225–26*
police/policing: activism for accountability of, 130–31; brutality and killings by, 20, 35, 94–96, 126–27, 129–32; in Critical Mass, 147–48; in International Hotel eviction, 155–56; of public space, 140; and real estate speculation, 32; in the SFSU strike of 1968, 143; in strikebreaking at Latham Square, 50–51; in student protests at Sproul Plaza, 69–70, 71; trans resistance to raids by, 183; violence by, 20, 35, 94–96, 126–27, 129–32; of youth of color, 84
politics, spatial, 139–40
Pollack, Andy, 182
pollution, mercury, 106. *See also* toxic landscapes
Port Chicago Sailors' Strike, 217–19, 241
Port of Oakland, 1, 55–58, *57*
Portuguese immigrants, 45–46, 92
Potrero Del Sol community garden and park, San Francisco, *181*
power: challenges to abuse of, 4; of community in the Gold Street Bridge, 90–91; in everyday places, 5–8; exclusion of immigrants from, 81; infrastructure in, 146; newspaper buildings symbolizing, 161; of organized labor, 51; political, 92, 172–73; of Tech CEOs, 88; Trans March and Pride weekend in, 183–84; white structures of, 81, 219
Precita Center, San Francisco, 164
Precita Eyes Muralists Association, 131
Prelinger Library, San Francisco, 177
Prince Hall Masons Firma Lodge No. 27, 219–20, *219*
prisons/prison industrial complex, 62, 196–98, 220–22, *221*

Prison University Project, 221–22
Proposition 6 (Briggs Initiative) of 1978, 183–84
Proposition 13, 128
Proposition 187, 84, 166
Proposition J, 129
"Protect Your People," *115*
protests: black power salute at Summer Olympics of 1968, 117–19; Black Seed Demonstration, 34–35; at Civic Center and UN Plazas, 144–45; Gold Street Bridge shutdown, 90–92; of "Google buses," 164; Hellyer Park, 94–96; of the House Un-American Activities Committee, 146; Lake Merritt, Sudan revolution, 49; Latham Square, *51*; March for Peace and a Bear Flag Alternative, 224–25; at Ogawa/Grant Plaza, 58–59; PARK(ING) Day, 139–40; Peoples Temple members in, 172–73; at the Port of Oakland, 56–57; of Proposition 187, 165; student, in Sproul Plaza, 69–71; student walkout at Mission Dolores High School, 166; youth direct action, 84–85
psychedelia, American, 172
public space: Civic Center and UN Plazas, 144–46; gentrification in rights to use, 174–75; houseless people in, 125, 144–46; in mobilizations and activism, 171–72; reclaiming and reusing of, 26–28, 139–40; use and policing of, 140
Puerto Rican migrants, 92, 101–2
Pulido, Laura: *A People's Guide to Los Angeles*, 5
Pullman Company, 2, 41–42
punk music, 24–25, 181–82
Purple Onion Bar, 168

Q

Quan, Frank, 200
queer people and communities. *See* LGBTQ people and communities
Quen Hing Tong, 93
Quicksilver Mine Company, 107

Founded in 1893,
UNIVERSITY OF CALIFORNIA PRESS
publishes bold, progressive books and journals
on topics in the arts, humanities, social sciences,
and natural sciences—with a focus on social
justice issues—that inspire thought and action
among readers worldwide.

The UC PRESS FOUNDATION
raises funds to uphold the press's vital role
as an independent, nonprofit publisher, and
receives philanthropic support from a wide
range of individuals and institutions—and from
committed readers like you. To learn more, visit
ucpress.edu/supportus.